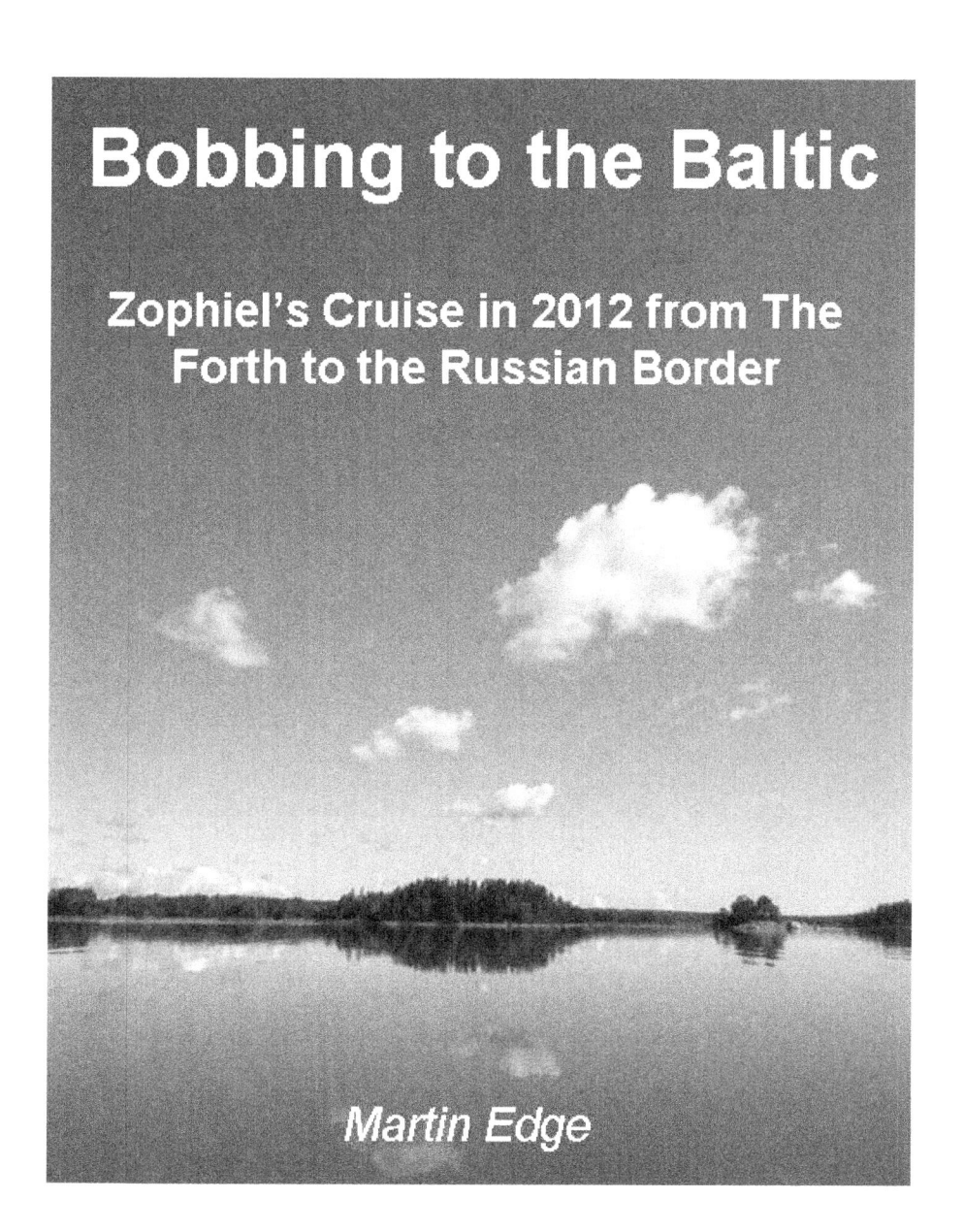

Bobbing to the Baltic

Zophiel's Cruise in 2012 from The Forth to the Russian Border

Martin Edge

Bobbing to the Baltic

Zophiel's Cruise in 2012 from The Forth to the Russian Border

Martin Edge

First Print Edition 2014
Published in Great Britain 2013 by Martin Edge.
Copyright © Martin Edge 2013

Martin Edge asserts the right under the Copyright, Designs and Patents Act 1988 to be identified as the author of this work.
All rights reserved. No part of this publication may be reproduced in any material form (including photocopying or storing in any medium by electronic means and whether or not transiently or incidentally to some other use of this publication) without the written permission of the copyright holder except in accordance with the provisions of the Copyright, Design and Patents Act 1988 or under the terms of a licence issued by the Copyright Licensing Agency Ltd. This book is sold subject to the conditions that it shall not, by way of trade or otherwise, be lent, re-sold, hired out, or otherwise circulated without the author's prior consent in any form binding or cover other than that in which it is published and without a similar condition, including this condition, being imposed on the subsequent purchaser.

The full sets of colour pictures from this and other volumes of Zophiel's travels are available free at:

http://www.edge.me.uk

Continents

	Page		Page
Preface		The Prison Ships	111
Waggling Wings	5	A Peeling	115
Denmark the Long Way	8	No 'U' Turns	121
Ice Cream or Road Cone?	13	Bloody Subscriber Identity Modules	127
Designer Holes	19		
Bloody Students	22	A Side Order of Eastland	134
First Clogging	25	Better out than In	140
Models on Bikes	30	The Phone was in the Oven	144
Tea Cup	33	Terrible Tidal Tales	149
Basket Case	36	Into the Yachts' Graveyard	154
Redundant Ditch	40	Self-Scrambling Eggs	160
Tide, What Tide?	45	Heroically Unsticking a German	165
Bridge, What Bridge?	45	Grungy Black Dreadlocked Hippy Fascists	169
Old Copper Nose	51		
Monster	55	Goulash Archipelago	174
Troll Hat	58	The Last Rock of the Year	180
Gotta Get to Gøta	63	Assimilation into the Hive of the Borg	186
A Fantasy for Lunatics	70		
Soda Shopping	76	Welsh Sweden	195
Broken	80	Hippyocrisy	200
Sölon Staff Association	85	Joy Spring	206
Goldilocks to Uist	90	Twinned with Hull	211
Lumparland	97	Mingunauld	216
Popular in the Summer	101	Fan	222
Wester Hailes	106	Lemming	228

Preface

"Bobbing to the Baltic" is the tale of Zophiel's cruise in the summer of 2012. 'Zophiel' is a Vancouver 27 – a wee, twenty seven foot, long-keeled, cutter rigged, fibreglass sloop. She's about thirty years old but designed more like the solid, slow, dependable, seaworthy craft of an earlier generation. In 2012 she travelled from the Forth Estuary to the Russian border with Finland then back, through the million rocky islands of the north shore of the Baltic – with a side order of Estonia – as far as Holland. The whole rambling shebang is published for various e-readers.

In 2003 Griff Rhys Jones published a book giving an account of a trip to the Baltic with the title "To the Baltic with Bob – An Epic Misadventure". 'Bobbing to the Baltic' is the story of a trip along a very similar route in a much smaller boat. It is better in four important respects. Firstly there's more pictures. Secondly I actually enjoyed the trip, for the most part. Griff Rhys Jones paints an altogether more gloomy and miserable picture of the Baltic. I hope I make it sound more like what it is – an idyllic summer cruising ground of infinite appeal. Thirdly, my book is cheaper. Fourthly, I need the money much more than Griff Rhys Jones does. After all, someone's got to pay for me to swan around sailing all summer.

On the other hand I make absolutely no claims as to literary merit or 'epicness'. It's just a wee story about an extended holiday. It joins three previous accounts of trips around the North Sea, to Arctic Norway and around Ireland, each of which has also been published for e-readers.

Zophiel Sailing under the Forth Bridge

Waggling Wings

"Ooo look, an aeroplane!" said Simon. "Yeah, very interesting" I replied a little testily. Since we were about ten miles from the Dutch coast and probably underneath the flight path from god knows where to Schiphol airport this scarcely seemed remarkable. Anyway I was more concerned with vessels at sea level than up in the sky. We were in the middle of negotiating the spaghetti junction of traffic separation schemes that litters the coast off the Dutch Frisian Islands and our AIS had packed up. Nearly all the goods coming into and out of Northern Europe pass along these shipping lanes and we were trying to cross them all in a twenty seven foot yacht. Visibility was fine and we didn't really need the AIS, but it was nevertheless annoying that Sod's Law had chosen that moment for our handy bit of ship-dodging kit to pack up. Anyway, AIS is becoming such a standard piece of kit for shipping that you can feel a bit bereft without it. Because of it you hardly hear any shipping on the VHF any more. For example we'd heard nothing at all on channel sixteen since leaving the Forth three days before.

"He's flying very low. And he's circling round again". "Uh huh". I dismissed him and continued trying to trace a break in the aerial cable that meant that the AIS could only detect ships less than ten yards away, when it was getting a bit late to take avoiding action. The choppy, grey following sea blown by a north-easterly onto a shallowing lee shore wasn't making the task, or anything on board, any easier.

"Ooo look, he's flying round again, even lower this time. I think he's trying to attract our attention. Come and look". This was getting annoying. I had developed a deep antipathy to leaving the saloon when it wasn't my watch. Ever since leaving our home berth at Port Edgar Marina, under the Forth Bridges, on the evening of May the first it had been bleeding freezing. Twelve hours of battering to windward heading for northern Denmark against a freezing easterly force five and a three metre chop had effectively soaked the three of us and everything on board with North Sea. Said sea, which Zoph's handy hull thermometer recorded at six degrees Celsius, continued to spray us with its icy shards of near frozen water on every wave. I was also acutely aware that arriving in the middle of Holland after aiming for northern Denmark was pretty poor navigation even by my standards.

The only thing that was making life bearable was the charcoal burning stove. This primitive, top loading steel drum had been stuffed to the brim with glowing charcoal since we passed under the Forth bridges and was managing to prevent the cabin from turning into a soaking fridge. Instead it kept it stable, with the temperature and humidity of a damp shed in winter.

"Yes, he's definitely trying to attract our attention". I steeled myself against the icy spray and climbed into the cockpit. This was ridiculous, why the hell would an aeroplane want to attract our attention? There were hundreds of huge ships out there and doubtless dozens of airliners zapping through the sky above the low damp clouds. Why would a wee twenty seven foot boat attract anybody's attention?

"Here he comes again". I had to admit he had a point. A twin engined prop-driven plane circled around us only a couple of hundred feet up. Suddenly it banked and headed straight towards us in a low dive. Headlights came on then flashed repeatedly and insistently at us. As it closed on us its wings started to waggle violently up and down. For a moment I had the surreal impression that we had wandered through a wormhole in the space-time continuum somewhere around the Dogger Bank and reappeared in the early 1940s. We were being attacked by a dive-bombing Stuka. Or perhaps The Netherlands had declared war on Britain and that's why there had been a radio silence. Something to do with the value of the Euro perhaps?

But he pulled up before hitting us and mercifully didn't machine gun us. He did however circle around and repeat the whole headlight flashing, wing waggling performance. "Yes, he's definitely trying to attract our attention" said Gordon, "Why not try and get him on the VHF?". "Well he's not contacted us on the radio. Anyway, do planes use Channel 16?". "Coastguard ones do and I imagine that's what he is" replied Gordon.

"Fair enough" I said and steeled myself for the frightening process of making official communications on the VHF. Now Zoph's radio is an ancient affair. None of your new fangled DSC facilities with automatic distress calls. This is a three knob job. One for the channel, one for volume and one called 'squelch', whatever that is. There's a speaker down below and another, nicked from a car stereo, sellotaped inside a Tesco ice cream tub in the cockpit. Very professional. The 'hand set' is simply an old fashioned black telephone handle, with a microphone at one end and a speaker at the other. The sort that used to sit on telephones that had a proper round dial on the front. A hole has been cut in the middle of this handle into which the 'transmit' button has been set. Soon before leaving home I had made a highly sophisticated improvement to this handset, which consisted of a couple of makeshift clips to hold it to the wall above the radio. I was pleased with my handiwork, as it stopped the handset from crashing about the cabin on its curly wire in a big sea. As I reached for the handle I realised that my improvement also had a small side effect. One of the clips holding it to the wall had, in the commotion of the three day passage, got jammed on the 'transmit' button.

For somewhere between twelve hours and three days – and certainly whilst we crossed all of northern Europe's busiest shipping lanes – we had been broadcasting to the world on the emergency channel. As the coastguard tried to broadcast strong wind warnings and anxious fishermen huddled round their radios, all they would hear was Gordon snoring or Simon saying how bloody cold it was. For days, as supertankers picked their way through the channels on passage from Germany to China, they would reach for the radio to call up other ships on converging courses and all they would hear was me moaning about the drip down the back of my neck, or swearing at crockery as it flew about the cabin.

I've occasionally heard of these cases in the past. "What sort of arse", I would think "would be stupid enough to broadcast Radio One on an emergency channel for hours? How dim witted would you have to be not to notice, apart from anything else, that you never heard anyone else on channel sixteen?". Now I knew exactly what sort of arse would do such a thing. Me. I made my apology to the Dutch Coastguard plane as grovellingly abject as was consistent with conventions for the use of VHF. But even though the chap on the radio was Dutch and therefore theoretically extremely laid back, he couldn't disguise the fact that he was fairly pissed off to be called out and have to fly about for hours trying to attract the attention of frigging idiots floating about in a plastic bucket.

Thus was my fairly inauspicious introduction to continental Europe at the start of Zophiel's 2012 cruise to the far end of the Baltic.

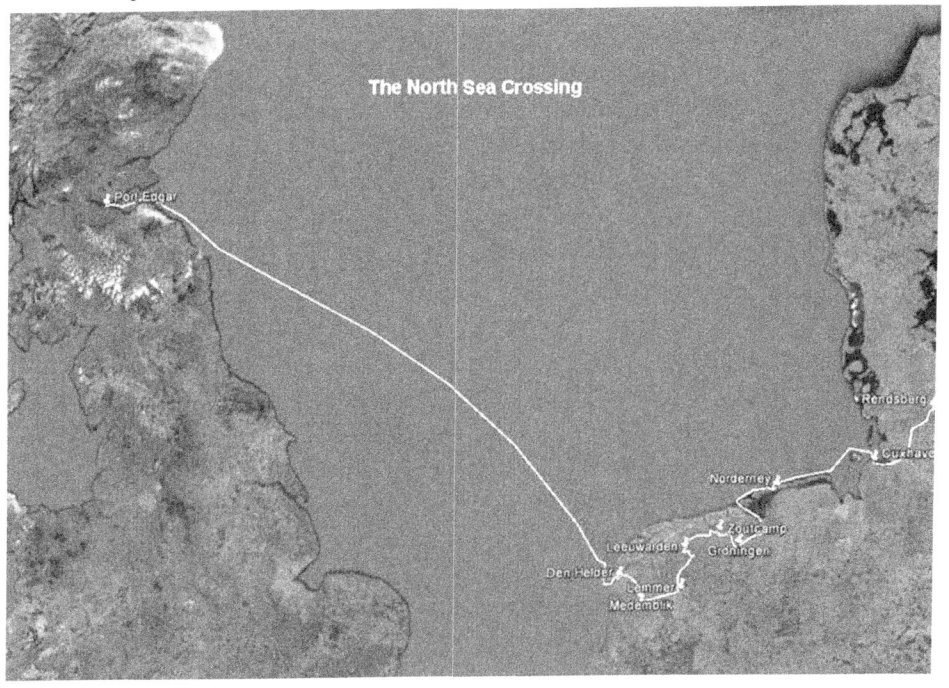

Denmark the Long Way

It was Ireland that made me decide to go to the Baltic. In 2011 I took Zophiel round Ireland anticlockwise and it was an interesting and mostly enjoyable cruise but – and they're quite big buts (or as the Americans would say 'big arses') – for the sea and the weather. On the west of Ireland there was a constant swell from the Atlantic that meant there were virtually no conditions of wind and sea in which you could actually sail. In the Irish Sea it's the moon driven, six hourly swell that causes problems. The tide seemed always to be against me and the huge rise and fall on its east side makes for inhospitable lee shore coasts with nowhere to go and a twelve metre tidal range. Coupled to this the constant depressions sweeping through every few days all summer meant that you had pleasant enough conditions for about one day in three. When I got decent weather I would take advantage of it by doing long passages that bypassed most of the good bits. The rest of the time I either battered into pissing rain and big swells or cowered in poor shelter in deserted harbours.

As I cowered I dreamed of other seas. I created a fantasy land in which there were no tides, no long fetches onto lee shores, no dangerous shallows and thousands of perfect island anchorages where Zoph could sit for free in perfect shelter. In my fantasy land there would be no Atlantic depressions bringing gales, but instead gentle summer breezes, reliable sunshine and warm summer seas in which we could float about at will. In short, I dreamed about a place where sailing was a pleasant leisure pursuit as opposed to a life-threatening and uncomfortable outward-bound challenge.

At home in the autumn I realised that my fantasy land actually existed. It had a name and was called 'The Baltic'. There, nobody has heard of passage planning. People just go for a sail in the sun without kitting themselves out in seventeen layers of fleeces and dry suits. There, they don't put on their serious faces and give full safety briefings to all crew before pottering out for a sail for an hour or two. Instead they leave all their footwear in the car, install their sprogs on the pulpit to get the most out of the cooling breeze, slap on some suntan cream and wander off under sail to a deserted island for a summer barbeque. By all accounts the Scottish use of the word 'baltic' simply to mean 'bloody freezing' is in fact a massive irony. I wanted to head to the Baltic for a taste of their ultra-reliable summer weather – thirty degrees Celsius every day and sea the temperature of bath water.

Plan 'A' was to head straight from Zoph's berth at Port Edgar to the sheltered waters of the Limfjord in northern Denmark. This sandy fjord has a shallow entrance which can be dodgy in onshore winds, but then provides a virtually riverine route through Denmark to the Skagerrak. Unfortunately there's the little matter of the North Sea between us and Scandinavia. This is, as I'm sure I don't have to tell you, far from being a calm and balmy duck pond and it's almost four hundred miles in a straight line from Port Ed to the entrance to the Limfjord. Though I'm happy to sail single-handed most of the time I really don't have the constitution or the temperament for a three day solo crossing of the North Sea, even in its most benign mood. Apart from anything else I am far too much of a fan of sleep to be satisfied with dozing in the cockpit and being woken by an egg timer to take a look around every ten minutes or so. At least three days of plodding across a cold North Sea in a weakened and semi-comatose state until I finally fetched up on a Danish sandbank did not appeal, so I set about looking for a crew.

Here is an odd fact about sailing in Britain. There are people who don't just laugh in your face when you offer them the tempting opportunity to be thrown around until their stomachs churn and be soaked to the skin by freezing salt water in a small plastic bucket. I sent out a few well directed emails and found two volunteers. I had been hoping for experienced, capable crew, but, as the Chegwin family have found to their cost, cheggers can't be boozers.

Living in the North Sea

The border guards waiting to pounce. Try keeping a photo of a customs ship as a way of repelling others

Gordon Campion had sailed his Moody 38, 'Equinox', from Edinburgh, round Spitsbergen, up to eighty degrees north and back. But he'd only done it once. Granted he'd also completely circumnavigated the globe in Equinox, Crossing the Pacific and returning via Pirate Alley off the coast of Somalia, but as I say I had hoped for a little more experience. The last time Simon Harrison crossed the North Sea, from the Elbe to the Forth, on that occasion aboard a Sadler 32, the mast fell down about fifty miles off Denmark. This didn't seem to phase him particularly and he was keen to have a go at a similar crossing in a smaller boat. I subsequently realised it was probably Simon's fault that the Sadler's mast fell off. He had the slightly disturbing and dangerous habit of tempting fate beyond endurance by saying stuff like 'Nothing can possibly go wrong now...' out loud. Aboard Zoph he would say such things without even touching wood and even whistled loudly at times when we already had plenty of wind. The RYA should mount a campaign against that sort of irresponsible behaviour.

So that was the crew. Both were available for the first week or so of May and both were practical engineers who could happily do things like strip engines down and put them back together at sea. The boat was as prepared as she was going to be. Most things were in reasonable working order, we had a full stock of scran, about 200 litres of diesel, 200 litres of water and 600 cans of beer aboard. This still left what I judged to be just about enough freeboard. The waterline was only a few inches above the level of the self-filling cockpit. All we needed now was a half decent forecast.

Annoyingly the North Sea is presided over by the Norse gods, who designed it to suit Vikings on raping and pillaging raids. So they gave it nice easterly winds all through the spring and early summer to blow the Vikings over to Britain. Later in the summer and in the autumn, once they had finished with the pillaging and so forth, Odin et al. obligingly provided nice westerlies to blow them back again. Though the Norsemen haven't done a lot of pillaging for a while now, the climate is still arranged in their favour, which is a pain in the arse for anyone wanting to head east in the spring and west in the autumn. It's a particular pain in the arse when, while you're waiting for your unlikely weather window, the headlines are confidently predicting 'The Coldest May for a Hundred Years'. I sat through the latter part of April watching the constant easterlies sweeping across the North Sea, blowing directly from the Limfjord to the Forth.

Only one circumstance led to anything other than easterlies all the way across the North Sea. That circumstance simply demonstrated that Thor and all his mates were just taking the piss. Sometimes the air flow turned a little to the north, giving north easterlies over the southern and western part of the North Sea and, ironically, north westerlies blowing straight into the Limfjord. All the pilot information on the entrance to this fjord is consistent. Whilst it's sheltered once you're in, you shouldn't attempt to enter it with anything over fifteen knots blowing from the north west. If we'd have headed there from Port Ed, by the time we were trying to cross the shallow bar into the fjord it would, according to xcweather.co.uk, have been blowing thirty five knots from the north west, gusting to over fifty knots. With a fetch of about 850 miles from Iceland pushing eight metre seas onto a three metre bar this would have been pretty much literal suicide, even if we could plug away on a beat for four hundred miles to get there. As May loomed closer it began to look increasingly like I wasn't going to get to Scandinavia before my selfish, inconsiderate crew were no longer available because they had, so they claimed, 'their own lives to lead'.

Faced with the prospect of remaining pinned to the east coast for months, my slow brain began to hatch another plan for getting to Scandinavia, based on the Gordon McEquinox school of weather forecasting. I had sailed with Gordon before – in northern Norway, across the Atlantic and, most recently, across Biscay, I knew he had a somewhat pedantic approach to passage planning.

Before heading anywhere Gordon downloads the most detailed, location-specific 'GRIB' files he can find for as far into the future as can reasonably be predicted without recourse to a medium. He then plans the passage in great detail and with massive certainty and states confidently exactly what the wind and sea will be doing every hour, for every mile of the route, for the next week. Four days into a passage Gordon whips out his GRIBs and pronounces that at three p.m. today, Tuesday, within a ten mile radius of this bit of the ocean, it should be blowing from the west north west at 15.3 knots, rising to 17.8 knots by half past four. If the anemometer says it's blowing from the west north west at 17.5 knots at three fifteen, there's either something wrong with the anemometer or a stiff letter of complaint to the Met Office is called for, since they've got the five day forecast wrong by over half an hour.

The astonishing thing is how well this approach seems to work, at least when you are properly offshore. With increasingly good forecast information available you no longer always have to look at the shipping forecast and say "Force seven in Forties and Dogger, so let's stay in port". Rather you have to ask "exactly when and exactly where will there be a force seven in Forties and Dogger. This year the first few days in May promised an easterly force four or five, going north easterly or northerly and up to force six or seven. But the strongest stuff was due to start near the Danish coast at round about the latitude of Edinburgh. Further south it was due to go round to the north and reach no more than twenty, or perhaps twenty five knots for a few days. This should be a good breeze to propel us south east down the bleak, shelterless coast of England, then across to Holland. If we spent thirty six hours or so tracking down the coast, we could get an updated forecast and decide whether to nip into somewhere grotesque like Hull, or turn further east to the Netherlands. A strong north easterly would, on the other hand, not give us a lot of options for nipping into ports along the shallow east coast.

I persuaded the crew that a trip to the Netherlands was preferable to a visit to Denmark and that the ironically named 'Easyjet' from Amsterdam was, if anything, a step up from Ryan Air from a field a hundred miles from Copenhagen. We agreed on a departure from Port Ed on the evening of May the first. This would mean battering against a bit of an easterly out of the Forth, but should get us to somewhere in Holland before any serious deterioration in the weather. The night before we left there was a near mutiny on the part of Gordon, who seemed to think that a family dinner and piss-up was preferable to battering through the night down a freezing estuary and that we could wait until the following morning. Having steeled myself for the trip I was reluctant to see the weather window slipping away and successfully shamed him into the evening departure.

So we waited on the fuel berth at Port Ed for my other half, Anna, and various hangers-on to turn up and send us on our way. At seven p.m. on May the first we slipped the lines, motored out into the Forth, raised a double-reefed main and battered under motor through the bridges. Two Hunter 707s belonging to Port Edgar Yacht Club were mucking about, sailing around the cans off South Queensferry with a couple of deep reefs in. I little realised how significant this sighting was and that I wouldn't see another British based boat of any sort until I arrived in Helsinki, sixty days and over sixteen hundred miles later.

The Dutch are obsessed with traditional boats

...Which fill the Ijsselmeer

Ice Cream or Road Cone?

I nervously wondered, as we pushed along due east at two and a half knots against the steep, easterly chop, whether Gordon might have had a point about waiting until the morning. But as we passed the small, sheltering Island of Inchmickery and bore away to motorsail on starboard tack, Zoph speeded up a little and we began to make a bit more respectable progress. Whatever the forecasts said about north easterlies, there was no way the wind was deviating at all from a straight east-west line as it blew up the Firth of Forth. At twenty degrees off the wind we weren't battering so directly against the waves, but even so, each steep two metre hill dumped a good few gallons of near-freezing brown estuary on us. The ancient top-loading charcoal stove enjoyed the stiff twenty five knot apparent breeze though and roared away. I had often wondered what sort of idiot would design a top loading fire, as the boat filled with thick smoke and black charcoal dust. But this time I didn't care. It was providing some much needed warmth and dryth, without which we would have become thoroughly miserable. Or rather, even more thoroughly miserable.

The crew were grateful enough for the warmth not to ask the usual incredulous questions about how you can have a solid fuel fire on a plastic boat. This question is usually asked by people with open fires in houses constructed primarily of wood. There was steak and tatties, precariously balanced on knees, for dinner, as Zoph bucked up and down on the short sea. A change to port tack as we passed Inchkeith island, then we settled down into a two hour watch system and Zoph plodded through the night at between three and four knots. I didn't do a great deal of tacking on this cruise. That shift to port tack lasted something over a week.

The fact that we were on port tack all the way turned out to be a happy accident. Zoph has only three berths – port and starboard saloon berths and a starboard pilot berth. Though the saloon berths have reasonable lee cloths it would have been extremely uncomfortable trying to kip on a port berth as your arse was constantly thrown sideways onto a straining lee cloth. Both starboard berths provided secure wedging spaces in which to jam yourself against the largest of the waves. There was the slight problem that each crashing wave sent a thin dribble of water under the sprayhood, across the main hatch and straight down your neck as you lay wedged into the pilot berth. But that was a minor inconvenience which it would have been churlish to complain about.

I was still nervous about whether I'd made the right decision in leaving when we did. I really didn't want to have to batter against wind and sea all the way to Holland. But when I went back on watch at six a.m. the motion was easier as the wind backed slightly to the north and we turned slightly to the south. In another hour we were on a fine reach. The jib and staysail went up, the engine was turned off and Zoph ploughed south east at over five knots.

As forecast the wind slowly increased during the day, but it backed a little further and we turned a little further south so that we bowled along reasonably comfortably in the three metre swell. It was still a fairly fine reach and the operation of cooking food or making coffee involved bearing away onto a near run so that the chef could put stuff in cups or bowls, as opposed to plastering the ceiling with it. For the purpose of changing course downwind I had rigged a permanent gybe preventer for the boom. This arrangement stays rigged most of the time when Zoph is cruising. Not only does it prevent people getting their heads stove in by gybes, but it stops the annoying effect of the boom thrashing about in a sloppy sea.

All changes in course on this passages were carried out by means of a few twiddles of Leo's knob. Leo was the fourth member of crew on board, the wind vane steering. His is the name that the human helm cries out when coming about. Having steered across the Atlantic on Gordon's boat 'Equinox' solely by means of her 'Hydrovane' wind vane steering, I was nervous of Leo's abilities on such a crossing. Being based on trim-tab steering attached to the transom hung rudder, Leo is a somewhat puny helmsman who's slow and lazy when it comes to correcting a course. In fluky, gusty breezes he's all over the place frankly, and even in a steady wind out at sea he tends to steer a course that wanders through about fifty degrees around where you actually want to be going. If you are having a wee sail near the shore and aiming at a bit of land this trait seems intolerably inaccurate as you see the boat snaking eccentrically about. But properly out at sea, with nothing to hit and nothing to aim at on the horizon, it scarcely seems to matter. This time Leo did a sterling job of steering us 375 miles across the North Sea. He was an absolute necessity on the passage, as the only crew member who could take the helm for more than a couple of minutes without his hands dropping off from frostbite. In short it was a bloody freezing and sodding sodden passage and having your well gloved hands thrust deep into warm pockets was a bare minimum for digit survival.

Though we had intended to track further down the coast, we didn't want to be headed when we did turn for Holland by having to head too far to the east. At around midday on May the second we were close enough to the coast to get a new forecast off the interweb. Little seemed to have changed, but the promised stronger winds for two days time seemed to be dropping a little. The forecast was looking OK for the Netherlands. A few quick phone calls home to explain the change of plan then we set a new course of 130 degrees for Den Helder. We twiddled with Leo's knob and sailed off on a snaking reach out towards the middle of the North Sea. We would not have been so relaxed and complacent had we known that, at seven thirty that evening, a major maritime disaster awaited us.

In an effort to cut down the likelihood of a mutiny on the passage I had taken the precaution of preparing three evenings worth of frozen meals. These sumptuous feasts were theoretically thawing in the fridge, which was at about ambient temperature – that is only marginally above absolute zero. Global warming and the retreat of the polar ice sheet are happening at a much faster rate than was the thawing of the rather fine chicken curry I had earmarked for the night's repast. So I bunged the frozen lump in a pan on the lit stove and poked at it with a stick for an hour or so until it began to thaw. The freezing process seemed to have done something very strange to it. All the lumps of chicken appeared to have vanished, leaving instead a thin, bland, fatty soup without a hint of spice. After some thought I realised that the reason for this phenomenon was that the chicken curry was still in the freezer at home. Tonight's dinner was in fact some stock left over from the goose we had last Christmas. Not having any dinner was, as I'm sure you'll agree, a maritime disaster of major proportions. There was much muttering from the mutinous Mad Jack Harrison and Redbeard Campion. I had visions of being cast adrift in the liferaft somewhere off the Dogger Bank with little chance of happening upon an exotic desert island. The Isle of Dogs perhaps.

We sailed on all night and into the next morning on a reach under reefed main and a jib with a couple of rolls in it. The breeze went a bit further to the north but stayed between eighteen and twenty five knots. A drawback of using chartplotters for navigation, especially small, cheap ones like mine, is that you have to zoom in to a ridiculously large scale before you see the detail. A spot of zooming and scrolling forward along our track revealed that we were heading straight for the shallowest bits of the Dogger Bank. These aren't shallow by some standards. A Dutch sailor used to sailing in puddles would feel most uneasy in the vertiginous depths of, in places, as little as sixteen metres. But with a three metre swell from the north pushing us down onto the shallowest bits and creating, in effect, a lee shore, I wasn't sure whether the sea might get a bit nasty. Given its size the North Sea is surprisingly shallow in places and it's worth remembering that people used to walk across the bloody thing only a very few thousand years ago.

So we freed off a bit and twiddled Leo's knob to change course and skirt round the south of the shallow bits. A few hours later, after a kip, I came on deck to find us hardened up again onto a finer reach. This was not caused, unfortunately, by a wind shift, but by a misunderstanding about where the bloody Dogger Bank was and, again, the stupid chartplotter not showing depths unless it was zoomed right in. We had changed course to pass up a channel in the middle of the Dogger Bank which would lead us straight to its shallowest part and not, as Simon thought, right round the north of it. Unless we motored north or retraced our steps it was a fait accompli. I was reminded of a passage aboard Equinox from mainland Portugal to Madeira. We were sailing on a fine reach in a force seven through five to six metre waves across an ocean whose depth varied between four thousand and five thousand metres. After a couple of days of this I noticed a spot depth on the chart, dead ahead, of forty metres. At first I thought it was an error and that there were a couple of missing zeros. But no, huge undersea mountains rise up in that area from sixteen thousand feet down to only just below the surface. Aware of what can happen to the sea on the edge of continental shelves, I had asked Gordon whether he thought we were likely to encounter huge foaming, breaking seas which would swamp the boat and send us to a watery grave. "We'll soon find out" he had replied, far too casually for my liking.

In both cases my fears proved groundless and on the Dogger Bank the breeze dropped slowly through the day. Reefs were shaken out and the engine was occasionally called upon to keep our speed up. South of Dogger we passed a couple of oil production platforms with attendant supply ships. Except for a single lobster pot on the Dogger Bank, forty eight hours into the passage these were the first vessels – and indeed signs that the human race still existed – we had seen since leaving the Forth.

Overnight the breeze both dropped and backed further and the sea state calmed down. We motorsailed on, with a force three abaft the beam, carrying on with a watch pattern which we had fallen into and was becoming natural. As I finished my watch and wedged myself into the corner of a bunk it struck me how surreally easily you fall into such habits. On deck we were in the middle of the grey, cold, uninviting North Sea in a twenty seven foot plastic bucket for which I was solely responsible. When I came off watch I had no more responsibilities and could retreat to an environment which felt snug and safe. The plastic bucket in the North Sea seemed far away and irrelevant.

By the morning we were pushing across the Traffic Separation Schemes and wondering why all the massive ships weren't appearing in the knackered AIS and why we'd not heard anything on the radio for nearly three days. Meanwhile a chorus of our snoring, farting and swearing echoed around the bridges of half the shipping in northern Europe. We were more or less through the shipping lanes by the time we were buzzed by the peeved coastguard plane and we pressed on towards Den Helder after this mortifying incident.

A few miles from the minor, northern entrance to Den Helder It came as no surprise at all when, just as I'd succeeded in getting the AIS to work again, a large coastguard ship hove into view over the horizon and appeared to be shadowing us. Clearly they intended to make us suffer for the VHF debacle. The ship passed us a couple of times and then appeared to be motoring off when Simon condemned us with his 'nothing can possibly go wrong' curse. "No, they've definitely lost interest in us now" he said. In a flash the coastguard launched a rib and three jack-booted, black clad border officials sped towards us. The rib bumped hard into Zoph's side as the helm vigorously evaded my attempts to introduce fenders between us and four of the jackboots clattered aboard.

It is an odd fact that, in most countries, it's only the police and the border guards who wear matt black wet gear and big black boots. All advice from the professionals is that you should wear bright, reflective gear. This applies even if you only sail about in the summer sun on a flat sea in nothing more than a force three. The border guards, on the other hand, presumably have to board large ships – the crews of which may be trying to avoid being boarded – in the middle of winter nights in big seas and near gales. As a safety precaution they all wear matt black so that, should they fall in, they will definitely drown because nobody will be able to see them. The only logical explanation for this is that they think they look cooler – and more threatening – in black. Boys like to play their 'Men in Black' games.

Anyway, these two weren't nearly as nasty as they might have been, given our VHF cockup. Even as the coastguard ship had been shadowing us it had struck me that, since we were motorsailing we should, theoretically, be showing a motoring cone. I had heard rumours that the Germen at least – and therefore possibly the Dutch – were sticklers for its use. I believed that I did have one of these devices, which nobody in Scotland ever, ever uses, aboard. I thought I could probably, given a bit of disruption, lay a hand on it. The only problem was that I couldn't for the life of me remember which way up the bloody thing went. Neither Simon nor Gordon knew, so I sent Anna a quick text asking her to Google the answer. She soon texted back… "Upside down". What in the hell was I supposed to make of that? Which way up is upside down you moron? Is it an upside down road cone or an upside down ice cream cone? I was none the wiser. But I had a strategy for avoiding my embarrassment. Sure enough, the more junior of the two rozzers, sitting in the cockpit and looking for something official to do, said "shouldn't you have a motoring cone?" By dint of removing from a cockpit locker the liferaft, five fenders and sixty litres of spare fuel cans I finally found the two black plywood triangles, slotted them together and asked Gordon to go forward and raise them on the staysail halyard. This done I waited for the lad to exclaim that it was the wrong way up. Had he done so my plan was to pretend not to have noticed, then to berate Gordon for his stupidity in not knowing which way up it went. Happily however, by sheer chance, it was the right way up. Should you not already know, which I'm sure you do, the right way up is with the pointy end pointing down.

After a modicum of form-filling most of the jackboots returned to the rib, leaving some of their black soles smeared indelibly on the deck. As a parting shot they pointed out that the northern entrance to Den Helder, towards which we were being carried nicely by the tide, was now unmarked and silted and not to be recommended. So we changed course towards the southern entrance. We could by now see Den Helder quite clearly only a very few miles away, but now we had to motor for mile after mile after mile against a three knot current to clear the long sandy spit that stretched way down along the coast. It took us about an extra three hours to get into port. In the great scheme of things and in the context of a long passage this doesn't seem much, but the last bits of passages, when you can see your destination for hours and hours but never seem to get any closer, can seem to take a lifetime.

We finally rounded the annoying spit and took the last of the tide up to the harbour at Den Helder. We picked up a pontoon in the marina at just after six p.m. local time, just over seventy hours and 376 miles after leaving Port Edgar. After briefly congratulating ourselves on a successful passage we hurriedly carried out essential maintenance tasks in the following order: Plug in leccy, switch on fan heater, beer, close all hatches, beer, plug in another fan heater, beer, beer, beer, very hot showers, beer, beer, food, beer, sleep. Oh, and between beers six and seven I erected Zoph's slightly ridiculous cockpit tent. This windowless edifice rises high above the cabin and has something of the look of a medieval jousting pavilion, though it's not actually stripy or large enough to conceal a knight on a white charger. But it was big enough to hang a huge mass of sodden clothing. Sealed in against the continuing cold, with the warming effect of showers, three kilowatts of electric heat, the ever trusty smoky charcoal stove and alcohol, the inevitable happened and we all began to think "well that wasn't so bad, was it?

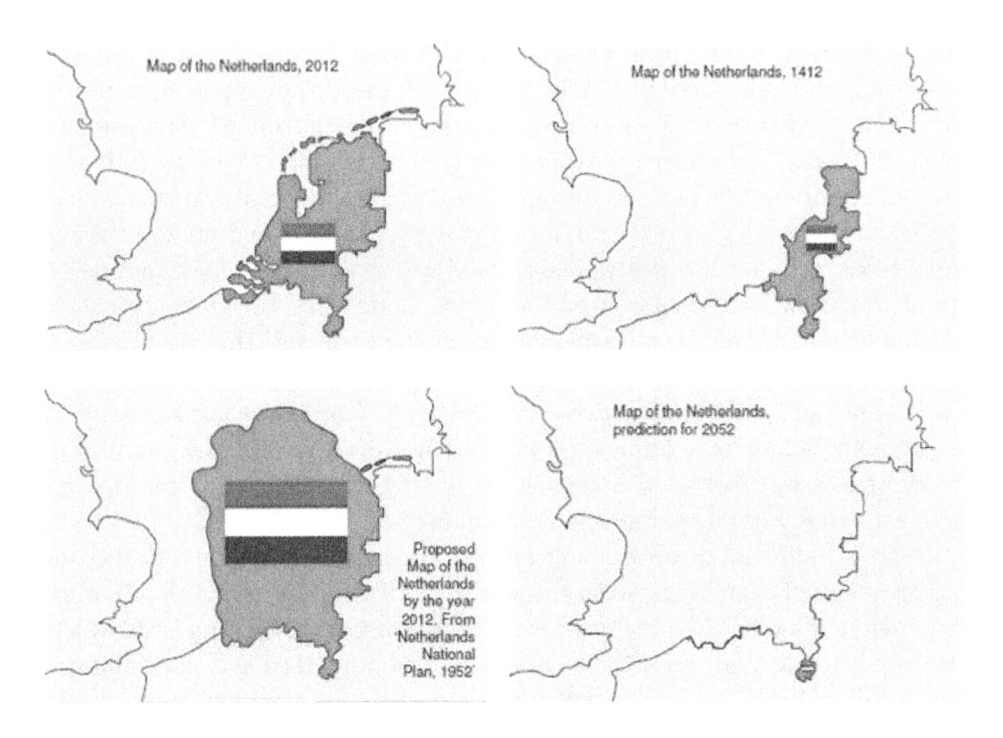

Map of the Netherlands, 2012

Map of the Netherlands, 1412

Proposed Map of the Netherlands by the year 2012. From 'Netherlands National Plan, 1952'

Map of the Netherlands, prediction for 2052

Designer Holes

Perhaps it hadn't been the most relaxed, pleasant and balmy passage, but Zoph had given us no cause for concern. It had been a reasonably well organised trip – albeit with a few glaring omissions in the planning process. Zoph's previous three North Sea crossings had been considerably shorter and had taken advantage of much more benign weather. In the past we had scuttled across the sea in a lull like a startled rabbit crossing a road. This had been Zoph's most grown up, proper, mature longer passage to date. It's a reasonably long passage for a twenty seven footer and I was interested in what Gordon, with his experience of proper ocean crossings aboard a thirty eight footer – and even an Atlantic crossing on a professionally crewed, brand new, eighty foot luxury cruising catamaran – had thought about it. Gratifyingly he thought Zoph had handled it really well. Like a proper cruiser and a much larger boat.

Unfortunately, his impressions were probably somewhat influenced by our most recent previous passage, across Biscay on the forty foot RoNautica 'Grand Slam'. In April 2012 Gordon Equinox, another sailor from Port Edgar and I had delivered Grand Slam from southern Portugal to Cardiff in a series of stages. After an easy passage up the west coast of Portugal and a couple of more disastrous attempts to round Finisterre, characterised by repeated engine failure and ropes round the prop, we set off to cross Biscay.

The forty foot RoNautica is billed as a cruiser-racer and Grand Slam is kitted out for extended cruising. In a force six and with four metre waves on the port bow the slamming of the flimsy flat-bottomed hull had us skittering and falling about all over the dance-floor-like cockpit. For five days the steering was all by autopilot, since the helming position, right aft, with your arse hanging out over the ocean and the wind and spray threatening to sweep you overboard, was more or less untenable. But these design flaws paled into insignificance beside the huge great hole that the designer – deliberately – had made in the front of the boat.

With her fine, low, vertical, racing bow, Grand Slam buried her front deep in every wave as we headed north on a fine reach. Because she is designed to race round the cans on a flat sea the genoa furler had been placed below deck, in the anchor locker. Apparently, having the jib set low across the deck might give her a 0.001 knot speed advantage in certain conditions. But it also left a large, permanent, unsealable hole through the deck, right in the bow. The hole to let water in was probably about eight or nine inches in diameter. The anchor locker probably had a capacity of about two hundred and fifty litres. By the time we'd gone through the second wave it was almost certainly completely full, with about a quarter of a tonne of sea. The anchor locker had a drain, of course. This hole was probably a bit less than half an inch in diameter. The 'IN' hole was therefore about 250 times the size of the 'OUT' hole. The yacht designers amongst you might have spotted a tiny flaw in this design. In fact anyone who is not in a coma can probably spot the problem.

So we ploughed on with the bow weighed down by a permanent quarter of a tonne of extra weight right at the front. Now factor in the influence of the consummate marine maintenance professionals based on the Forth in Port Edgar. One of these dedicated craftsmen, several years before, had been charged with installing a navigation light in the bow. He had facilitated this by drilling a dirty great hole halfway up the starboard side of the bulkhead between the anchor locker and the fore cabin. On port tack this hole, which was impossible to get at whilst at sea, was probably a couple of feet below the level of the water in the anchor locker. There was a permanent spout of water the size of a bath tap with a two foot head flooding the boat.

About three hours out from La Coruna this minor design flaw became apparent, since the boat was rapidly filling up with water, via Gordon's bunk in the forepeak. A few minutes of panic then a bucket chain ensued. Some thought was given to the possibility of giving up and returning to La Coruna, as opposed to continuing with a four day passage across Biscay in a seriously leaky boat. But with the wind backing we were able to bear away a little and as long as we didn't get too many splashes over the bow or go too hard to windward it seemed to be possible to stem the flow. In the end we somewhat reluctantly decided to continue.

Plenty of other design flaws made themselves apparent by rendering life damp and uncomfortable on that trip, along with others which might have had serious consequences. The boom falling off was just one. But the one that got me was the unsealable hole deliberately moulded into the front. It struck me that the designer was faced with a choice. He could design the genoa system so that it gave a 0.001 knot speed advantage in certain conditions on a flat sea. Or he could design it so that the boat didn't sink. I decided that I didn't, ever, want a boat designed by the bloke who thought that the 0.001 knots was more important than the boat not sinking.

The Vancouver 27 is of course the obverse of the lightweight racer. Often it's frustrating to plod about more slowly that other boats on a wee sail in gentle conditions on a summer Sunday. Sometimes I wish Zophiel was a bit closer winded. Sometimes it might be nice to plane about under spinnaker. But on that passage from Port Ed to Den Helder it would be hard to imagine a twenty seven foot boat that could have handled it better. Except perhaps a Vancouver 27 with a different skipper.

We hung about in Den Helder that evening and the next morning, marvelling at the fantastic facilities thrown in with the cheap berthing fees. The luxurious showers, the friendly staff and the fine, perfectly sheltered pontoons were something of a contrast to the dangerously exposed, ramshackle staging and communal, superannuated school changing rooms of Port Edgar. Unusually, we were again visited by border officials. This time they wandered out of an office and casually asked if we'd already been done by the Customs. We explained that we had. They asked which ship had stopped us and I fished about on my camera and showed them a photo I'd taken of it, which seemed to satisfy them. This might be a handy tip for any would be drug smugglers or human traffickers out there. When stopped by Customs tell them you've already been searched. Keep a photo of a likely looking coastguard vessel about your person and if they appear to doubt your word just show them the photo. I've sent two groups of inquisitive customs men off by this method.

Gordon and Simon had a couple of days before their flight home so in the afternoon we caught the rising tide and sailed under jib up to Den Oever, where there is a lock through the huge sea wall into the Ijsselmeer. At times we hit eight and a half knots over the bottom as the tide swept us to the lock with about six other boats. As usual it was somewhat disconcerting to feel the lock drop us down instead of up, from sea level approaching high tide to the lower, inland, freshwater lake.

The Netherlands is a product of concerted engineering effort. The natural coast of the country is something of a moveable feast and huge areas have been reclaimed – or in fact just 'claimed' – from the sea over the centuries. Why do we refer to bits of sea that we drain and turn into farmland as being 'reclaimed' when, as far as we know, it has always been sea? The modern map of the country looks very different to that of a few hundred years ago. Plans to claim more and more land from the sea seem to have been curtailed in the latter part of the twentieth century, as first a greater ecological awareness and then global warming have come to the fore. The original plan was to reclaim the whole of the Zuiderzee – what is now the Ijsselmeer and Markermeer – as farmland. The future shape of the country would seem to depend on who wins, global warming or Dutch engineering.

Bloody Students

The last time I'd crossed this lock was one Easter in the early 1990s. I had been taking a coach load of about fifty quantity surveying students, mostly from places like Elgin and Peterhead, to see the sophisticated civil engineering works. It had been a hell of a trip. The bloody students were an entirely desocialised set of lager louts and I had got virtually no sleep for several days. On the ferry from Hull they had managed to annoy and scandalise most of the other passengers. Several of them had been locked up by security, requiring me to free them at about four in the morning. One had had his passport stolen by a prostitute. Every night I was on call to pacify hotel managers and the local police until about four a.m.. When I finally did get to sleep the foreign student contingent – Malaysian and Hong Kong folk who had the good sense to be in bed by ten – were getting up and knocking on my door at five a.m. asking about breakfast.

The coach deposited the students on the windswept new Ijsselmeer barrage and a friendly engineer led us down below the roads into the tunnels at the heart of the massive concrete structure. We walked for what seemed like hours down a dank, dripping tunnel that stretched as far as the eye could see ahead and behind us. Our feet echoed along this surreal, alien Dr. Who set of a tunnel. This was of course before the age of the mobile phone, so when a phone rang, also echoing along the corridor, it came as something of a surprise. How could there be a phone in this uninhabitable concrete wasteland? The engineer kept walking for a hundred yards or so then went to an almost hidden panel on one damp wall. He plucked out an old fashioned phone receiver of the same type as Zoph's VHF set. My colleague, standing behind me and aware of the sheer volume of problems which can be generated by a group of students joked "It'll probably be for you". We laughed. The engineer said "Dr. Edge, it's for you". Even in the middle of the dank, dripping, uninhabitable tunnels, deep underground, in the middle of a windswept dam, in the middle of nowhere, with ostensibly no means of communication, the bastards had found me. And yes, it was a lost student.

This time I was glad to be sailing out of the lock instead of driving down the dam. There was a fresh eighteen to twenty knot breeze on the Ijsselmeer and we reached south under jib at five to six knots. We picked up a berth between wooden piles in one of the four large marinas in the town of Medemblik. It was the first time I'd been on a pile mooring for about five years so I was pleased not to have made a complete arse of it. Gordon and Simon were once again amazed at the scale and quality of the facilities for yachts in a small Dutch town. It was too early in the season for anyone to bother charging us for berthing. Well there gusting up to. If we were still in the Forth this would have been my last chance to get to Denmark. After that my crew would no longer have been available. It was taking me a long time to get to Scandinavia, but I reckoned that, by getting across the North Sea anywhere, I'd done as well as could be expected from that crewed leg of my journey.

First Clogging

My plan for getting to Denmark by the long route via Holland didn't, by the way, involve battering further eastwards through the North Sea, getting all cold and wet again. Zoph was becoming a canal boat now. I was heading through the Netherlands along what the Dutch call the Staande Mastroute and what they would, if they could speak their own language, call the Staandemast Route. Obviously it is the mast that is standing, not the route that is masting. Get your language sorted out, Dutchsters!

In Britain we seem to have the idea that there is something extraordinary about Amsterdam. We think of it as Canal Central and find it entirely remarkable that it has a few aesthetically pleasing canals and houseboats. If anything, in a Dutch context, Hamsterjam is remarkable for its lack of canals. The entire country is in fact riddled with waterways of all sorts. Since most of it is below sea level you could look at it the other way round and say that the entire sea is filled with low islands with narrow channels between them. Unfortunately a lot of the millions of channels have quite low bridges across them, but there is one route by which a boat with a mast can travel from one end of the Netherlands to the other. From Lemmer I headed north east on the Frisian part of that route.

And it was Frisian too, let me tell you. Bloody Frisian. The predictions of the coldest May for a hundred years still seemed to be spot on. As I waited for the lifting bridges to let me out of Lemmer and motored slowly through them I experienced the year's first clogging. The fantastically complex. Intricate and expensively maintained Dutch canal system is more or less free to use. You can nip into the inland waterways and travel the length and breadth of the Netherlands without anyone asking you for paperwork or money or insurance documents or evidence of your competence to drive a boat. Which is a relief. The only exception to this is the cloggings. As you approach the first bridge in various small Dutch towns there is sometimes a toll to pay. Usually the toll is a one-off payment that covers you for passage through all the lifting bridges in that town. It might cost you between two and five Euros to get through the two to ten bridges. Since you'd be unlucky to come across more than one of these toll points per day it's a pretty good deal.

Cheap though it may be we all resent paying money for anything, but the Dutch canal tolls are such a clichéd, cultural self-parody that I actually look forward to being charged. The bloke operating one of the bridges is responsible for collecting the toll and he does so, inevitably and always, using a wooden clog. A perfect, miniaturised wooden clog – presumably manufactured for the purpose – is suspended from the end of a makeshift fishing rod. As you pass through the bridge he releases this footwear at the end of the rod and swings it out into the middle of the canal. You have to grab it and bung the right change into the clog. If you've not got the right money the shoe swings out across the canal again with your change in it. It's a wholly remarkable, efficient system and presumably demonstrates that the Dutch don't mind playing up to their stereotypes. It's the equivalent of paying the old Forth Bridge toll by flinging money into a gaping kilt, or paying your bus fare by introducing the right change into the end of a set of bagpipes.

I paid the Lemmer clogging – or the Lemming, as it isn't known – and was on my way. I unfurled the jib as I emerged from the canal onto the first of a series of shallow, marshy lakes. In high summer these lakes would be hooching with boats of all sorts, but on a cold, damp, windy Tuesday in May I didn't have a lot of company. As I passed the town of Grouw, which seemed to have grouwn since I was last there, I negotiated what amounted to a five junction canal roundabout. Here the signage to the Staande Mastroute was a little ambiguous But for once I had detailed paper charts. I was using my book of charts of the area which I bought in 2007 and which shows the route and everything on it in some detail. I pressed on. A couple of hours and a few bridges later I arrived at another major road bridge. The lights were red so I hovered about, staying within a hundred metres or so of the bridge. I waited. Nothing happened. I moved closer to the bridge to make sure I was in line of sight of the CCTV camera. Most of these bridges are now operated remotely by a bloke stationed at one bridge and generally speaking, if they are awake and it's not a railway bridge with a fixed schedule, they open for you within a couple of minutes. But this time nothing happened. I waited for about half an hour, but still nothing happened.

There was a large, commercial, cargo carrying barge moored to the bank nearby – yes, such things still exist in mainland Europe – and a bloke on deck seemed to be trying to attract my attention. I motored over for a chat. He told me that this bridge would never open and that the Staande Mastroute had now been moved. I had taken a wrong turn about two hours ago in Grouw. This, of course, is the downside of a country filled with a complex canal system. It's pretty difficult to get lost on the Crinan Canal but by no means impossible in Holland. I was not to despair however. There was a shortcut just a couple of miles back. A small back-lane canal with a couple of opening bridges. Thanking him I plodded back down the road.

The wee side turning led to an unmanned bascule bridge at the edge of the world's tweest village, with a phone number and some instructions in double Dutch on a sign. I phoned the number and got the only bloke in the Netherlands who doesn't speak English at least as well as a Glaswegian, if not better. But he seemed to get the idea and soon an old manny tottered into view on a bicycle and opened the bridge. I motored down a narrower and narrower, tree lined canal into the heart of a picture on a biscuit tin. The tweenery was extraordinary. Another bridge appeared and this time, even though we were in perfect shelter, the channel was too narrow just to hold position in the middle. My first attempt to tie to the bank was thwarted by an overhanging tree growing in the middle of the local traditional wooden boat museum. Having extricated the rigging from the branches I tied up a yard or two away, on the other side, in front of a rather appealing looking, but closed, restaurant. I promised myself that if I ever came back this way I'd tie the boat to the side of this restaurant and have a meal sitting some eight feet away from the boat.

Unfortunately the exertion of pressing the button to open the last bridge had proved too much for the old manny, who was now on his lunch break. There was no question, of course, of just pressing another button for the only boat likely to appear today and having his lunch a minute later. Lunch was lunch and it took an hour. It was an extremely pleasant place to wander around however and an hour later we were on our way. At the end of the shortcut it became clear why they had moved the route. To avoid having to open a bridge and disrupt a major road they had dug a tunnel several miles further west. Now the main road went underneath the canal, which bore no relation to the one on my five year old chart. There were several new channels and a whole new suburb of 'Grand Designs' modern houses, each with a forty foot yacht in its own personal harbour. Civil engineering is something that the Dutch seem almost addicted to and new canals, roads, towns, islands and lakes appear all the time all over the place. I suspect somebody in Holland had carnal relations with a beaver a few centuries ago and they are just genetically predisposed to building stuff and altering the landscape. It's just an instinctive reaction they have no control over.

Back on the proper route I motored rapidly onwards, concerned to try and get somewhere decent to moor before the bridge mannies clocked off for the night. This endeavour was thwarted at one railway bridge. This the manny failed to open in any of the interminable gaps between trains for about an hour. I arrived on the outskirts of the town of Leeuwarden just in time to be too late for the bridges. Damn. I was stuck outside the first bridge to the town, between an industrial estate and a field of sheep. I found a bit of grassy bank to tie to next to a factory. The only dwelling in sight was a houseboat with an extraordinarily woofy, mentally disturbed Alsatian aboard. Great. It was still bloody freezing and had started raining. This was the first night since the middle of the North Sea when I'd not been able to plug into a handy leccy supply. I lit the charcoal stove and made the best of it.

Later I cycled into the town aboard my folding bike, Bertie the Brompton. Leeuwarden. Have you ever heard of it? I hadn't. It must be a nondescript wee market town. In fact it's the capital city of the region of Friesland. The historic centre is as canal ridden and chocolate-box as you'd expect, but it's also big. It even has – get this – a hill in the middle. It must be a good ten feet high. Some of the buildings must actually be above sea level! Beyond the historic centre lie shopping streets and a civic square in which they are building a massive new museum. The Friesland Museum is a modernist construction that towers about eight storeys high. It makes the museum of Scotland look like a wee corner shop. Beyond this the massive skyscrapers of the business district rise thirty storeys high and house head offices of various household name companies. The tallest is apparently 380 feet high. The whole town was busy and prosperous and had all the trappings of a capital city. Yet it's the capital of what amounts to a county that you probably couldn't place on a map and I suspect I'm not alone in never having heard of it.

All summer I was to see more and more evidence of how backward, depressed and scruffy everywhere in Britain is compared to elsewhere in northern Europe. I don't wish to depress you but we are careering downhill and will soon flash past a load of countries that we used to call 'developing' a very few years ago, which are on their way up.

Tied to a restaurant at Wartena. I must go back there for a meal some day

My musings on the subject of Leeuwarden and international development were interrupted by the onset of some of the heaviest rain I have ever experienced. In a trice I was soaked to the skin as I pedalled furiously back to where I thought Zoph was. Continuing the day's theme of getting lost on canals I had cycled off on the wrong radial route from the town centre. Swearing a lot I cycled back and tried again. Wrong again. For about an hour I frantically cycled up and down the wrong canals in the freezing, pissing rain. Finally I hit upon the right one by accident and the cabin steamed dramatically all night as the charcoal stove worked hard to dry out all my clothes.

Models on Bikes

The next morning I paid a clogging and motored through the leafy, parkland centre of Leeuwarden, muttering darkly at the few boats moored in the pleasant surroundings where I should have been last night. After the night's excesses of damp the sun was out for a change and I had a pleasant motor up still more pleasant suburban and rural canals. As the landscape opened out so did the jib and I sailed and motorsailed throughout the day. It remains a normal pursuit to sail up even quite narrow canals in the Netherlands, though you are often supposed to keep the engine ticking over on standby. I arrived at the village of Burdaard just in time for the clogging bloke to go off for lunch, so had to wait for an hour again. But it was scarcely an imposition as I had my own lunch and wandered around the predictably lovely village.

A motor boat full of Germen was also waiting. I had been quite impressed by a lot of the Dutch motor cruisers. They were seaworthy looking steel boats with deep hulls, proper decks with handrails and gleaming, mostly dark blue paintwork on their hulls. They varied in size but were often quite palatial. They looked like they could confidently be taken out to sea and cross at least the English Channel, if not the North Sea. It had taken me a while to realise, incredulously, that these posh gentlemen's motor yachts were all charter boats. Nearly all the crews were Germen and they were available for hire at about the same rate as the scuffed, dented, knackered, ugly plastic bumper-boats that ply their way up and down the Caley Canal, banging into people's yachts with their dirty great black rubber bumpers fixed all round. The Dutch definitely have a more civilised approach to canal boating

I passed through the fortified market town of Dokkum. I took a mental note of another perfect mooring on the main street. On the Lauwermeer the engine went off for a while and I had a pleasant, gentle sail. I stopped for the night in Zoutcamp in a more or less random two hundred boat marina. It was a slightly scruffy and worn one but nonetheless pleasant. The Lauwermeer was, after all, a stretch of water half a mile across, so it stood to reason that there would be at least ten large marinas around it. Zoutcamp had a couple of pubs and the inevitable traditional boat museum. Strangely, so far from the sea, it was home to a large number of trawlers. Some were local boats whilst others were from far flung parts of the North Sea coast and in one of the canal side yards for maintenance. It was a surreal sight in this inland, rural farming village.

At Zoutcamp the next day I passed through a massive sea wall and a large lock complex. But the lock and the wall were redundant, the water level the same both sides and the sea now some five or six miles away. In the blowy, gusty, cold conditions I saw no other boats on the move at all for the first three hours as I motored on, in wind gusting up to nearly thirty knots. It was an annoyingly tortuous route, down a canal which followed the course of what had been a meandering river. Negotiating one bend Zoph turned through fully 270 degrees, so the wind seemed to be coming from all over the place. Birds of prey soared over the flat fields on either side. The lack of traffic meant that one bridge manny had presumably nodded off, as I had to call up on the VHF to get a bridge to open. After the first one he was on the ball however and opened them on my approach so that I scarcely had to slow down.

I entered a large lock a few miles before Groningen and my rather lax tying on technique was found wanting. Expecting the usual two inch rise or fall I was taken by surprise by the water level rising four or five feet. Almost like a proper lock. Groningen must actually be on a bit of real land, above sea level. The ability of trees and buildings to ameliorate the wind is amazing and as I passed from the wild, woolly, freezing countryside into the calm, windless, sunny, warm town I felt a bit overdressed in my full wet gear, woolly hat and multiple fleeces. The route through the town passes myriad houseboats and traditional barges lining the canals and rafted on one another. After this pictureskew tour of the town I tied up for the night to a short pontoon in the municipal visitors' marina near the centre. I was in the company of only a few motor boats. The summer rush had definitely not started yet.

Grand design barges in Groningen

I wandered round the town. The long-suffering burghers who live in the centre of Groningen seem to have to put up with an extraordinary amount of noise. Last time I was there a full scale rock festival was in progress. This time there was a superabundance of fairs and street entertainment, engaged in an insane competition to see which could be the loudest. This imposition is compensated for by the local university's rather dubious student recruitment policy. Groningen is very much a student town. But the university seems only to accept female students who look like fashion models. Since it's a Dutch town of course they all travel about on bicycles. So the whole town seems to be populated almost entirely by models on bikes. I'm not sure what the rationale is for this policy, whether such discrimination is legal or whether this feature is highlighted in the tourist brochures, but it's not an unpleasant look for a city.

A further, though less glamorous oddity was the floating basement bogs. We are quite used to being below sea level aboard boats, but there's something different about a floating building. If you step into a glorified portacabin on a low floating platform it seems somehow fundamentally wrong that it should have a basement. As wrong as a dugong in a thong, as the old saying doesn't go.

I was made to feel more at home by the posters displayed in a lot of the shop windows saying, in English, "No Trams!" In Edinburgh, of course, we have no trams either. A strong evocation of what now seems like the distant past is the smoking in pubs. I was surprised to see this as I thought the smoking bans were now Europe-wide. But not in Holland it seems. There, everybody continues to light up wherever they please. It wasn't just in the pubs. In one marina toilet the bog roll holder had an integral ash tray which was clearly still in use. The Dutch have a particular love affair with tobacco and you still see a lot of people rolling their own. Ah, them was the days.

The stage from Zoutcamp to Groningen had been a short one and I had deliberately not pressed on because I knew I would have to wait for a suitable forecast to head out into the North Sea again. So the next day was just a three hour motor down the dead straight commercial barge canal to the seaport of Delfzijl. Aside from waiting for a few bridges the only incident of note was in the locking back to sea level at Delfzijl. I was in the lock behind a large, low tanker barge. All was well until the barge engaged gear and jammed on the throttle to leave the lock. It thrust most of the water in the lock backwards into Zoph, pinning her hard against the rough concrete wall for a while. Little was seriously damaged but my cool however, as I wrestled to fend her off.

Delfzijl is an unremarkable town and the home of several oil refineries. It is the Dutch equivalent of Grangemouth or Runcorn and as such you'd imagine it not to be the loveliest place to stay. But of course it has a large, sheltered, friendly, cheap marina with fantastic facilities. The town, about a hundred yards from the marina, has pleasant shops and pubs.

From here I had to head back out to sea and the forecast for the following day was exactly wrong – north west force six to seven. So I settled in to wait a day in Delfzijl. Zoph has a capacious gas locker and I carry three large, 4.5 kilo Calor Gas butane cylinders. It is of course impossible to get these filled outside the UK and I was worried that my gas supplies might not last a long summer. So in Delfzijl I bought a small, cheap electric kettle and a single electric hob ring. The idea was to use these wherever possible when in port and connected to the leccy. The downside of this otherwise useful arrangement being that I was to become pathetically addicted to plugging into the leccy wherever I went, suffering from withdrawal symptoms at anchor on deserted islands.

Tea Cup

Failing to live up to the efforts of their Dutch neighbours the lazy, shiftless Deutsche have not even bothered to dig a canal from the Ems, on which Delfzijl sits, to the Elbe and the start of the Kiel Canal to the Baltic. Well, they have actually, but there's fixed bridges across it and sailing boats can't go that way with their masts up. So from Delfzijl you need to go out into the big, nasty North Sea and outside a load of sandy islands and drying sandbanks to the difficult, choppy, strongly tidal Elbe Estuary.

A handy halfway point on this journey is the pleasant old German resort island of Norderney. Now there's two routes from Delfzijl to Norderney. You can take the short route, across the drying banks behind the islands of Borkum and Juist, or the long route, north west past Borkum and east outside the islands. Back to Delfzijl from the Elbe the inside route is easy enough if you time it right, because you can cross the shallowest bits as soon as you've enough water, then take the fast flow of the flood all the way to Delfzijl. The way I was going was more difficult. It's hard to plug against the three knot tide so you end up crossing the shallowest bits, which are near the end of the trip, on a low and falling tide. Or you can take the falling tide to Borkum, then go ten miles back the way you've come on a rising tide and stem the flood over the shallows to Norderney. Are you with me so far? The problem with the outer route is that you have either to head a long, long way out of the estuary to the west, or cross a shallow, shifting bar straight into a North Sea swell. When you get to Norderney you have to cross another, even shallower bar which shifts about on a weekly basis just as the fancy takes it. The short route is about thirty five miles, the longer, outside route about fifty five.

Every house has a yacht parked outside

A force seven from the north west was forecast, with the wind going down the following day, but still from the same direction. With a fetch from that direction of about four hundred miles this would make the shallow bars untenable for a day and probably pretty dodgy thereafter. Which route to take? The inside route or the bars... Bars! That's nearly always the answer to everything. I repaired to the marina bar to quiz the local Dutch and German sailors about the best route.

One of Friesland's wackier bridges

Throughout the world all marinas are littered with blokes who model themselves on Harry Enfield's character "You didn't want to do that". From time to time I thought I had made a decision on the route, based on the absolute unshakeable certainty of one local expert's views. But when I voiced my decision it was greeted with disbelief and derision by other experts who, with equal conviction, told me to do the opposite.

I eventually came across an eccentric septuagenarian Dutchster who was also planning on going to the Elbe via Norderney. He was convinced that the outside way was best. He had access to some obscure subscription website where the exact positions of all the sandbanks in the world were updated on a daily basis. There was a foolproof short cut across the Borkum bar, as long as you followed the waypoints exactly. Over a small sherry aboard his rather nice moulded ply yacht I finally decided that outside was the way to go. He was a little eccentric and, though a Dutchman who spoke perfect English, insisted on talking in German to me all the time until his wife, periodically, reminded him that I was an English speaking monoglot.

Relieved at having made a decision I repaired back to the bar, where my plan was greeted by hoots of derision from a very pissed German and his mates. There would be breaking waves over the Borkum bar. But the worst thing was that the sea would be breaking over the Norderney bar so I would be trapped outside. And anyway he had it on good authority that all the Norderney channel buoys were in the wrong place. Bollocks. But I had made my decision so sod them.

I wandered the pontoons. There were various boats for sale. I wandered in the town. I looked in a few estate agents' windows just out of idle curiosity. The boats and houses were all marked 'Te Kuyp', which is Dutch for 'For Sale'. Unfortunately and by a lamentable lapse of the imagination it also means 'Tea Cup'. Historically, the confusion created by this was the reason for the invention so much as a bath chair, wearing a thick woolly jumper, with a tartan rug pulled over her legs against the cold. And that was on an advert for a beach resort. It would have been an effective way of emptying a British resort entirely.

I repaired to the marina bar for a beer. Somehow I managed to get involved in buying rounds with the barman and the other two mannies in the place. Between the three of them they spoke approximately no words of English, but it was a friendly sort of crew nevertheless. As I sat looking out over the marina just after sunset two more boats came in. The first was some sort of grotesque parody of a naval shooty-ship. It was a brand new, battleship grey, luxury gin palace about eighty feet long, twenty five feet wide and, oddly, forty feet high. It was probably crewed by a professional delivery crew and despite its cruising speed being about twelve knots it would shadow me for many days to come. The clue to its Zoph-like slow progress was in its name, 'Escarg'o'.

Alcohol abuse amongst architects is a common problem in Groningen

The second was a cruising catamaran. Well, I say a cruising catamaran. Actually it was a dinghy. It was a racing dinghy catamaran about fourteen feet long with a netting trampoline between the hulls. The solo sailor tied it to a vacant pontoon and proceeded to erect a one man ridge tent on the netting. Later I spoke to him. He was cruising the length and breadth of the Frisian Islands, which continued to live up to their name and were. Very. Back down below on Zoph I reflected on the range of different experiences that the word 'cruising' can encompass. With Zoph's relatively comfortable cabin and reassuring five tonne, long keeled bulk I felt quite spoiled compared to the bloke shivering in his floating tent six inches above the freezing briny.

The wind always sounds stronger in a marina than anywhere else. Even in the most benign conditions some git's rigging will be clanking and dreadful ghostly howling sounds will be emanating from one idiot's in-mast furling system. When you know you have to get up and head out into an unfriendly sea at the crack of dawn the howling and clanking seems the more threatening. After a broken sleep I staggered up at seven and headed down the channel. The forecast was much more favourable than the day before. There might be a force six around, but it was from the south west, off the land, as opposed to the north west. The sea state should have decayed and the wind was due to go down later in the day. Bars shouldn't be a problem and I ought to get a nice reach up the Elbe with its famously strong and awkward tide. Nonetheless the low cloud and freezing twenty five knot breeze were not inviting as I joined one other yacht outside the harbour. With two reefs in the main and full genoa and staysail I headed off at six knots on a reach. The other poor bugger, surprisingly, turned west. He was going the opposite way and would be beating into the force six. There was no sign of my septuagenarian Dutch chums of the previous day, who were due to be embarking on the same passage.

Following a Dutch loony out of Delfzijl

And surviving it

You've got to stay a good few miles offshore to bypass the shallows around the Jade and Weser. That meant that the wind was creating waves at right angles to the decaying swell from yesterday. So there was still a two metre chop as we bowled along on quite a fast, exciting reach. There wasn't a lot of traffic about inshore of the busy shipping lanes to the Elbe but I was passed by the bulk of the grey pseudo-shooty-ship. Ahead of me a small ship was moving slowly from starboard on a converging course. The AIS said she was engaged in survey work – and therefore probably showing 'restricted manoeuvrability' shapes – and doing about two knots. I'd cross easily in front of her. What with steering down the swell I was only dimly aware of a ship calling someone on channel sixteen. I thought I'd only heard half of the conversation, but the bloke seemed to be saying, in English, that he wasn't in a hurry so would slow down to let the other vessel pass in front. I never heard a response. How dim am I? It was only a couple of hours later that I realised that it was almost certainly the survey ship calling me on sixteen and offering to let me go first. What a rude bastard I was not even to acknowledge his call. Sorry Cap'n Survey Ship.

After about mid-day the wind began to veer from south to south west and go down as predicted. We got those slightly annoying conditions where the sea state doesn't decay as fast as the wind drops so you can't sail effectively even in a half decent breeze. The engine went on, the reefs came out and we motorsailed in the sloppy sea. It was a perfectly organised passage for once and the last three hours was spent motoring rapidly up the notorious Elbe estuary with a strong tide and absolutely bugger all waves. I'd seen none of the several yachts that had supposed to be coming on this passage from Norderney. I had taken a

Gordon Equinox approach to passage planning and followed the fine detail of the forecasts for exactly where I would be at particular times during the day. If you'd just followed the German Bight shipping forecast you might have got a fright and stayed in port.

There was a lot of big shipping on its way into the estuary, but it was easy to skirt along the edge of the main channel and keep out of their way. It seemed as though even the bigger ships, whose skippers generally ignore minutiae like weather and tides, were queueing up to take the rising tide up the estuary. It struck me that lots of the really major ports of the nineteenth century and earlier, from which the Euros had conquered the world, were in really difficult and crappy places, where strong tides made life as difficult as possible and at low tide the mud banks stretched as far as the eye could see. In the UK we had Liverpool and Bristol with their impossible twelve metre tides. The Thames was also a pretty dodgy bit of water. The Dutch ports, from where Indonesia had been conquered, were all along shallow, drying coasts. And here, in the corner of the North Sea, the estuaries of the Elbe, Jade, Ems and other rivers made for potentially thoroughly unpleasant passages to and from the ports. Seeing the shipping queueing waiting for the tide made me realise that perhaps, in the age of sail, these difficult tidal conditions were a positive advantage. If you didn't get a favourable wind you could simply anchor over the shallow sandy bottom, them drift up or down channel with the tide for six hours, anchoring again to wait for the next tide. What now appears like a bloody awkward, problematic tide was the engine that drove the port and sent us off on our global looting and pillaging sprees.

One of the ships passing me rapidly from behind gloried in the category 'Law' on the AIS and had the legend 'Schifffahrtwache' emblazoned along her side. The Germen really are astonishingly organised. Imagine having a whole Government department solely dedicated to watching sheep fart. We arrived in Cuxhaven's large marina after a passage of sixty five miles in ten and a half hours. Zoph was really speeding towards the Baltic.

Redundant Ditch

Cuxhaven is supposed to be a pleasant enough seaside town. The beaches I passed were certainly littered with enough sofa baskets to suggest that it had, like everywhere else in Germany that faces a bit of water, or is even a bit damp, a thriving tourist industry. To be frank I couldn't be arsed exploring all its exciting possibilities and just had a few beers on board. Early the next morning I motored with the tide up the estuary to Brunsbuttel and the lock into the Kiel Canal. On the way I was passed by the grey pseudo-shooty-ship, which nipped into one of the massive locks. One pair of these gargantuan affairs is used for yachts, the other, even larger pair for the large amount of shipping which, according to Griff Rhys Jones, doesn't ply its trade along the canal to and from the Baltic. Inevitably the lock gates slammed shut behind the gin palace and Zoph was left outside. The powers that be chose that time to commence very slow dredging operations in the entrance channel, so I had to muck about for about an hour, motoring in small circles out in the tide. This would have been fine were it not for the pilot boats. These made a sport out of speeding towards the canal at twenty knots then jamming the brakes on just before hitting the sea wall. The aim of the game seemed to be to create a breaking wash steep enough to crash over the four metre high lock walls. A side effect was the near swamping of Zoph.

Strandkorbs - Eccentric beachware on Norderney

Which of os hasn't suffered from this condition

After an hour or so of this I entered the lock in company with a Swiss yacht which had just arrived from Cuxhaven where they'd doubtless had an extra hour in bed. Jammy buggers. The locks at either end of the Kiel Canal are so large that you can motor half way up them at six knots before cutting your revs and will still stop way before the end. There are pontoons either side to tie to, but these are waterlogged, solid wood affairs with no cleats of any sort, which float only about three inches above the surface and are studded with steel bolts and other nasties. Back in fresh water again I motored off down the redundant canal.

I knew it was redundant because Griff Rhys Jones, in his book entitled 'To the Baltic With Bob' had told me as much. To quote, him "…The canal was largely redundant now… The granite blocks had an industrial museum charm". Apparently ships were far too big to use the piddling ditch nowadays and the whole thing was an anachronism, just used by a few yachts. Having motored up the thing he ought to know. But I did wonder how he could have missed the sheer, efficient grey concrete of the truly gargantuan pair of ship locks, just beside the huge, but dwarfed, old granite ones now used for yachts.

I motored on, passing a redundant oil refinery loading redundant oil into redundant tankers. Redundant car carriers and container ships bustled in the opposite direction at the rate of about one every five minutes. A redundant cruise liner filled with passengers overtook me. One redundant, heavily loaded bulk carrier, which the AIS said was 680 feet long, overtook me at nine knots then promptly stopped, so that I had to overtake it again. This seemed to be a popular pastime with some of the largest ships, which battered on then had to stop for long periods on the wider straights to wait for vessels coming the other way. Just going a bit slower seemed not to have occurred to their pilots.

Wikipedia tells me that there are around 43,000 commercial ships a year transiting the Kiel Canal, as well as god knows how many yachts. The total tonnage of goods carried is about twenty to twenty five percent as much as the total tonnage arriving at and leaving the whole of the UK. The largest ship ever to go through was 225 metres long. So yes, Griff, redundant, absolutely. This selective maritime blindness seems to be endemic amongst your traditional maritime Brits. It's quite common for sailing accounts to take as a given – as a baseline assumption – that Britannia still rules the waves and that other countries look on in envy at our impressive marine feats and unparalleled maritime economy. This untenable view is clung onto despite the evidence of many other more active, modern and thriving economies amongst other European countries and elsewhere in the world. They look at the few rotting hulks littering the ports of Britain and see a dazzling armada. They are dimly aware of the gleaming leviathans plying their trade under other flags amongst the efficient, modern ports elsewhere, but see only a poor fleet of second rate barges. It's a National disease amongst, in particular, the English maritime posh. The total blindness to the huge amount of traffic heading down the bustling, thriving canal into the Baltic is a good example. Not only that but he clearly nicked the title of his book from me.

I motored on into a freezing light drizzle. The fashion conscious amongst you might be interested in knowing what I was wearing over my underwear. I was modelling long johns, a thermal base layer, thick trousers, a shirt, a woolly jumper, a thick quilted body warmer with an astronomical tog rating, a large, thick fleece, a woollen scarf, a thick fleece hat pulled over my ears, a pair of thin socks, two pairs of thick fleece socks, wellies, salopettes, offshore coat with upturned collar, hood and skiing gauntlets. It was mid-day in the middle of May. There was no wind and it wasn't even raining hard. Yet I was still cold.

I noticed that the land on either side of the canal was not merely a bit lower. There were rolling hills, stretching as far as the eye could see, the tops of all of which were below me – and I was a couple of feet below sea level. The bottoms of the pleasant wooded valleys must have been thirty or forty feet below sea level at least. How in the hell is such a weird landscape created? And for how long can it be sustained?

I passed a large number of scuttlers. These are the small car ferries which ply their trade crabwise across the wide canal every few miles. Scandinavia is full of scuttlers as well and all the drivers have been to Scuttlerskipperschule. Here they are trained in the cardinal rules of cross-channel scuttling. The main rule is always to make sure you start motoring across the stream just in time to be on collision course with a small yacht. Preferably Zophiel. The Scuttlerskippers at the top of their game are able to lull you into a false sense of security. You feel that you must have gone far enough to have passed them, but just at the last possible moment they whizz across the channel straight at you. This ploy works best when the yacht is the stand-on vessel, leaving the skipper in an agony of indecision about exactly when to break ranks and change course. Many scuttler drivers take their work very seriously and wouldn't dream of casting off until there is a small boat to terrorise. But the Kiel Canal scuttlers had perhaps all been out on the booze the previous night. Hardly any of them threatened to ram us at all. It was a very poor show and I wondered about writing a stiff letter of complaint.

Probably Germany's wackiest bridge

It was about thirty five miles to Rendsburg, a pleasant town just off the main canal and the only really decent place to moor along the course of the canal. The Kiel Canal is a bit of a lost opportunity in that respect. There's various pubs and restaurants along its banks, which attract hundreds of camper trucks, but nobody has bothered putting in a few piles to give protection from the shipping wash and a place to tie up and have a pint. I arrived in Rendsburg with chattering teeth that evening and successfully negotiated a pile mooring quite near the grey, pseudo-shooty-ship Escarg'o. Zoph had done 173 miles in twenty seven hours over the past three days, averaging nearly six and a half knots with the help of the tide. We were making progress now and nearly in the Baltic.

The forecast for the following day was utterly shite, with strong winds and torrential rain. So though it would have been perfectly possible to press on in the sheltered waters of the canal, I decided to stay put for a while. I amused myself with the great spectator sport of watching other boats make an arse of mooring. The Dutch, Germen and Scandians can appear to be quite expert at picking up pile moorings, motoring between the tree trunks, dropping a loop of line over them and hopping ashore from the bow. But they generally rely on benign, windless, millpond conditions for this manoeuvre, as well as volunteers on shore to lend a hand. With a good, strong, vicious crosswind it's a different story and it was great fun to watch everyone rushing about throwing ropes into the water and generally failing to fend off things.

...on the redundant Kiel Canal

The lock at Kiel

Your Scandian, in particular, only ever deploys the lines that will form the final dock lines. Since there are rarely any cleats available, just small steel rings which lines have to be fed through, finger loss in blowy conditions is routine. If a Scandian approaching a berth happens to have the leeward line in his hand he will pass it to you. Often it is about three feet long with a carabiner clip on the end. You are supposed to clip it to a steel ring. Meanwhile the windage on the boat has sent it crashing downwind into its neighbour. If you attempt to pull it upwind with your short line you are given short shrift and told to fasten it downwind. The crew then leap around fending off and wondering why they keep hitting things. On no account will they rig a long, temporary line which could be thrown and taken around a handy pier or stanchion in the meantime while they sort themselves out. The utterly benign conditions they are used to do not prepare them for the least docking difficulty.

Twenty four hours after my arrival in Rendsburg the Dutch Septuagenarians from the Borkum bar showed up. I asked why they had taken so long and they told me that there was no way they were leaving Norderney the day I did because it was a bit blowy. This highlighted for me the danger of taking for granted the expertise of others. The bloke had been quite happy to attempt shallow bars on a lee shore after a near gale had been blowing from the north west for a day or two. But a forecast of twenty five knots of breeze off the land and a broad reach off a weather shore with both sea state and wind decreasing all the time had him staying in port. I realised that he was probably a bit of an old loony and that I was lucky not to have come a cropper in following his advice so blindly.

In Rendsburg I was invited aboard one of the only two Australian boats I saw all year. This was a slightly scruffy steel yacht called 'Sahula' whose solo skipper had come all the way from Oz, with various crew, via somewhere like Great Yarmouth. Having traversed half the world, including Pirate Alley, he was most proud of having navigated up the Danube and down the Rhine, from the Med to northern Europe. He claimed to be the only Australian boat to have ever done so. He got me thinking about this and other routes through the massive European inland waterways system. For such an ordinary, inland town Rendsburg had a surreal mix of boats of many nationalities, all on the way through eastwards or westwards. There was one flag I didn't recognise. I asked the skipper where it was from. "East Land" was the reply. It took me a while to realise that he was translating the name of the country into English, trying to be helpful, but merely confusing my small brain. He was of course from Estonia.

I wandered the pleasant inland town looking for food shops. Rendsburg is a good example of a universal law. There are no useful shops in towns. A village is likely to have a wee co-op shop or a Spar where you can buy food. The 'shopping streets' of towns, internationally, only sell shoes and mobile phones. There are national variations. So for example in each German town, as well as shoe and mobile phone shops there are also loads of pharmacies, in Holland, as well as shoes and phones, you can buy bicycles and in Norway there are also fishing tackle and lifejacket shops. But no food shops. The food shops are located about ten miles from the centre, but a stranger has no idea in what direction. I systematically walked every single street in Rendsburg several times in both directions in search of a loaf of bread and a bottle of milk. But to no avail.

Strande

The Pilot station for Kiel is a shed about ten miles from land

Tide, What Tide?

The next day, Thursday May the seventeenth, dawned sunny for a change and after a fraught couple of minutes disentangling Zoph from the pile mooring in the gusty crosswind I headed off east the twenty miles or so to the Baltic. It was apparently a bank holiday to mark some sort of obscure christian occasion – the "Day of the Great Pretend Magic Trick", or "Levitation Day" or something - and Germany was out in force to celebrate. The Germen are drawn to the edge of water like creeping hydrophilic roots and the youth of the country was gathered in large parties on the canal banks every couple of miles or so. They were, to a man, woman, boy and girl, as pissed as fährts. I passed them along the canal to rousing drunken cheers and bad taste oompah music. As time wore on to the afternoon the knots of the pissed I passed seemed more and more inebriated and could only manage weak shouts as they lay around on the grass. At one point I passed a rock band tuning up loudly for a gig in front of an audience of several fire engines. I knew that in France they had mid-week bank holidays, but I was surprised that the famously efficient Germen would have an official holiday on a Thursday. It seemed highly unlikely that many of the girls and boys would be efficient cogs in an economic engine on Friday.

As I came within a mile or so of the lock at the end of the canal I could see a number of yachts slowly manoeuvring themselves into it. I jammed the throttle forward and sped along, trying to nip in before the gate closed. This 'gate' is a single sliding door about ten feet thick that appears from the bank and closes infinitesimally slowly. They seemed to be waiting for me and I just nipped in time. As was the case the last time I was there five years before, I could find no way of paying a fee for the canal transit. It was impossible, as a solo sailor, to leave Zoph on the dodgy, low, cleatless pontoon while I wandered off to find the Canal Conductor. Surprisingly, the Germen seem remarkably laid back about things like being paid for stuff. The lock operated – upwards to the sea of course – and I emerged, finally, into the Baltic. The sun was out, it was a bank holiday and all Germany was out sailing in the gentle breeze on the sheltered, tideless waters. This was more like it.

I unfurled the genoa and reached off to the north. The waters round Kiel are sort of Germany's Solent and are of course filled with marinas. The village of Strande has two. One was built for the Olympics in the 1930s but I repaired to the other one. This was the busiest I'd seen any waters so far this year and sailing – or even motoring – up to the marina was extremely fraught. There seemed to be about ten different fleets of yachts, keel boats and dinghies racing around different, interlocking courses. Hundreds of kids were tacking back and forth across the entrance in toppers and the like. With some difficulty I managed to get into the marina and berth in the pleasant afternoon sun. Summer was coming and I'd made it to the Baltic. It felt like a real arrival. The end of one phase and the start of something new and exciting.

Strande was not in the least like the Solent as regards the berthing fee, which was nine Euros – about £7.50 – including unlimited electricity. As its beachy name suggests, Strande was another sandy resort littered with a million Strandkorbs. I wandered the beaches and admired the thousands of Halberg Rassys and suchlike that were ranged up in rows on the pontoons and the classic old wooden yachts sailing around in the bay. The Germen seemed to have a penchant for naming their boats in English. Unfortunately they seem to choose some pretty stupid names. I saw a 'Down Under', a 'Bruce' and a 'Gammy Bird'. I'm not sure if this last was meant to be 'Game Bird' or 'Gammy Leg'. Either way it was pretty daft.

Shadowed by this truncated, pseudo-military gin palace for several days

Is this the single worst taste vessel ever, in the history of seafaring?

At half six the next morning I motorsailed north in a gentle easterly. The breeze slowly increased until I could turn off the engine. Progress was good for a while and I was enjoying the tideless waters until we got a one and a half knot tide against us. What? Why was there one and a half knots of contrary tide? The pilotage information seems inconsistent on this. Sometimes it says that currents in the Baltic are caused by persistent wind from particular directions. If that was what this was, then why had it suddenly kicked in against a south easterly? Some sources do admit to there being six hourly tidal flows, but no bugger can tell you when the bloody thing will change.

Later I realised that this part of the Baltic – the relatively narrow bits between the Skagerrak and the south – do have some tidal flow. There are some channels where it flows at two knots in one direction for six hours, then at two knots in the other direction for six hours. But – and it's a big but – the Scandigermians don't bother to work out when the tide will change or to publish any tidal information at all. I later asked a Dane how I could tell when the tide would be favourable to plan a passage. He looked at me as if I was particularly dim and said "Well, if the speed on the GPS is greater than the speed on the log, the tide is with you". I explained that I knew how to tell what the current was actually doing, but that I wanted to be able to predict it. He laughed incredulously as if I had asked for the recipe for making gold out of shit. They simply do not bother with any tidal information at all. They just put up with it.

We plugged away against the tide up the Langelandes Belt for hours, doing six and a half knots through the water but less than five over the ground. A variety of boats passed going in the opposite direction. The bloody grey pseudo-shooty-ship overtook me yet again and one yacht appeared going in my direction. In the early afternoon the Germanian courtesy flag was lowered and the Danish one raised. Another landmark. I was in Scandinavia. Almost immediately I passed a selection of open boats drifting about in the chop and dangling fishing rods over the side. I was definitely in Scandinavia, with its ubiquitous obsession with fish. A whole grid of massive wind turbines rose out of the sea ahead of me. They weren't on the four week old chart on the chartplotter and I had to choose the most likely way round them. By about half past four the contrary tide abated a little but the motor went on in the increasing wind as I battered more to windward. At six p.m. I picked up a pile mooring in the harbour of the small island of Vejrø, joining about four other boats.

Bank Holiday afternoon off Strande

The harbour was exposed to the east and uncomfortable in the force five breeze, which sent quite a significant chop in through the entrance. It was pleasant enough wandering over the wasteland of the rather scruffy, run down island, consisting of a farm and a few holiday cottages however, and the bog and shower facilities were brand new and stunningly posh. Far too worryingly posh in fact. After an hour or so two lads turned up and demanded thirty five Euros for the night for Zoph. Of the larger boats they were demanding forty or fifty kroner. The Danes and Germen were outraged. How the hell could they justify these prices? The lads were apologetic but explained that the berthing fee included the use of bicycles for all my family, I could use the tennis courts and that the kids could use the swings and the sand pit. I explained that I was by myself, had no kids, no desire to play tennis, had my own bike and had left my bucket and spade at home. But to no avail. It seems that the entire island has been bought by a German bloke with big ideas and a touch of megalomania, who was trying to turn it into a luxury resort. At the moment it's a not very luxurious field of pigs, so good luck with that. I had a somewhat uncomfortable night thinking about Denmark's indeed Scandinavia's - most expensive mooring and how I'd got stung. Zoph continued to buck and roll about in the exposed harbour.

Bridge, What Bridge?

I was having problems with my tiny chartplotter. It was always difficult navigating using a screen four inches square, but now that I was heading towards some more intricate channels it was becoming more problematic. It was a difficulty which would be compounded a hundredfold in the surreally tortuous and complex channels around the Swedish and Finnish islands. The main problem was the need to zoom in to a ridiculous degree before the bloody thing deigned to show all the charted details. By the time the scale was sufficiently large to begin to show, say, a harbour or marina, said marina entirely filled the screen. I was trying to work out the best route west through the shallow Storstrømmen and past the large island of Møn.

The main question was whether to pass north or south of Møn. I was somewhat confused by the pilotage information in both the dreadful 'Germany and Denmark' pilot and the equally useless 'Baltic Sea' pilot. I couldn't make sense of their recommendations in the context of the chart. For a start the number of bridges didn't add up and It wasn't at all clear whether the shorter, shallow northern route, about which dire warnings were given, was passable at all. According to the Imray pilots, not only was it extraordinarily shallow but, at unspecified times in this tideless sea, a six knot tide ripped up and down it. I asked the ebullient skipper of a Swedish boat which route was the best and he simply said "There's only one way, east!" I explained that to the east of us there were two options, either side of Møn. He looked puzzled and repeated his assertion. I strongly suspected that everyone else would head down the shorter, shallower channel. But in the light of this advice I decided that the route round the south of Møn, which was more directly east, was the safer option.

I sailed, then motorsailed east, as the breeze dropped slowly from twelve to seven knots. A bridge appeared which was not on my four week old chartplotter chart. I knew that it wasn't because I have minutely investigated the route the night before. It was clearly high enough for Zoph to pass under, but had I been on a much larger boat I would have had problems.

Not only was Vejro a rip off, but the wildlife was extremely rude

As I passed under the bridge I zoomed in and in. It definitely wasn't shown. I wondered if the bridge was less than a month old. Its rusty steelwork and stained, thirty year old concrete suggested otherwise. It was only when I came back that way, two months later, that I again zoomed in even further on the chartplotter. If you zoomed in so far that the area of chart on the screen was only about fifty metres across, the bloody bridge suddenly appeared. The extent of the chart you were working on had to be only a few boat lengths before bleedin' Navionics bothered to show any impediment to navigation at all.

This feature of the crap charts was particularly annoying in Denmark. I'd paid about £170 for all the charts of Scandinavia. These would take me throughout the Baltic, up the Gulf of Bothnia and, if I wanted, up the coast of Norway beyond the North Cape. They covered a huge area. But they didn't include Denmark. For a couple of days cruising through the Danish Islands I'd had to pay another £170. Something to do with the licensing by the various National hydrographic agencies. The charts 'app' on my mobile phone was even more annoying. For this the charts of 'Europe' cost eighteen quid. This covered the area from Russia and Spitsbergen in the north and east to Egypt and the Canary Islands in the south and west. It covered the entire Mediterranean and all the inland waterways of the whole of Europe. But it didn't cover Denmark. For this you had to pay another thirty five squid. Denmark was twice the price of the whole of Europe and north Africa put together. Musing on the unfairness of life I pressed on south of Møn in the increasingly warm sunshine. Looking behind me, of course, I saw every other boat on the water – including the ebullient Swede – head off north though the shallow channels the pilots had warned about. Sod's law was alive and fully functional.

In the shelter of the narrower channels the wind dropped further and the sun became warmer. Astonishingly, my waterproof gear came off for the first time since southern Portugal in March. Well, I'd taken it off to sleep and for the odd bath, you understand, but had worn it pretty much all the rest of the time until then. With the water by now flat calm, the visibility fairly poor and the sun burning down out of a pale blue sky the red and green channel marks seemed to be floating in mid air as I approached them. In the absence of a horizon the one or two passing yachts seemed detached from the sea and in a holding pattern on the flight path to Copenhagen airport. Summer, it seemed, was arriving.

I spotted a couple of boats on the AIS which seemed to be approaching Klintholm, where I was heading. In front of the harbour they both stopped and seemed to motor back and forth outside for a while before entering. As I got closer I saw the reason for their hesitation. A mass of long sticks protruded from the sea in chaotic lines stretching far out into the bay and seemingly blocking the entrance. They were presumably poles for stretching fishing nets between. It was not at all clear which side of them was the bona fide route into the harbour.

These were a feature of a lot of the shallower bits of the southern Baltic. I guessed at a route and entered the harbour.

Klintholm was a very pleasant, if somewhat manufactured and false environment. It consisted of a sheltered visitors' harbour surrounded by neatly painted rows of holiday cottages. A couple of handlebar moustachioed, quintessential Germen took my lines and I wandered round the pleasant, if somewhat sterile village. They told me that in the middle of summer this place would be hooching with boats. Now, in the middle of May, there were only three or four.

Klintholm

Copenhagen's surreal link to Sweden. Half brdge half tunnel

I had reached something of a crossroads. The ultimate aim was to head up the Baltic and the east coast of Sweden and Finland. But the south east coast of Sweden is quite exposed and the forecast for the next week was for east-north-easterlies of between twenty and twenty five knots. This would make for a rather unpleasant batter, straight into the wind, for several hundred miles. Though not an ocean, there is a three hundred mile fetch in the Baltic for north east winds. I was also getting a bit knackered from the long – albeit mostly quite easy – passages every day. In addition I had something of a cold coming on. The alternative to eastern Sweden was to bear away to the north and head up the west coast of Sweden to Gothenburg, then head into the large canal and lake system which passes through the middle of Sweden to the east coast. With a snottery head and faced with the onset of a dread denise, I decided on the latter course of action.

A memorial plaque to Denmark's smuggest man

Old Copper Nose

Heading north the next day I had a great sail on a reach in the easterly force three to force four for four hours or so. (Is writing three 'fours' in a row in a reasonably grammatically correct sentence a record?) But in the late morning the breeze died to nothing then came back at five knots from the south. With zero knots apparent wind I motored with a motorsailing cone (the right way up, which according to Anna is upside down) along the increasingly busy shipping lanes past Copenhagen. I bypassed the surreally huge bridge on which the road spans from Sweden then dives below the sea. Half of the crossing is by bridge, the other half tunnel. This gargantuan scheme has created a fantastically handy shortcut to the rest of western Europe for the Swedes and the Norges. Previously, to go by land, they would have had to head hundreds of miles north into the Arctic, round the Gulf of Bothnia, through Finland and into Russia, then through the Baltic States and Poland. This bridge/tunnel combo has effectively turned the virtual island of Scandinavia into a part of mainland western Europe.

It being a Sunday and summer having decided to start, the waters around Copenhagen were hooching with pleasure boats of all description. There were yachts, wee speed boats and folk out fishing. The air was also hooching with flies of all description, which were less pleasant. Wee midgelets, mossies, wapses, greenfly, daddy short-legs, mini-beetles, sea-bees, aerobatic ants and others filled the air all around. About half a million settled on the windless main sail. I made the mistake of shaking it to dislodge them. All half a million fell on my head and down my neck. They weren't nasty biting midges or anything, but this explosion of insects occurred a few times while I was in the Baltic and was a mild annoyance.

About fifteen miles past Copenhagen the Danish flag was struck and the Swedonian raised as I arrived at the Swedish island of Ven and tied up alongside. It being Sunday evening most other boats were busy untying from the pleasant guest harbour and heading back across to the many marinas on the Danish side. The boat parked next door was flying a very odd flag. An ensign with a Union Jack and a ground of horizontal red, white and blue stripes. It was a rather cheap, tacky, flashy sort of flag. I asked the Swedish sounding wifey on board where it was from. Her obviously American hubby said it was from Hawaii. I asked if the boat was in fact Swedish. If so then there's no law about having to fly a National flag. You can fly a skull and crossbones if you like. No, the Hunter 33 had been

Oddly, the Danish navigational authority celebrates Christmas in May

shipped across the Atlantic on a cargo ship and was USA registered. I pointed out that as a foreign vessel they ought, by law I'm afraid, to be flying a National flag, not one representing a small district with the population of a medium sized English county. They might want independence for Hawaii, which after all was violently colonised by the Americans, but they've not yet got it. I did try to explain that my concern was just that they should be flying a National flag. I had no antipathy towards Hawaiian Nationalism per se. Indeed I thought it would be an excellent idea if the whole of the USA broke up into its constituent parts. But their daft stripy Union Jack was not, currently, a bony fido National flag. I have to say they were unimpressed.

If you want to know where Ven is I haven't got a chart but I could draw you a diagram. It sits in the middle of the Øresund, the narrowing channel between Denmark and Sweden and gives a satisfying view of both countries and of most of the traffic heading into and out of the Baltic. Having travelled far to the south of Edinburgh, then way back up north, in the harbour on Ven Zoph was now exactly two hundred metres south of my house in Edinburgh. I wandered over the pleasant, pastoral island. It was nice to be able to walk up a hill for a change, albeit one only about a hundred feet high. Nowhere else I had been in the last three weeks had been more than a foot above sea level.

Ven was the home of the sixteenth century scientist Tycho Brahe, he of the metal nose. I wandered the island being fed tourist tit-bits by the various plaques on various buildings. It seemed that old Tycho lost his nose in a duel, which struck me as being pretty careless. He had a metal one made and went about with it glued in place. It's generally said to have been made of gold or silver or both, but apparently someone investigating his long dead skull – well we all need a hobby – noticed a lot of green staining, suggesting copper. Apparently he may have had several noses for use on different types of occasion. My guess is that the thing was made of copper and he was just bigging up his conk bling by claiming to have a gold neb. Old Coppernose should not be confused with the nearly contemporaneous Polish astronomer Coppernickers, who first invented the preposterous idea that the earth goes round the sun.

The sun was shining hotly on the earth the next day and after an hour or so of motorsailing I had a fast reach north for a while. I was pleased to see that the scuttler skippers here were right on their game. Two of them competed to ram Zoph from opposite directions as they plied between Helsingborg in Sweden and Helsingør in Denmark. The wind, which I expected to increase as rounded Kullen point – home of the famous lizard-based soup, Kullen skink – actually died.

It seemed that the law of comeuppances applied in Scandinavia as it does in Scotland. If you get one decent day of summer you can expect to pay for it with a load of shit. By two p.m. large thunderclouds were developing and at four the heavens opened with a massive thundery cloudburst. Distressingly I could see the forks of lightning striking the sea not far away. The thunderstorm didn't bring much wind, but I never like lightning at sea, especially when Zoph's is the only big, inviting metal spike sticking up in the air.

As I neared my destination a small freighter played cat and mouse with me. No matter how hard I tried to give way to the bugger as he came up behind me, he kept altering onto a converging course. In the end, with the sodding ship fifty metres behind and closing fast, I had to turn hard to starboard and do a full 360 degree turn, then follow behind him. At this point of course he slowed down to two knots, determined to continue being an annoying bastard.

The port of Falkenberg had been recommended as a lovely town by the Rough Planet Guide, which if anything was worse than the pilot books. The entry to the port was about a mile up quite a fast flowing river, past a long row of large freighters, all of the same shipping line, in port for major maintenance. It was quite surprising that they'd all managed to get up the shallow river, which was only half as wide as they were long. The yacht club, complete with visitors' berths, was just next to this industrial scene. With the help of a couple of blokes on local boats I managed to come alongside the upstream side of a jetty which stuck out into the strong stream. This was very much your local boat club and reminded me more of harbours on the Forth than anywhere I'd been so far. Except that the leisure boats were cheek by jowl with commercial shipping. In Britain of course – and only in Britain – where the port authorities are limited companies with the sole aim of making a profit, the local boat club would not be allowed to survive. Everyone was friendly and interested in where I'd been. It was, of course, not the season yet, so nobody appeared to take any money off me. Nevertheless the locals were happy to give me the code to the lock on the club house, with its showers, kitchen and other facilities.

Symptomatic of the arrival of summer was the condition of the butter. Ever since leaving home this had been outside the fridge and when I'd needed any I'd practically had to chip shards of it off the block with an axe. Now it was running into the bilge. The long johns had long gone and the very ideas of thick fleecy jumpers and woolly hats was repellent. The locals said that the temperature in Falkenberg had reached twenty nine degrees Celsius that afternoon. About a week before and considerably further south it never rose above about four.

The trip from Strande to Falkenberg had covered 232 miles in four days. I was looking forward to putting the shallow, sandy, exposed coast of the south behind me and arriving at the rocky, island strewn coast where distances shrink and its never more than a couple of miles between perfect anchorages.

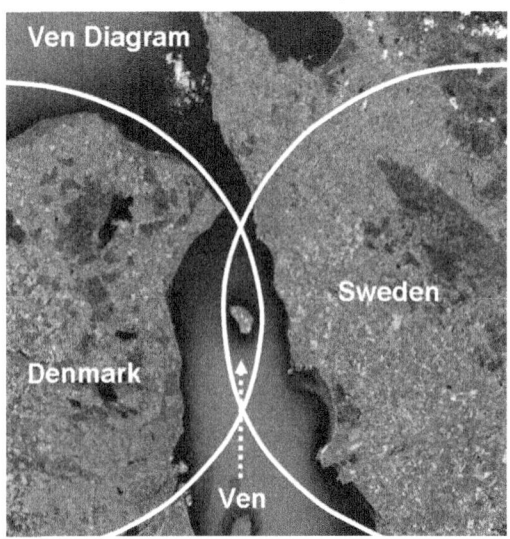

Monster

To celebrate arriving in what I, rather swingeingly, think of as 'proper' Scandinavia I was given the best day so far since leaving Port Ed. The sun shone all day and the fluky easterly soon turned into eight to sixteen knots from the east north east. On a perfect reach in a smooth sea Zoph seemed to be on rails.

Just about the only thing I ever heard on the VHF was someone periodically telling me that I could hear navigation warnings "on the main channels". No matter how much I shouted at the radio he never bothered to say what these 'main channels' were. But today by chance I found one, channel twenty four. Of course these warnings are for the whole of the Swedish coast. The Skagerrak, Baltic and Gulf of Bothnia. They cover thousands of miles of coastline and were extremely unlikely to affect me. But I listened anyway. The very first navigation warning I heard was that Falkenberg light, two miles behind, was currently unlit.

I sat sweltering, trying to maximise exposure to the cooling breeze in the summer heat. Another warning was broadcast. I was told that the ice had just receded from the main parts of the Baltic, but that half the buoyage had been destroyed or moved out of position during the winter and would take several weeks to fix. I dipped a bucket of water to chuck on my face and cool me down.

We sailed past the town of Glommen which, as are all towns in Scandinavia, was probably a popular holiday centre. If they wanted to go a bit up market in their holiday trade it struck me that they could market themselves under the slogan 'Don't be Common, Come to Glommen'. I may offer my services as a marketing consultant.

After thirty seven miles I sailed right into a deserted island anchorage at the end of a perfect sail during which we'd even had half a knot of tide with us all day. I headed right in to the most sheltered part of the anchorage, a tiny bay on a small, rocky island reminiscent of the southern Hebrides, with two or three deserted holiday cottages. I picked up a stern buoy – the first time I'd seen this typical Scandinavian mooring on this trip – and tied the bow to a rickety landing stage. I stepped ashore onto a perfect island, on which the rocks and trees and grass tumbled right down to a perfect sandy beach a yard across, which fringed the clear sea. At three weeks to the minute after I had left Port Ed. I sat on a rock in the evening sun with a glass of wine, surveying the scene. This was the life. I had arrived and an idyllic summer stretched for months ahead of me.

The name of this idyllic, deserted island was Mönster. Pronounced, as far as I can make out, Monster.

From the inappropriately named Mönster I continued north the next day towards Gothenburg. Again a warm, summertime easterly gave me a perfect reach on a flat calm sea in the sun. Now I was in behind the Skaergaard, the sheltering fringe of rocky islands that makes most of Scandinavia the best cruising ground in the world. The Skaergaard stretches from south of Gothenburg, north up Sweden and Norway almost to the North Cape. In the east it runs from a hundred miles south of Stockholm up to the Åland Islands, across to Finland and all the way to the Russian border. It would give me almost perfect shelter for most of the next two and a half months and almost two thousand miles.

Mönster

Not only does this fringe of islands provide sheltered snailing conditions. It also offers an almost infinite number of perfect anchorages where a boat could sit out a hurricane without ruffling its feathers. The anchorages are often so perfect it becomes difficult at times to believe that they've not been the subject of design. Douglas Adams tells us that the coastline was designed by Slartibartfast and as a confirmed atheist I'd rather the Scandian coast didn't come up in arguments with nutty, certifiable monotheists about intelligent design.

A slight downside of this island perfection is that people have the sense to live on these island paradises and commute from their posh, idyllic suburbs across the sea. In this case to Gothenburg, to make Volvos. They do so on fast hydrofoils which suddenly zoom out from narrow, tortuous channels between islands and say 'boo'. The craven, worrying pilot books are full of dire warnings about them. But actually the sea is filled with leisure sailors of no greater ability than you or I and the zoomer drivers are quite used to dealing with boats travelling at a tenth of their speed. The narrow, tortuous rocky channels between the islands are a challenge however and my index finger was soon worn out from zooming in to see individual rocks and zooming out to see where the bloody hell I was going.

Gothenburg is a big town and the waters at the entrance to its river port were already busy on a sunny Wednesday afternoon. The character of the boats was different to what I'd seen elsewhere, with racier, fully crewed yachts speeding round short courses in the baking sun. Of course the area is studded with large marinas. I chose one more or less at random and picked up a vacant berth - with a green tab to show that it was available – between tree-trunk piles.

I intended to leave Zoph in Gothenburg for a week or two. It had been a long haul to cover over a thousand miles in just over three weeks and almost two thirds of the trip had been solo. Not only was I feeling generally knackered, but the dread denise, which was turning into a disturbing man-flu, was weakening my resolve.

I had booked a flight with, I'm afraid, the execrable Ryanair, who fly to Edinburgh from a ploughed field which is, surprisingly, less that a hundred miles from Gothenburg. Annoyingly, however, one of their myriad ways of ripping off and pissing off their customers is to charge them sixty quid if they arrive at the appointed field without a printed boarding pass. When a bit strapped for cash they have even been known to turn their website off for the whole of a bank holiday weekend so that every single passenger has to pay an extra sixty quid I was, naturally, determined to avoid this scam.

The rather nice thirty two foot Vindo in the next berth to Zoph's was occupied by a pleasantly chatty old Swedish manny who's plan was to circumnavigate southern Sweden the opposite way to me – anticlockwise. He was from Vänersborg on Lake Vänern, where I was soon to be heading, but he had family in Gothenburg. He was trying to fix some plumbing and the judicious investment by me of a few inches of PTFE tape into this endeavour paid immediate dividends. Within the hour his son had printed off the boarding card at home. We spent about half an hour on the phone as I gave him all my details for Mr Ryan, including a full DNA test and blood sample. I explained how to avoid the many traps for the unwary, where they trick you into paying extra for bags, insurance, reserving a seat and air to breathe.

Cap'n Vindo's puny reward for this service was a can of beer in Zoph's cockpit. It was sunset yet still swelteringly hot. I was only forced to wear a shirt since huge, tropical sized mossies were biting. Down below in the cabin it was oppressive and airless. It seemed incredible that this was the same continent as hundreds of miles further south a week before.

Troll Hat

I reflected on the last time I had been in Gothenburg, in May 1983. I had hitched from Aberdeen – where I was a student at the time – to Harwich. Thence to Denmark and by ferry to Gothenburg. There I had got a lift in an ice cream delivery van driven by a nice young chap rather worryingly named Bengt. He had gone so far as to offer me a bed for the night in the swish holiday bungalow he was borrowing. So, followed by a day of sightseeing on his delivery route around the main holiday spots, we repaired to Bengt's pad. On my first ever night in Sweden he switched on the telly. The first thing that met my eye was footage of gaggles of drunken, kilt-and-jimmy-hat wearing Aberdeen supporters. He changed the channel. More of them were waving cans of Tennants about and falling over. Another channel. "Here we go, here we go, here we go" they bellowed tunelessly. Every single channel on Swedish telly was solely occupied by pissed Aberdonians. It was possibly the most surreal moment of my life up to that point. Not having the slightest interest in football I had missed the fact that Aberdeen had actually made it through to the final of the European Cup Winners' Cup, which was taking place that very night in Gothenburg.

This time the area seemed to be mercifully free of stereotypical Scots. I had a whole day to spare before my flight and was wondering about pressing on beyond Gothenburg a bit. Cap'n Vindo had offered me the use of his berth in Vänersborg, at the entrance to Lake Vänern, for a fortnight, for nothing. I decided however that it was too far to take Zoph there and be at the landing strip in time for my flight. He did persuade me that it was worth heading on up river as far as the enticingly named Trollhätte Canal. First Monster, now Troll Hat. These were proper Viking names from mythical lands. I confidently expected to see Norse gods flinging hammers about the sky. Perhaps that's what the thunderstorm yesterday had been about.

The Trollhätte Canal is the start of the long and somewhat expensive route through the middle of Sweden. I was told that there was a quiet, secure wee set of moorings at a place called Lilla Edet , some thirty miles upstream from Gothenburg. The moorings were inside the first lock and officially part of Trollhätte Canal, but they were before the point where you had to pay and - in all probability - nobody could be arsed chasing me up for money. The prospect of a fortnight's free berthing was too good to resist, so next morning I motored off up river through Gothenburg.

The large port was busy with freighters, the prison ships of the cruise lines, tankers and scuttlers, tugs, ferries and yachts. The waters of the sheltered, almost windless river were a frenetic chop of old bow waves bouncing off walls and creating little harmonic peaks. It's amazing how much disturbance a few boats can cause. Zoph picked her way past the moving traffic and the moored ships on either side. As elsewhere in mainland Europe, Gothenburg was not scared of mixing up its functions. Huge shipbuilding cranes towered over new, modernist yuppie flat developments. Office blocks rose high above a multitude of yachts. From old square riggers to billionaire gin palaces to sailing boats of all ages and sizes.

Despite the alarmist pilot book, the hydrofoil drivers know what they are doing

Typical Gothenburg suburbs

I was going the wrong way, of course. All the advice was that it was better to use the canal and lake system to pass westward, avoiding south westerly winds in the more exposed Baltic. The other reason was the three knot tide which was flowing down the thirty miles of the Gøta River in the spring, when melt water was still feeding the rivers from hundreds of miles to the north. Should you be interested in how to pronounce 'Gøta, a 'Gøta yacht' is alliterative. There's no hard 'G'.

I motored out of the city up the increasingly fast flowing river. The shipping traffic decreased in size and number the further I went. Soon the river felt like a dead backwater. There were more rotting hulks than extant ships. One that, unfortunately, didn't seem to be out of commission, had a large banner on the side reading 'Sailing for Jesus'. So presumably his water-walking abilities are exaggerated.

The first bridge that was too low for Zoph was a railway one and I waited impatiently for a while for nothing to happen. One of the few good things about motoring against a strong current is that staying still is easy. You just keep going forwards slowly at the speed of the current.

Pressing a big red button on a staging next to the bridge didn't make it blow up, but it didn't achieve anything else either. After half an hour or so I looked up a phone number for the canal management in the pilot book. I was concerned that, early in the season, nobody might be watching the CCTV. On the phone I was shunted from pillar to post by various bemused office phone girlies. It seemed that this bridge was not part of anybody's department. Eventually however a bored operative pressed a button and I motored through.

Cranes dwarfing both boats and blocks of flats

Concerned that I might have the same problem with the next bridge I checked out its height on the inaccurate and eccentric electronic charts. Eleven metres. Zoph's air draft is about twelve and a half. But as I approached the bridge I saw that its centre rose slightly above the main part. Right in the middle, where the two opening sections met, the road base was thinner and there was a narrow slot, a foot or so wide, where the bridge was higher. A sign proclaimed that it was thirteen metres at this point. Stemming the tide and hoping that the spring thaw hadn't significantly raised the water level, I inched forward and Zoph's VHF and AIS aerials just slid through the narrow, thirteen metre high slot. A twelve and a half metre high boat under an eleven metre bridge was a first for me.

Aside from hitting bridges my main concern on this trip was staying cool. Literally, of course. I have long ago abandoned attempts at metaphorical cool. I was wearing a pair of swimming shorts - and nothing else. Calm down ladies. It was far too hot for a shirt. I spent much of the trip rigging up a variety of sun shades from the backstays. If I kept completely out of the sun and chucked a bucket of water over my head periodically it was just about bearable. I remembered incredulously motoring down the Kiel Canal, way down south and eight days before, dressed in Scott of the Antarctic's entire wardrobe. Now the thought of long johns, woolly socks and fleecy hats was utterly repellent.

After I left the outer suburbs I only saw one commercial ship. It was a small bulk carrier that, inevitably, decided to leave its makeshift dock next to some roadworks, where it had been delivering hardcore, just as I approached. On the transom of the scruffy, rusty old tramp coaster was the unlikely name and port of registration "Sheltand Cement, Nassau". I suspected that the ship may not be a familiar sight in Nassau. As the countryside grew more wild the current grew stronger. I occupied myself with guessing which side of the river would have the least current. I opted for the inside of the bends, reasoning that the water would be swept to the outside, scouring that bank. The tactic seemed to work more often than not. By hammering the engine somewhat I managed to average four knots for the whole trip, but it felt like a slow one.

Finally I reached the first lock into the Trollhätte Canal. Unlike Dutch and Deutsch locks these beggars do actually lift boats up and down. A lot. About twenty five feet in fact. They are oppressively deep, dripping gorges which the mast barely protrudes out of. Despite this they are a piece of piss to negotiate. With a bit of luck you can just hold onto a ladder amidships as you rise. Unlike most of our locks in Scotland the water wells up from gratings at the bottom, instead of rushing from sluices at one end. This means there's virtually no turbulence, just a surreally rapid rise.

The Lilla Edet moorings were just at the top of the first lock. I picked up two of the big red stern buoys and made fast to the quay in the bow. There were only a couple of boats in, including a long, low, sleek, beautifully painted and varnished wooden sloop. Obsessively I tied Zoph on with about a hundred lines, making sure she was an unreasonably large distance from everything, including the quay I had to leap onto.

I took a critical look at her. I had spent a prodigious amount of time and effort over the winter applying layer after layer of polish. I hoped that this would prevent her going rapidly a shitty yellow colour with whitish patches, a result of her age and a couple of repairs occasioned by me ramming things. But not a bit of it. Shitty yellow with whitish patches she undoubtedly was.

Mind you, she'd been through a lot. Since leaving the Forth twenty four days earlier she'd covered 1041 miles. Unfortunately however Port Ed. was still only 550 miles away. I'd taken a massive ten day tack south on port tack, then another one north on starboard. I raked back through my logs and discovered that this was only the second time she'd done over a thousand miles in a calendar month. The first was June 2008, when she'd done 1021 miles in Norway. Yes, result! I felt stupidly competitive against my former self and vowed to beat that bastard 2008 Edge and do more miles than him this year. This is why I don't race. I'm so competitive I can practically give myself a seizure trying to beat some imagined other incarnation of myself. I began heartily to dislike 2008 Edge. God knows what would happen if I actually raced against other people in other boats.

In the evening the owner of the sleek sloop turned up to polish or varnish something he'd missed. A bit of anchor chain or something. I remarked how nice his boat looked. "Yes, it does, doesn't it?" he replied, nose in the air at a haughty angle. Not a good start. I pointed out that Zoph had been almost as pristine and white at the start of the month. With lip curled in a grotesque sneer of disbelief and disgust he said "Well she's certainly VERY dirty now". Resisting the temptation to push him in the canal I asked him where he was from. He explained that, at the start of the month the boat had been craned in to that berth, exactly where she now was. Since then she had moved not one single, solitary inch from the mirror flat canal berth.

"Well you supercilious, smug, self-satisfied bugger. A boat is for sailing about you know, not just polishing and keeping preserved in aspic. My boat would be all gleaming as well if I did nothing but polish it, but Zoph and I have come over a thousand miles, so stick that in your pipe and smoke it.... By the way you've missed a bit". These were all the things I didn't in fact say to him.

The next morning I hopped on a bus to a field within a hundred miles of Gothenburg and left Zoph on her slightly dodgy free mooring.

Zoph stayed at Lilla Edet for two weeks

Trollhätte

Gotta Get to Gøta

Two weeks later I returned with Anna. At that time she had just grabbed voluntary redundancy eagerly, with both hands. A newly redundified lady of leisure, Anna was easily persuaded that a June holiday in Scandinavia was the perfect way of celebrating release from wage slavery. Little did she realise that she was being press-ganged into unwaged slavery before the mast. The Trollhätte was easy, but I needed someone to chuck lines to, in the 'up' section of the Gøta canal.

Zoph had fared well on her free mooring for a fortnight and hadn't sunk or been nicked. In the afternoon we cast off and headed up the canal. Unfortunately it was still a canalised river at this point and we had between one and two knots of tide against us. We negotiated a couple of the very deep, cavernous locks, overtook a small Danish yacht and were chased by a couple of larger ones. In company with a Halberg Rassy 43 we entered the last lock before the town of Trollhätte and took an alongside berth in the small guest harbour at the top.

Though the locks are easy to negotiate the Troll Hat is a somewhat impersonal canal. The only time we got to see any of its employees was when a student girlie arrived at the top of one lock to take the rather steep eighty five quid fee for the short transit. As expensive as the overpriced Crinan Canal, if about a hundredth of the effort to get through. The girlie managed to be considerably more helpful and less rude and unpleasant than some of the Crinan crew as well.

The Troll Hat is also still a commercial canal. Small ships use it to ply their trade into Lake Vänern and deliver goods right into the heart of Sweden. The canal system doesn't only pass right through the country. An offshoot also winds three hundred miles north to the border with Norway. In common with, it seems, every country in Europe apart from Britain, the Swedes actually use their waterway system as it was intended, for commercial goods traffic. Only in Britain is there an unwritten law that says that all goods must travel by road. Witness for example the recent argy-bargy about the delivery of turbines to a hydro scheme right next to the Caley Canal. In all the argument about how they could be got down the winding, twisting A82 there was never any suggestion of using the waterway alongside it, which is designed specifically for carrying a large tonnage of goods. On reflection it is probably a good thing that no commercial traffic uses any British inland waterways, which are solely for the use of narrow boats and discarded shopping trolleys. If it did then – consistent with the policy of 'never the twain' – all leisure traffic would be banned outright.

Our arrival at our alongside berth in Troll Hat was greeted by the eruption of a full-on fanfare from a full scale brass band on the quay about a yard away. We took a bow but it seemed the band had not turned out in our honour. An appealing feature of a lot of Scandinavia is the propensity for small festivals of nothing-in-particular to pop up in the smallest villages at seemingly random times. As well as the brass band the area around the harbour was littered with all manner of gleaming, obsessively polished vintage cars. The fields and verges were full of genuinely ancient 1930s models, stupidly wide american things with wings from the 1950s and, disturbingly, quite a number of 'vintage' cars which were, with the exception of the degree of polish, identical to the sorts of cars my mates and I drove around in our youth. My mate Tony's bull-nosed Saab was there for instance, as was my Mini. It is distressing to discover that your own youth is now the subject of ancient history. On a pleasant, calm, sunny evening we joined the motley assortment of Swedes – and indeed Turnips – wandering around the pleasantly pointless event. This felt like the start of a summer holiday.

The annoyingly impersonal nature of the Trollhätte became evident the next day as we waited for interminable hours for bridges to open. I had intended that we would razz along the few remaining miles of the canal to Lake Vänern, then nip thirty or so miles up this large body of water before nightfall. In the event we had to wait for nearly two hours for some more boats to catch us up before they deigned to open the first bridge. This would have been more bearable if they had bothered to tell us – on the VHF or the large neon noticeboard next to the bridge – what was going on and how long we would have to wait. But not a word was spoken. In any language. Instead we waited with yesterday's large Halberg for three more boats, including, oddly, a German Moody, to reach us travelling up in convoy – seemingly from somewhere in Denmark.

Finally we arrived at the small town of Vänersborg. It had taken us four hours to go eight miles and, faced with the prospect of a long trip up an exposed and very large lake – Lake Vänern has been re-categorised by the Swedes as a sea, purely based on its size – we decided to call it a day. We tied to a pontoon in Vänersborg guest harbour. Here I was surprised to be stung for a berthing fee, having been assured that all harbours on the canal were included in the passage price. With a gentle smile of condescension the harbour manny explained that this didn't apply to his marina, so cough up you bugger.

Near Zoph were the first proper British yachts I'd seen since under the Forth bridges. There had been a British flagged ocean racer berthed near Gothenburg, claiming its home port as Glasgow, but it was one of a permanent fleet of oddities available for hire by the day. Indeed it was so firmly based in Gothenburg as to have an illustrated plaque about it on a stand next to its berth. But in Vänersborg were a Westerly from Beaumaris and a large, scruffy British ketch. At the start of what was to become a comprehensive survey I interviewed both skippers. Both boats had been based in the Baltic for a number of years and were not on an annual cruise from the UK. This was to become a recurrent theme. Very nearly every British boat I met had not come from Britain that year.

In the evening we wandered the town, investing in one of our rare beers from a bar, as opposed to from Zoph's stash of cheap Tesco stuff. Again there was something of a festive, summer feel in the air. But this time the festival atmosphere mostly involved a local band churning out some old rock and roll favourites in English and a few Swedonian numbers for a small crowd of drunken karaokers.

The local exponents of the bridge-lifters' art didn't seem to have improved their performance the next day as we waited at the last railway bridge before Lake Vänern. It didn't bode well for the rest of our trip through Sweden, which would involve getting through several hundred lifting bridges. Eventually however the bridge monkey awoke and pressed a button – presumably in exchange for a small amount of food or some other treat from a dispenser – and we emerged onto Sweden's, and the EU's, largest lake. Lake Vänern, about fifty metres above sea level. is over two thousand square miles in area and we had to sail about half way up it and over to its eastern edge to reach the entrance to the Gøta Canal.

We were heading north east and Sod's Law dictated that the wind was blowing from exactly there. At first at about eight knots, but rising to twelve to fifteen knots for most of the day. With a sixty mile fetch from that direction an annoying chop developed on the freshwater lake. We motorsailed into it all day, tacking about three times. For a few hours the German Moody sailed and, annoyingly, almost kept pace with our motorsailing. It was bright and sunny, but cold and after about seven hours of damp battering into the chop we were glad to enter the Skaergaard which fringes the long peninsula stretching northwards up the middle of the lake.

Läckö Slott

Leaving the main body of water and entering the narrow channels between the islands was like entering a different world. Dressed in our full wet gear, together with woolly hats and gloves, we passed the crews of open speedboats lying around on the lee side of rocky islands in their swimming gear, luxuriating in the sun. A north easterly breeze being, of course, the perfect wind direction for afternoon sunbathing in the northern hemisphere.

We followed tortuous channels to the holiday camp and moorings at Spiken. Finding it a bit of a soulless caravan site we pressed on a couple of miles to Läckö Slott. This is an impressive old castle on a small peninsula with, crucially, a whole pile of about sixty stern buoy moorings for visitors. There were so few boats around this early in the season that we didn't bother picking up a buoy but simply went alongside the quay, joining the big Halberg from the day before and being joined by a rather nice small local wooden yacht. It was here for a concert the following day at which the wifey of the couple was playing. We were treated to a series of practice sessions on the recorder, which weren't too painful.

We wandered up to the castle. The Scandian approach to the seasons is an odd one and I've still not quite grasped it. The moorings were empty because, on June the eighth, it was still out of season. There were guided tours of the castle for two days a week during May and up until the eighth of June, then no more for the rest of the year. The castle was open to the public from June to

August, then shut for the rest of the year. The other nine months were out of season. I understand that the Scandian sailing season is a short one, but can the weather really be too inclement to visit a bloody castle for nine months of the year? What the hell do they do during these nine months? Hibernate?

Läckö Slott's main claim to fame, as the photo shows, was to have been home to the world's largest ever woman. With a length of twenty four metres, a beam of five and a half metres and a weight of seventeen tonnes, Sigrid Storråda was not a bint to be trifled with. The next morning we were presented with some fresh cinnamon croissants for breakfast by the generous crew of the wooden yacht. The need for some sort of fresh bread for breakfast seems to be something of a National obsession in Sweden and it's often the only thing you can buy in marinas and small villages.

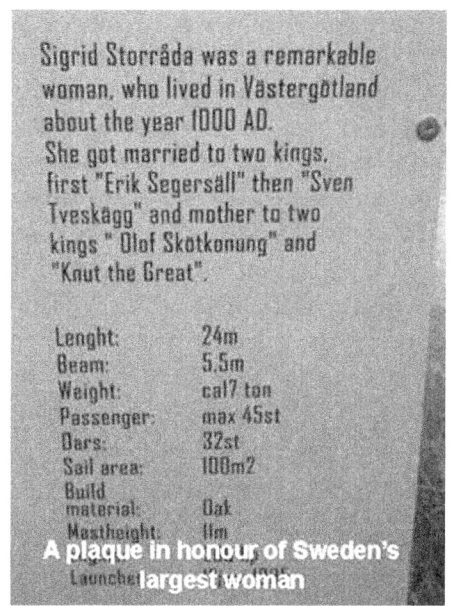

A plaque in honour of Sweden's largest woman

We squeezed out of the narrow harbour past the rather appealing wee cruise ship 'Diana', which had docked at the castle overnight. She then followed us as we motored and sailed across the lake to the narrows on the approach to Mariestad. The Diana was one of a number of small, old fashioned, but posh and expensive river boats that plied the length of the Trollhätte and Gøta canals, fleecing posh people for cruises. These wee ships looked, nevertheless, almost infinitely preferable to the Baltic cruise prison ships we would come across later.

The wind went from nothing to fifteen knots and from nowhere to south west then immediately north as a series of huge, threatening rain clouds chased us down the loch. For the last half hour before we motored into Mariestad we were comprehensively pissed upon. Though billed as an interesting wee place and not without its aesthetic appeal, Mariestad was an extraordinarily dull little town. For some reason there wasn't a festival of any sort going on and a half an hour wander was enough to have seen every last corner. We wandered the streets in the pale sun, which appeared between the downpours. The only remarkable thing about Mariestad was the presence, on the hard, of a couple of Albin Vegas which appeared to have been modified to have twin rudders. You don't find that interesting? Well fair enough, but it may be to someone.

The less excerable cruise ships of the Göta Canal

In the morning we motorsailed and sailed north in a force four, down the channels and under a high bridge, for ten miles to the start of the Gøta canal at Sjötorp. We tied up in the tiny, painfully pretty basin while I went, accompanied by a cheque book, a full set of financial accounts and my bank manager to find one of the Canal Elves. The Gøta canal is not cheap. It cost us over five hundred quid to transit it one way in a twenty seven foot boat over a period of six days. Had I gone back the same way the return trip would only have been half price, but even so. The powers that be justify their pricing by saying that my five hundred squid entitles me to stay in the canal for up to a hundred and twenty days. But why the hell would I want to do that? The fee includes up to five nights stay in each of the many 'marinas' along the way. These are fine but most consist basically of a bit of canal bank to tie to and an unheated bog block, opened by a universal key that gets you into all of them. I had decided to bite the bullet, pay up and not resent this extraordinary expense in what was, in most other respects, a cheap trip.

A series of huge, threatening rain clouds chased us down the loch

I paid the canal elf. In common with the University of Groningen's student recruitment, the Gøta Canal's policy seems to be only to give jobs to unemployed fashion models. These are all students on their summer holidays. The ludicrously short summer season fits neatly into these holidays. Given the weather they mostly looked like the models in your mum's mail order Fair Isle jumper catalogue. Like most models, even when dressed in woolly jumpers and hats, they sported bare feet. This is part of the programmed response of the Scandians to the seasons. The actual temperature is not important. It is June so they will have bare feet or sandals, come what may. Having a system that relied for its smooth operation on a bunch of students did not bode well, but I have to say the canal elves were universally efficient, smiley and helpful all the way along the Gøta.

The elf opened the lock gate and we slid into the Gøta Canal. Its character is very unlike the Trollhätte . The latter is a ship canal which operates year-round. The former is like a British canal. Designed by Thomas Telford it is pleasantly old and small scale and now takes only leisure traffic. The locks are commensurately smaller and progress through them is mostly pleasant. Unlike the Trollhätte they are operated by human beings – well, students – who actually talk to you. As such it is much less impersonal. Unlike Scotland's most overpriced canal, the Crinan, they actually do stuff for you. You don't need to manhandle the locks, which are automated. On a couple of occasions I recounted my experience of Scottish canals and the elves stared open mouthed as I described how you had to push open the lock gates with your own actual body.

We rose up a few feet, the other end of the lock opened and we slid into the Gøta Canal. We'd been and got to Gøta.

A Fantasy for Lunatics

We headed off down the canal in the company of a brand new Halberg Rassy 31, a large Norwegian Hanse and a posh gin palace of a motorboat covered in acres of teak. This last was obviously being delivered somewhere by a professional crew and was the only boat we were not in danger of being rammed by. It left us after a few locks and the Norgian stopped after a few more. The Halberg and Zoph pressed on as far as we could before closing time. In fact the Halberg skipper was so keen to get to the top of the canal that he bribed the elves to keep working after their normal knocking off time. In the event we managed to get through nineteen locks, almost to the top level of the canal. This was one advantage of transiting from west to east. It's generally easier and less fraught going down locks than up. Because the easy Trollhätte locks are so deep we were starting out pretty high up and would have a lot more down locks than up locks. The transit was relatively zoomular because it was still early season. By June the tenth the canal had only been properly opened for a few days and was almost empty. We could command the full attention of the canal elves. In July, we were told, we'd be queueing up for hours to get through the locks.

We tied up for the night next to the bog block in Hajstorp. This was a pleasant, agricultural environment with a couple of canal side cafes and craft shops. Everything was, of course, shut, but we had a pleasant evening wandering about in the decidedly non-maritime environment. We chatted to the skipper of the brand new Halberg, tied up near us. This was a delivery trip for him. He had just bought the boat – his long-time dream come true – with his retirement lump sum and was taking her home. 'Home' was the very far north of the Gulf of Bothnia, some five hundred miles north of the end of the canal and way up near the Arctic. Up there in the middle of June things were only just thawing. I can only imagine that the 'sailing season' up there is about four days long.

Speaking to the man from the north of the Gulf of Bothnia gave me an introduction to a strange, primitive, netherworld of ill-educated buffoons with a culture so far removed from that of the civilised world as to beggar belief. That's right, he introduced me to the world of the Frederick Forsyth readership. Since we were English speakers he reasoned that we would be grateful for books written in English, so gave us a Frederick Forsyth novel he had lying around called "The Fist of God". I flicked through the misguided thing. At first I was just amused at the nonsensical plot, but then began to get a small window into the minds of the sorts of cretins who read this nonsense. The premise of "The Fist of God", published in 1994, is that Saddam Hussein has access to a new secret weapon – a weapon of mass destruction – that can "rain death and destruction on the allied forces". Our hero, Major Mike Martin who can, in Forsyth's words "pass for an Arab" is sent off to find it. No question, of course, of our hero being perhaps of middle eastern extraction to help him 'pass for an Arab'. No, his name is 'Major Mike Martin'. I think that's what I called my Action Man when I was eight years old.

Of course this childish drivel just had me tittering a bit, until I read the reviews at the front. The Daily Express says "Often there's more truth in one of his explosive 'faction' novels than there is in a dozen contemporary biographies or histories". 'Today' wrote: "Forsyth's works are avidly read by the CIA... and the British SIS". Apparently 'SIS' isn't a misprint and stands for 'Secret Intelligence Service'. Wow. I cast my mind back to all the 'weapons of mass destruction' bollocks we were subjected to under the Blair administration. The absolute certainty that, somewhere, the Iraqis had the power to destroy us all if we didn't invade the hell out of them. I recollected that there turned out to be no truth at all in the self-serving mythology spouted by the politicians and military leaders and that grotesque war crimes were committed on the thinnest of pretexts. Could it really be true that the paranoid fantasies of our leaders were generated, at least in part, by the semi-literature of the insanely jingoistic, paranoid fantasist Frederick Forsyth? Surely they can't be mad enough to think that these daft wee cowboys-and-indians stories for twelve year old boys are real, can they? Not wanting to start burning books I made a mental note to give it away to someone who was unlikely to find him or herself the leader of a powerful country or in command of an army.

Happily the rural idyll was still in place the next morning as we pressed on up the canal. Here Sweden was reminiscent of rural France, with rows of tall, straight poplars and horse chestnuts and deep hedgerows framing lush green pastures. We were on exactly the latitude of Dounreay where, coincidentally, the man from the Gulf of Bothnia's son apparently worked. It looked not one tiny little bit like Dounreay. Given the lush, verdant growth it was difficult to believe that the summer was really as short as people claimed. It looked like it had been in full swing for months.

Lake Viken

Channels on Lake Vänern designed for hauling sailing ships through

Every half an hour or so we came upon a road bridge and waited a minute or two for it to open. We had to wait for forty five minutes for a railway bridge, but there was a constant procession of trains across it. The lock at Tåtorp was actually operated by hand, but had an ingenious ratchet system for opening the gates which could be operated by a small child leaning on the handle. To open the gates on the Crinan Canal, by contrast, you need several medium sized elephants. One more lock and we emerged at the top of the canal, ninety metres or so above sea level, on Lake Viken. We motorsailed down this relatively small lake, with a sharp dog-leg half way up, through another bridge and into the semi-canalised channels towards Forsvik.

The eastern end of Lake Viken is almost certainly the tweest, most surreal section of an extraordinarily twee canal. As the lake narrows and shallows and you pass down tortuous side channels, winding walls have been built by ancient giants out into the lake to guide you. Dry stone walls of huge stone blocks have been constructed, just up to lake level, right out into the shallow waters. The giants have placed huge stone bollards at intervals along the walls. In the days before diesel, ships would be pulled along these walls down the convoluted natural channels of the lake towards the canal. The walls were strangely surreal in the context of what looked, in other respects, like a highland loch.

Walls built by giants

Soon after the lake had turned into a tall pine lined, winding canal, we arrived in the small, preserved-in-aspic, industrial heritage village of Forsvik. Watched by a small crowd of bus tour spectators we entered the first down lock – and the oldest lock on the whole canal – and tied up to the quay at the bottom. Forsvik was basically just a literal museum of old wooden buildings portraying the early, small scale production of iron goods in the days of watermills. In the evening, when we didn't have to pay, we wandered around the damp site, peering into buildings at massive old timber beams supporting water wheels and ancient, nameless equipment. In the pissing down rain Zoph's jousting tent awning was deployed for the first time since Den Helder.

On a damp morning we decided to leave the awning up as we motored down the narrow, convoluted loch towards Karlsborg, probably not the best town in Sweden. Peering through the narrow slit between awning and sprayhood I was just about able to see a bit of water ahead of us and was glad that there was bugger-all traffic or wind to complicate matters. No sooner had we tied up in Karlsborg than I was accosted for a chat by an elderly manny. After I had bragged smugly about how far we'd come, he told me that he had spent sixteen years circumnavigating the world, single handed, on his long keeled Allegro 33. He now stalks the canal side at Karlsborg, putting upstarts like me in their place. And fair enough.

I was then quizzed by another old manny who thought, like many Scandians, that we were from Australia or New Zealand. They naturally assume that every country just flies its national flag. Since a red ensign is clearly not just a union jack and they have a vague idea that the Australian flag is blue, many assume that Zoph is a Kiwi boat. Though I have no objection to being accused of being from the antipodes, this must really piss off Kiwis when it happens the other way round. Imagine you've sweated blood to sail your wee boat half way round the world from antipodean New Zealand to the podes – and Sweden. Half the people you meet will assume your flag is just an unusual brand of British ensign and that you've just nipped across the North Sea. Very annoying

Our Rough Planet guide pointed to the attraction of the ancient fort in Karlsborg and for a spot of sightseeing we went off in search of it, via a rather bemused wifey in the tourist information office. After walking for miles we discovered that the fort appeared to be an actual, extant, modern military base, still in the business of repelling invaders. We gave it a miss. Thankfully it also missed us... just.

Back aboard we motored out onto the second largest lake of our transit, Lake Vättern. Vättern is less than half the size of Vänern, but long and relatively narrow, much deeper, more highland and forbidding, with fewer good anchorages and no skaergaard. But we just had to get across it so sailed on a beam reach in a gentle breeze the seventeen miles to the other side. Both chart and pilot book warned of the firing range in the middle of the loch, but neither gave any clue as to what one should do about it. There seemed to be no particular exclusion area, no communication by VHF and no other means of finding out what was happening. As we headed out onto the lake there were, of course, various flashing yellow lights on buoys either side of us, but no means of telling where we were or were not allowed to be.

Reasoning that the Swedes were far too nice, surely, to blast visiting boats on the main channel through their country out of the

water, we just carried straight on. It was disconcerting that, for the duration of the trip, loud explosions rent the air around us, emanating from the fort we had just left. But we never actually saw any shells hit either the water, or any of the few boats which, reassuringly, also seemed to be crossing the lake. With a vast country, largely unpopulated in its northern two thirds, it did seem odd that the Swedonians were so keen to blow stuff up in one of their most populated and popular areas. The busy marina near Gothenburg had also been beset by constant gunfire. I suppose the military of all countries enjoy making a lot of noise and reminding the rest of us how butch and scary they can be.

The spires of the town of Motala, on the other side of the lake, stood out on the horizon as we approached. This domination of the works of humankind over those of nature was a striking feature of the whole summer cruise. It was much more striking in the Netherlands, but all the way through the Baltic the sense of scale was different from our experience of Scottish waters. The lack of real mountains and high hills meant that the works of man – be they old churches, tall buildings or industrial cranes – stood out high above those of nature. Despite the size of the countries and the amount of land in Sweden and Finland, there is not the sense of being dwarfed by nature that you experience on the west coast of Scotland. In the Baltic people seem somehow much more in control. Perhaps this phenomenon provides some explanation for both austere Calvinism and our "oh fuck it, what can you do?" fatalistic, 'can't do' attitude to more or less everything.

Talking of doing things, a huge new bridge was being constructed high above Motala harbour. We motored under its thirty metre high span and berthed on a pontoon in the large and almost empty guest harbour. We were soon joined by a big, posh Malo yacht. The Malo ignored the vast number of pontoon berths to squeeze unnecessarily into the narrow berth next to us. All night she rubbed up and down against Zoph's fenders in the substantially empty harbour. They were lucky that Zoph chose not to pursue a sexual harassment case against them.

In common with most Swedonian towns museums were high on the agenda and in common with most Swedish places vintage cars were a major obsession. Pottering about in a venerable, veteran Volvo or a senior, superannuated Saab seems to be a popular summer occupation. There were also several displays celebrating the Gøta Canal and its 'twinning' with the Grand Canal in Jiangsu, China and the Caley Canal, Scotland. Embarrassingly, the Scottish contribution to this cultural exchange was a deeply naff wooden 'sculpture' of the Loch Ness monster. I parenthesise the word 'sculpture' because it was a large piece of cartoon-like tat, crudely fashioned by a chainsaw into a huge version of the kind of tourist knick-knacks for sale at Drumnadrochit. How our chests swelled with pride as we gazed upon it.

Whilst completing the log that evening, June the twelfth, I noticed that we were just two cables ahead of that bastard, 2008 Edge on the same date four years earlier. With this slow progress down a canal it seemed likely that the bugger would push ahead of us soon. Damn him!

Soda Shopping

After consulting with the canal elves we left sharpish and on time in the morning to get through the first bridge, which had restricted and scheduled opening times. With a gentle following breeze we pressed on, sunbathing in the shelter and getting cold again in the breeze. Progress wasn't bad, except at one bridge, where the stupid elves evidently weren't watching the CCTV, as we circled around, waving and gesticulating in the full glare of the camera. Judging by their body language when we met them at the next lock, the male elf and the female elf had found something better to occupy themselves than waiting about for the odd boat to turn up.

We had to wait a short while at the top of the canal's longest 'staircase' of locks at Berg. The elves were not persuaded by my argument that on the Caley Canal they can lock boats up and down a staircase at the same time, getting them to pass in the middle. In fact they were openly sceptical about the practicality of this simple technique. When we did get going we zoomed down the locks however and were tied to a stern buoy and a quay in Lake Roxen by four thirty in the afternoon.

Back in the large basin, half way up the staircase, the Norwegian Hanse from a couple of days ago arrived. As did a couple of the expensive wee cruise boats that ply the canals, and seething masses of Swedonian youth. This mass mooched about the lake side feigning to chuck each other in, razzing about in ribs and generally having a youthful time. We wandered around the strangely suburban landscape in the setting sun.

On a cloudy morning we motorsailed up Lake Roxen in an increasing breeze, then passed back into the canal at Norsholm. Griff Rhys Jones recounts how he had somehow managed to get lost on Lake Roxen, which you enter at one end and leave, thirteen miles later, at the other. This was an impressive feat and I found it hard to imagine how it could be achieved in reasonable visibility, even in the complete absence of charts and any navigational aid at all apart from eye balls.

Our arrival at the locks was well timed. We found them mostly the right way round for us – that is they were full – and made good progress. At one point we passed a red cutter, moored at the side of the canal next to an overwintering yard, with "Lerwick Boating Club" written on her transom. We had to wait a while for the scheduled hourly opening of the main road bridge near Söderkoping. But soon we grabbed the last really handy alongside space on the pleasant town quay, narrowly missing the eccentric hire boat that was vacating it. Söderkoping, pronounced, of course, something like 'Soda Shopping', was a pleasant, attractive, quite lively town with a bit of a holiday atmosphere and a bizarre, shingle covered bell tower. This last reminded me, oddly, of the architecture of East Timor more than anywhere in Europe.

Forsvik

Scotland's embarrassing cultural contribution to the Göta Canal

The town was pleasantly lively enough for us to resolve to eat out that evening, and hang the huge Scandinavian expense. In the event of course, once we had wandered the streets doing our sightseeing thing for an hour or two and a sensible time to eat had arrived, all the waterfront cafes and city restaurants had closed for the evening. The many touros in town were left to wander aimlessly around looking vainly for something to eat. The Scandians aren't, by and large, great ones for restaurants. If they do eat out it tends to be long, extended lunches. Since none of them get up until about ten, they are in bed by ten thirty in the evening and it takes them from about six to ten p.m. to prepare their barbeques, a two hour lunch leaves very little day to play with.

More usefully Soda Shopping, or 'Tonic Buying' as it isn't known locally, did have a rarity for the canal, a decent chandler. I had been getting a bit worried about the level of information I had available about the eastern Baltic. Information is usually the single most expensive thing about a summer cruise and the insanely complex, island strewn Baltic waters created a particular problem. Though I am nowadays converted to electronic navigation I don't like going anywhere without at least back-up paper charts. It has been my custom to buy old, cancelled paper charts online. These set me back about three quid each instead of about twenty quid.

If you are used to navigating along, say, the east coast of the UK you may think me a cheapskate. There, a couple of 1:200,000 Imray charts and Reeds Nautical Almanac will take you hundreds of miles. In Scandinavia it's different. A 1:200,000 chart is next to useless in the rock-strewn inshore channels of the Skaergaard. For paper charts to be any use they need to be at the largest possible scale. Some Admiralty charts of Scandinavian waters provide an acceptable level of detail whilst others, even at the same scale, just give you acres of pale blue nothing. They also, helpfully, often print a statement in the middle of the pale blue telling you to go away and buy a larger scale chart. But for this trip I hadn't even been able to find large scale Admiralty Charts. I had bought over twenty, but they were nearly all the useless, 'there be dragons' variety at a scale of 1:200,000.

I was coming to the conclusion that the information in Imray's Baltic Sea pilot book was even less useful than this. I had been reading its entry on the first bit of the Baltic we were going to traverse, northwards from the end of the canal towards Stockholm. To paraphrase freely, the book said this: "There is an infinite number of gorgeous places to anchor, so go and buy an entirely different book, written only in Swedish and available only in Stockholm, which will tell you about them. Whatever you do, don't go anywhere that's not mentioned in that book, none of the contents of which are reproduced here. Instead, we are going to tell you only about one, large, unpleasant industrial town with an oil terminal which you really don't want to go to. There now follows a series of dire and frightening, generalised warnings about sailing in the Baltic to put the willies up you. Now fuck off and go and find your information elsewhere".

I must say I found this approach somewhat less than helpful. I scanned the publications in the chandlery and the assistant was incredulous that I didn't have a fully comprehensive set of up to date, large scale charts for everywhere I was going. I looked at some of the Swedish charts. These came in A2 sized ring-bound books containing charts of various scales and covering tiny areas. At least when navigating the coast of Norway a few years before I had been on a more or less linear track, so I could just go from chart to chart. Here the books of charts covered a whole body of water, as wide as it was long. So any one route across it would necessarily avoid touching on about three quarters of the charts.

In the end I invested in one book of charts, for the first section of the Stockholm skaergaard we would reach. It cost about seventy five squid. In the event we razzed across this small area in double quick time, spending only two nights in the bit of sea covered by the charts. It was in fact a huge waste of money. On reflection I think I'd advise just going with the electronic info, as long as you've got more than one system as a back-up. Then it's just a matter of getting used to working at least two distinct scales, the hugely huge and the normal, keeping both sorts of information in your head at the same time. Do, though, buy pilots and harbour guides wrote by Swedes. Don't bother with guides written by Brits who, like me, have just wandered through an area once and decided that they can write the definitive book about it. Clutching my purchase and trying not to think of my bank balance I repaired to Zoph for a cheap beer.

In the morning we motored down the canal, passed easily down the last three locks to Mem and, after filling with diesel at the automated fuel pump, finally, one thousand two hundred and ten miles from Port Edgar, motored out into the big, bad, beastly Baltic Sea. We were finally on the East of Sweden. Good title for a novel that, though I can't help feeling that I've seen it before somewhere.

Söderköping's bell tower is more reminiscent of East Timor than anywhere in Europe

Söderköping

Broken

I am aware that the title of this section might be disturbing to those of a nervous disposition. Let me make it clear in advance, therefore, that no bones or vitally important ship's systems were actually broken in the course of this chapter. In fact nothing terribly bad is about to happen at all.

And the Baltic wasn't big and bad and beastly. In fact it scarcely seemed like a sea at all. It didn't smell of the sea and up near the head of the sea loch it was as flat as a duck pond. Where it wasn't lined with tall, straight pines the green pasture came down to within six inches of its tideless shore. Cattle waded around grazing in it. It was probably the most benign bit of sea I had ever seen.

The landscape didn't get any less sheltered and benign as we headed east along the loch, past two sets of narrows, one overlooked by a castle, at the foot of which was, of course, a large marina. Once we reached the 'open' sea we were still, of course, magnificently sheltered by islands, as we would be for almost all our time in the Baltic. Although perfectly sheltered by rocky islands, they are not terribly high or mountainous islands, so typically the breeze is reasonably true and reliable. So we had a pleasant sail in a gentle southerly towards Arkösund.

It was my introduction to a couple of months of Baltic sailing in a landscape which could perhaps have become monotonous, were it not so perfect. The channels wound between endless low, rocky, tree-clad islands. Many had wooden houses nestling in their sheltered bays, with wooden quays to which were tied a variety of boats. They ranged from wee open boats and speedboats to gin palaces and large, posh Malos, Najads and Halberg Rassys. From sleek, long, classy looking sailing boats with low freeboards to chunky leisure fishing boats. The houses ranged from tumbledown sheds to large, spreading bungalow complexes. From traditional larch clad holiday homes to swish, modern glass summer palaces. All the time reverberating in my head was the word 'Baltic' in a strong Edinburgh accent. The use of the word as an adjective to describe somewhere quintessentially wild, cold, uninviting and freezing. It was difficult to reconcile this image with the perfect scenes of benign nature we sailed through that day and continued to sail through for most of the rest of the summer.

As we approached Arkösund I noticed three moorings behind a sheltering, uninhabited island off a mainland bay. One of the moorings had a small yacht on it, on which a manny was in evidence. I decided to test the water, so to speak, as regards moorings. Were these publicly available or private? What was the deal in this part of the Baltic? We sidled up and asked the manny, who was very chatty and assured us that we would be fine on one of the moorings. We picked one up and settled in for the night. A mere five minutes later another small yacht turned up and her occupants, politely but firmly, suggested that we bugger off. We transferred onto the other free mooring and the chatty manny, motoring across in his dinghy, assured us we would be fine there and told us lots of snailing tales.

Once he had buggered off and motored ashore I went off for a wee row in the dinghy. By the time I was fifty yards or so from Zoph another bloke appeared in a small rowing boat with, for some reason, a massive poodle in it. He explained that this was his mooring and that we were welcome to stay, though it was in fact designed for a small canoe made entirely of feathers and weighing fifty grammes. But if we wanted to risk our five tonne boat on it that was fine, honest. Clearly he wanted us to bugger off, so we did. It had been an error of judgement to trust the opinion of the chatty old manny as regards the use of moorings. I clearly had a lot to learn about the way things operated on this coast. We unfurled the jib and sailed off into Arkösund.

Our best information was that there were at least five marinas in Arkösund which welcomed visitors. We took a 'boom' or 'strut' mooring in the local sailing club. Your boom mooring is sort of like a very sub-standard pontoon. It consists of a 'U' shape formed of two galvanised poles with small floats, sticking out from a main pontoon. The poles are rarely as long as the boat and you are supposed to tie warps to loops at their outer ends. Since you can't usually walk on the struts this is well nigh impossible from a boat with any sort of freeboard. However we made fast and had a wander. The marina seemed to want around twenty five squid for a night's berthing. Unapologetically I was informed that, though there wasn't actually a hot shower, there was a cold hosepipe in a shed without a roof. I was really beginning to feel at home. This was the level of both pricing and facilities I would expect in Britain.

Out into the wilds of the Baltic

Briefly on a mooring near Arkösund

The huge new complex of pontoons next to the sailing club wasn't shown on any charts and seemed not yet to be quite complete. All the other marinas in Arkösund had big new signs up, facing seaward, proclaiming that they no longer accepted visitors. This seems to be a worrying trend in the Swedish part of the Baltic. A company called 'Promarina', which seemed to be universally detested by the small sample of sailors I spoke to, is trying to anglicise the market. That is, they are charging almost twice what has been the going rate for a visitor's berth. Casual observation suggests that they are trying to maintain demand for their services by buying up – and shutting down – the competition. They may be entering into price-fixing agreements with them. Given the number of mooring options open to the Swedes it is fervently to be hoped that they fail in any ambitions they may have to create monopolies.

Though a pleasant enough place to wander around, Arkösund was an inauspicious start to our Baltic adventures. Happily however it proved atypical and, as I learned more about mooring in that part of the world, life got easier and more rewarding as time went on.

The forecast for the next day was for pissy rain to clear, so we waited in Arkösund all morning until the sky showed signs of brightening. We were not yet in the area which was covered by the new book of charts I'd taken a mortgage out to buy, so we spent much of the morning printing out screenshots of the 'C Map' charts from the laptop. We had invested in an onboard printer after the last debacle with Ryanair. I was determined not to afford Michael O'Leary the satisfaction of charging me sixty squid for a bloody boarding card. But the printer came in useful as a way of creating a paper-based backup to the chart plotter.

Armed with our bits of A4 we cast off at one forty five and headed north and east up more narrow channels. A south easterly had been blowing and, though it had now subsided, we could see the white breakers on reefs to our east. Oxelösund was the unpleasant industrial port detailed in the pilot book. I don't mind the odd unpleasant industrial port, but when you've an embarrassment of gorgeous, perfect anchorages, why the hell would you tell everyone to go to Grangemouth? So we skirted Oxelösund and continued north and east in the hope of spotting somewhere better.

A handy spot for a G&T on Broken

A Broken View

We passed a couple of vacant blue mooring buoys in a sheltered bay. I thought these were probably visitors' buoys but wasn't sure, so we carried on. In fact they were moorings of the Swedish Cruising Association, the 'Svenska Kryssarklubben'. So yes, they were visitors' moorings, but you were supposed to have paid your subscription and could be chucked off if a couple of bony fido members' boats came along. We carried on down more perfectly sheltered channels past perfectly proportioned, pretty islands.

Ahead I saw a large Beneteau motoring purposefully. It had an AIS so I followed it on the chartplotter. Suddenly it veered off the narrow channel and headed between two small islands and into a hidden bay. On the AIS I saw it slow down and stop a mile or so away. On an off chance we followed it between the islands and into the bay. The sky cleared, the sun came out, we rounded a corner and there, in the early evening sun, was a long pontoon with twenty or thirty boats tied to it by their bows. Their sterns held off the pontoon by anchors. I hailed somebody on one of the boats who confirmed that this was a guest harbour and we could stop there. For the first of about a hundred times that summer I flung Zoph's kedge anchor, with its brand new, gleaming anchor braid attached, off the stern and we tied her bow to the pontoon. We wandered ashore past the other boats. A wooden sign on the shore bade us 'Welcome to Broken'.

Broken was the most appealing place I'd stayed since Mönster. Ashore we found bog blocks and a club house filled with folk having picnics. We found a handy picnic table a hundred yards away on the other side of the island where we could watch the sun go down with a gin and tonic. The only thing to disturb the idyll was just a slight feeling of disquiet that we weren't really supposed to be there. One bloke had said we were welcome, but practically nobody else spoke to us. They seemed somehow disapproving and putting up with us reluctantly. I came to the conclusion that this was a private club island that we'd muscled in on and that we shouldn't really be there.

Some six weeks later, when I was passing that way on the return journey, I chatted to a bloke in a harbour near Broken gained an insight into the character of the place. Suffice to say that we were, in fact, quite entitled to berth there, despite the somewhat cold shoulder. Nevertheless we had a very pleasant evening watching the wee model boat races and drinking gin in a perfect anchorage on an island perfect in every respect, except for its indigenous dour bastards.

Sölon Staff Association

From Broken we sailed further east up more complex, convoluted channels. The wind was fickle and we needed so many course changes to follow the channel that we mostly had to motorsail. Following the minor channels in the Skaergaard is a piece of piss, potentially extremely dangerous and would have your traditional old British salt turning in his grave. Swedish charts don't just show the buoyage, they are criss-crossed by winding black lines. In the case of Navionics electronic charts the lines are an annoyingly easily confused shade of pink. These lines are drawn along the recommended channels. So you don't even have to interpret where the channel is from the buoyage. You just follow the line. It makes navigation ridiculously easy.

Too easy. The danger comes when thousands of boat drivers – the most likely candidates are the drivers of local motorboats – enter courses in their chart plotters which exactly follow the squiggly lines on the chart. Most worryingly of course, with many systems now you can set the autopilot to follow such a course automatically. When you set your waypoints somewhere within a wide channel this is a relatively low risk strategy. But when you can place them exactly on a precise, recommended course line on the map and then, with hundreds of other Sunday drivers, zoom along the course at twenty knots, it's obviously a recipe for disaster. You will be disappointed to learn that I didn't, nevertheless, abandon such unseamanlike techniques and rely only on a sextant and the position of the stars. We continued motorsailing along the wavy line on the chartplotter. Now we were also on my new, expensive paper version as well and within four hours had travelled a third of the way through the seventy five quid book of charts.

We wondered briefly about heading due north, up the back route inland to the centre of Stockholm, but decided in the end to keep to the outer, island route. We passed through a narrow slot and to the north of the landmark Island of Landsort. We wended our way through some of the narrowest channels so far, between riverine tree-lined banks and past perfect anchorages. Our information level was slowly improving. In Arkösund we had found a free guide to the commercial visitors' berths along the coast. We had also found the website of the Archipelago Foundation. This organisation details a whole series of islands in the Stockholm Archipelago and provides some simple maps showing the best anchorages. We were now just within the southern extent of the Stockholm Archie and we began to explore a couple of places to anchor. In the second half of June it still counted as out of season so there was no competition for anchorages which are said to be extraordinarily busy at times.

But on the other hand there was nobody to give us a lead or indicate what was a bona fide anchorage and what was a no-go zone.

We passed down a partly canalised, partly natural channel which took the prize for the narrowest and most extraordinary of the whole summer. The Dragera channel was under two metres deep and less than a Zoph's length wide. I've just tried to find it on Göøglë Eårth and have difficulty doing so because it seems to be completely obscured by overhanging oak trees. If so much as a canoe had come the other way while we were going down it, there is no way the two boats could have passed each other. If another boat like Zoph with a long keel, uncontrollable in reverse, had turned up, we'd probably still be stuck there now, shouting at one another to get out of the way. This was the narrowest channel I have ever seen.

A handy restaurant stop on a Baltic channel

Landsort

Just round the corner we checked out a couple of likely anchorages. Then I saw a small wooden quay, off which was a single stern buoy, on an island with a single hut. We went over to check it out. A sign on the shore said in large letters "Personal Föreningan Sölon Klubbholme". This turned out to mean that it was the clubhouse of the Staff Association of a company called Sölon. It was getting late. There was no-one about. We took a chance and picked up the stern mooring. As an added bonus I was able to nick a leccy supply from the shed, which was about thirty metres from the boat.

We settled down to a pleasant and comfortable evening in our quietest and cosiest anchorage yet, praying that if someone from Sölon arrived they would be reasonably friendly and that Sölon wasn't a company manufacturing torture equipment or cattle prods. Later we wandered around the small island. The only vaguely distressing thing was finding some quite large and unidentifiable poos littering the top of the island. These were the product of some beast which we hoped was reasonably benign and not genetically modified by the evil geniuses at Sölon to eat trespassing yachts crews.

The next morning we sailed gently past Nynäshamn with a following wind. This substantial town had some fine old buildings around the front, with the usual mass of yachts of all descriptions. There were signs of more mega-marina developments just off the main channel and to the north of the town a major port and the tanks of an industrial area. The tanks all had the familiar name 'Nynas' on them. I'm sure I've seen that on ships going into Grangemouth. It seems that Nynäshamn was the site of the first oil refinery in Sweden, in 1928. For a country with a small population Sweden manages a lot of major, international company names.

The wind increased to a force four to five and we sailed downwind all day, gybing frequently as we changed course to pass between the gorgeous wooded islands. For mile after mile we passed the holiday homes of Stockholm's rich, nestling in the perfect natural environment of a million rocky, pine forested islands. We dodged the hydrofoils and scuttlers that plied their way to the islands. It was astonishing to zoom out on the chart and realise that we came that day within fifteen miles – as the crow flies – of the very centre of a major capital city. This was commuterville, less than an hour from the office. By rights it should be blasted earth and monotonous suburbs. Or at the very least large rectangular fields of stubble and fallow. The Swedonians have inhabited this landscape for thousands of years and somehow managed to avoid chopping down all the trees. Nowadays they can brag about their environmental policies, but surely when Vikings were rowing down these channels on the way to a spot of pillaging they weren't that concerned with the eco-system. Yet the entire Stockholm Archie looks like an untouched wilderness whose sole purpose is to provide a backdrop for the metropolitan Swedish middle classes to brood morosely in front of their pine-fringed modernist glass boxes filled with sleek pine furniture.

There was more sailing traffic about than previously and we were, annoyingly, passed all day by faster boats. One of them was bright yellow, with a yellow arch in the stern for its radar, a wide, open transom and a large main on a swept back mast. When I first saw it was about two miles away. Without the use of binoculars I immediately said to Anna "That's a French boat". As it got closer and we could see the flag it became obvious that it was. This was not a lucky guess and there were very few French boats around. It is just amazing how national characteristics are somehow displayed in the design of a boat. Obviously lots of people sail about in Beneteaux and Jeanneaux. But the French don't. Not when they are cruising abroad.

How do you remember the difference between the French and Dutch flags? Well there's two ways. Firstly, think in national stereotypes. The Dutch are a practical, pragmatic people, the French more romantic and quixotic. So the Dutch flag has horizontal stripes. That way, as it wears down over the years they don't need to replace it. It can fray and fray for years, but as long as it's still an inch long you can still tell that it's red, white and blue. The French live more for the moment and have vertical stripes. That way as soon as a third of the flag has frayed away it's just blue and white stripes and needs to be replaced.

The world record narrowest Baltic channel at Dragera

This really is a navigable channel at sea

The other method for distinguishing between a Dutch and a French flag is to see what sort of boat it's on. If it's on a chunky, black painted steel cutter with a canoe stern, high freeboard, a sturdy pilot house and an immaculate paint job, it's a Dutch flag. If it's on an aluminium sloop the shape of a surfboard with a wide, open stern, a low coachroof with a single 'eye' window, a huge racy rig held up with two bits of string and a paint job in primary colours it's a French flag. Here endeth the lesson.

We sailed close past the small port of Dalarö looking for a handy place to stop and a shop to replenish our dwindling food stocks. But we couldn't see a shop or anywhere handy to tie up so we sailed on. We were aiming at a waypoint from our new, free harbour guide, which was reputed to mark a small guest harbour. For once we sailed all day without having recourse to the engine. As we sailed up the narrow channel towards the harbour of Malma Kvarn in a wind made fluky by the sheltering rocks and trees it looked for a while like the bloody harbour didn't in fact exist. In the end however we rounded a corner and there were the stern buoys and a rickety wooden quay.

We tied up in what would have been a half empty harbour, were it not for a huge Halberg Rassy 46, which had chosen to moor beam on to the quay, instead of picking up a buoy and going bow-to. This is a no-no in Baltic harbours, some of which are likely to charge you four times as much for the privilege. The skipper of this one had bought the Halberg in England and was busy kitting it out for a trip across the Atlantic on the ARC. He was already flying the ARC flag and had managed completely to fill the quay, picnic tables and adjoining shelter with mountains of equipment, provisions and an extended family of hundreds of squealing grandchildren. The rest of us just had to pick our way over the mountains and sit in our cockpits, which were the only spaces the Halberg had not – as yet – colonised.

In the search for a shop I made an effort to cycle over the hill, down the lane, across the fields to the main road to try and find the harbour and the shop that reputedly lurked there. After cycling about fifty miles down a series of dead ends I gave up and we subsisted on gruel for the night. On your Swedish rural road the asphalt tends to run out quite early on and you are left with a gravel and pine needle track through the woods. Periodically you come across a series of eight or ten post boxes on, appropriately enough, posts. The boxes are painted up with the names of householders. The lane then winds off round the back of houses spaced about a quarter of a mile apart, eventually ending in the back garden of one of them. Wayfinding is severely affected by the thickness of the forest and the fact that, by and large, the hills are never high enough that you can see over the trees. The only place in Sweden from where you can get a long-distance perspective is looking across the sea. Either from a point on the shore or, if you want a decent view, from a boat. Perhaps this explains somewhat the great Scandinavian enthusiasm for boats, compared to the indifference of the Scots to all things maritime. It's the only way the Scandians get to see out. We, by contrast, have nothing but long distance panoramas. After a whole summer in Scandinavia it was quite striking to come home and find that I could often see thirty or forty miles from the side of quite small hills.

In Malma Kvarn I thought about joining the Swedish Cruising Association so that we could use their moorings – blue buoys dotted here and there around the coast. The wifey was happy to take my money but didn't have any of the requisite documentation. Crucially she didn't have the book which showed where all the moorings were. Without this the membership would have been useless so I didn't bother.

Goldilocks to Uist

The next day we motored around to the Port of Stavsnäs and tied up next to the fuel berth in search of a food shop. I had heard that this was the 'winter harbour', from where the ferries operated all year round and that the village also had a 'summer harbour', on the other side of the headland. I asked the girlie behind the counter in the petrol station if this was the case. She genuinely didn't know. A mechanic confirmed that there was another harbour but there was no shop there. Can it be that some people are so insular that they are not aware of the existence of a whole harbour in a different part of the small village they actually live in? On the mechanic's advice we walked a mile or so to a small supermarket to stock up on essentials.

We sailed off in an increasing westerly breeze up first wide then increasingly narrow channels between islands. These islands were like a modernist interpretation of Little Red Riding Hood. The thick, dripping forest was there, but Granny got all her furniture from IKEA and the Big Bad Wolf was an architect with a god complex and a penchant for huge, sleek, low, rambling, wood and glass, Grand Designs bungalows. Sorry, I've just realised there was a tautology there. It was wholly unnecessary to mention that the architect had a god complex.

The fourteen knot breeze in the morning was gusting up to twenty seven knots in the afternoon as we skirted the Stockholm Archie. We turned to port to beat past the island of Goldilocks and the Three Graphic Designers. Following the twisting channel we bore away past the holiday home of Snow White and her vertically challenged chums. The motor went on as we pushed westward and glimpsed Kevin McCloud and his crew filming the successful Swedish media couple, Hansel and Gretel, as they put the finishing touches to their dream gingerbread home. The wind died in the lee of Sleeping Beauty's massive glass-fronted bungalow then gusted strongly as we passed out from behind the island.

The general pattern on most of the small islands of Sweden and Finland seems to be the same. You build a large wooden house which you use for a maximum of two months every year. The rest of the time it is firmly boarded up and in most cases – especially on the smaller islands where transport is by private boat – is completely inaccessible during the frozen winter. A year later the project is to build a large extension. The next year you build an impressive guest house – basically the same as the main house but half the size – down the bottom of the garden. The next year you build another extension. Then a large boathouse. Then an extension to the guest house. Then a double or triple garage. Then an extension to the boat house. After about ten years of this the whole lot is demoted to be a massive guest house complex and you get an architect to design a huge, rambling glass box which completes dwarfs the original complex. Then the whole process starts again. The landscape is of pine clad islands and gorgeous, sheltered bays. But there's a whole pile of money invested in this fairy tale environment. All that Griff Rhys Jones saw when he travelled down this lovely coast, by the way was, to quote "A monotony of lumber".

We beat on port tack down a west north west facing channel, leaving the engine on as I knew we would have to motor to windward down a narrow channel in a few minutes. I was suddenly jolted out of my fairy tale reverie by the high, shrieking whistle of the engine's overheating alarm. Bugger. We turned off the motor and furled the jib to slow us down and take stock. Crap in the water filter? Broken impeller? I checked both of these and they were fine. I came to the conclusion that it was beating on port tack with the engine on that had caused the problem. As a narrow beamed long-keeler Zoph heels a lot when beating. It's easy to get her over at forty five degrees or more. Paradoxically that's part of her stiffness. She doesn't broach and you don't need to spill the wind from the sails as they are self-spilling. In the gusts Zoph just heels a bit more, the sails present less area to the wind and she carries on. But this means that, potentially, the raw water intake for the engine can rise above the waterline and the engine sucks air. Twenty minutes of this might have been enough to get the engine overheating.

This diagnosis made sense, except that it seemed incredible to me that it had not happened before. Surely in over twenty thousand miles over the past ten years there must have been other occasions when we were heeling on port tack with the engine on. The odd time when I've had to motorsail hard against a big chop, for example. But the problem hasn't recurred and I think my diagnosis was, for once, correct.

But not trusting to the engine we sailed slowly up the increasingly narrow, relatively high sided cleft between the islands of Yxland and Blidö. I managed with some difficulty to turn Zoph into the wind and berth inside the long pontoon attached to the restaurant at Stämmarsund. Again there were stern buoys, but with only three boats around, alongside berthing was the order of the day. The pontoon was exposed to a half mile fetch to the west and it was choppy with a force six blowing, but facing the wind and on the leeward side of the pontoon Zoph blew off nicely and was quite cosy.

A friendly old local told us stories about how crap the restaurant was, so we gave it a miss and wandered in the thick woods. In Sweden you can head down a winding, unpaved track into the darkest, thickest of forests and come across some housing or a small factory or a shop. Unlike us the Scandians don't seem to zone all their land and concentrate particular uses together in ghettos. In this case it was a two storey office complex we came across in the woods. Four by fours sat in the car park whilst folk in linen suits did graphic design, or engineering or some such, in the depths of the primæval forest.

From the boat I could hear the low drone of motors all through the night. This was odd because we were on an island with no proper roads or industry. The noises also conformed to an odd pattern. They seemed to begin over in the south west and move very, very slowly north and east. We could hear each one for about half an hour, then it would be replaced by another. Occasionally we would get one going in the opposite direction. There was no sign of lights or any activity anywhere. Eventually I switched on the chart plotter and realised that we could track the engine noises on the AIS. The long, narrow, sheltering island to the west was only half a mile wide. Just the other side of it was the main channel out of Stockholm to the east. Ferries and freighters, tankers and tugs were heading to and from Finland, Russia, Estonia and elsewhere in a constant procession.

It was obvious that the staff of the restaurant weren't interested in us and I was all for just heading off in the morning without paying. We hadn't managed to get access to the shower block, after all. But Anna insisted on going to find someone to pay. This was not so much driven by any moral code or attachment to honesty as a superstitious idea that not to do so would be tempting fate and angering the gods. We were, after all, about to embark on a sea crossing, albeit an easy and short one. In the event, of course, when she found someone it was a chef who had no idea what to do with the money and was bemused that she had presented him with it. A waste of a few Swedish Kronks.

Overnight the wind had decreased and in the morning we motorsailed north east up the channel and dodged the traffic across the main shipping lane. This was easy enough and a string of other yachts was doing the same. But in Sweden it's never just as simple as the one channel. There's a million islands with channels between them and something like a fast hydrofoil ferry is likely to whip out of a side turning without warning at any time. The pilot book is full of dire warnings and insanely stupid advice on this, about which more later. But actually it's easy to negotiate these channels. There's a million wee yachts in high summer and the ferry skippers know how not to ram you.

It is said that the best way to get across the Gulf of Åland to the Åland Islands in high summer is to follow the boat in front. On that day the traffic wasn't very heavy, but there were a few yachts that had the same idea as us as we headed out towards a clear horizon. It's about thirty miles from the last bit of Sweden to the first bit of Finland and we crossed it in brilliant sunshine on a sea with only a gentle swell, motorsailing all the way with about ten knots of true breeze behind us. In the middle we negotiated the quite busy lanes of ships entering and leaving the four hundred mile long Gulf of Bothnia. We were passed by a number of large ferries delivering boatloads of touros between Stockholm and the Åland Islands. Åland is a region of Finland with a degree of autonomy, where everyone speaks Swedish. It was our easy, stepwise introduction to Finland.

The low, treeless islands on the western fringes of Åland hove into view and we approached the island of Rodhamn, where there was a guest harbour. The contrast with the Swedish coast was striking. We had come from a land of tall, straight, dark green pines clustered together to make impenetrable primæval forest. It was a central European land of fairy tales. In thirty odd miles we had travelled from the land of Goldilocks to the outer Hebridean island of South Uist or Mingulay. The islands were equally as rocky as the Swedish ones, but more recognisably bleak. In the Scottish psyche this seemed somehow more fitting for maritime rocks at sixty degrees north. The bare red rocks were attractive in their way, but it was a more bleak, unforgiving, hard way.

I later found that Scandians, presumably like Griff Rhys Jones bored with the monotony of perfectly sheltered, tree covered islands, often recommended these few western Åland islands as particular beauty spots. The bleakness, which to us seems depressingly familiar, is exotic to your Scandian and to be sought out. We motored round the island of Rodhamn and into its sheltered bay, picking up a stern mooring and tying the bow to the rickety quay. This was easier said than done as the buoys were evidently designed for hundred and twenty foot superyachts with, oddly, a two foot draught. Having tied several warps together to allow us to reach the quay from the buoy we then hit an unmarked rock a yard or so before arriving. But with a bit of adjustment we made it and hopped ashore on what was basically, sort of, Finland.

I wandered the island. It was quite nice in fact to have the uninterrupted views that such a rocky island afforded. The harbour was run by the sort of middle class hippies who believe that people should pay to keep them in the lifestyle to which they have become accustomed. They believe this irrespective of the fact that they can't be bothered to provide anything for the money. The rock lurking below the surface along the quayside was symptomatic. There was no water or electricity available, no showers and only a sputtering candle in the long-drop bog. Needless to say the hippy couple who demanded the full commercial marina rate lived in a big house next to the marina which did have electricity and plumbing. They were just engaging in the eco-experiments with us. In retrospect I rather wished I'd just anchored in the bay and rowed ashore.

The museum in the old pilot station was interesting though. A big two storey house sat on the highest point in the middle of the island. It had been the site of a huge clunky radio transmitter for much of the twentieth century, but now it celebrated the former life of the island as a pilot station. This was a repeated theme in Finland. As far as I could make out, half the country traditionally made its living by acting as pilots to guide people through the channels of the impossibly rocky coast. Aside from the pilots the history of settlement in the area seems to have been fairly short, difficult and possibly brutish, if not actually nasty.

There was another British flagged boat in town. A Rustler 36 with two old mannies aboard. As usual the boat was based in the Baltic – in the unappealing town of Oxelösund, which we had passed a few days before. The retired skipper told us that he managed two weeks cruising every year. The rest of the time the boat was on the hard. He had no idea how much they charged to look after it, which seemed odd. Even more oddly they told us that, because of their wind vane steering gear, they could never deploy a kedge anchor from the stern and always had to find somewhere to go alongside or anchor from the bow in the traditional British way. This seemed an extraordinary disability to have in the Baltic, where you nearly always moor bows-to, with either an anchor or a buoy in the stern. And since most of the sailing is up narrow channels in fickle breezes and he wasn't doing any solo sailing, the wind vane was almost redundant anyway. It struck me as a peculiarly post-colonial approach to remaining defiantly British in the face of funny, uncivilized foreign ways. Stiff upper lip and all that!

Without the aid of a pilot we motorsailed the next day the nine miles up well marked channels from Mingulay to Bournemouth. That is, we picked up a pile mooring in the large, three quarters empty guest harbour in the capital of the Åland Islands, Mariehamn. I recognised one of the boats moored near us and wandered over for a chat. The skipper was reasonably impressed that I remembered having seen his wee yacht in Strande, the day I entered the Baltic. I didn't like to tell him that I only remembered it because 'Gammy Bird' was probably the silliest name for a boat I'd ever seen.

The pilot book, the Rough Planet and Griff Rhys Jones had all been fairly scathing about Mariehamn. They said it was just a regimented grid of streets. Well yes. So is Edinburgh's New Town. They characterised it as being a dull, mostly industrial town rammed with the zombies from the prison ships... Sorry, I mean the passengers from the cruise ships. We actually found it a pleasant, mature town with nicely planned Victorian streets and tree-lined avenues. Evidently it had been pretty prosperous for a long time, with some Åland islanders making a mint out of shipping. The old money showed in the quite genteel streets which seemed a million miles from both the Hebridean landscape of Rodhamn and the thick, central European forests of Stockholm. Mariehamn sits at almost exactly the same latitude as Lerwick and freezes up completely all winter, yet it is verdant and prosperous and bright, with avenues of tall deciduous trees and suburbs with industry of all kinds. It's a constant theme of my travels in the north I know, but why the hell is there no industry in the north west of Scotland? And why, apart from the obvious religious nutters, isn't Stornoway a bright, lively, prosperous market town like Mariehamn?

I searched long and hard in Mariehamn for a book which was rumoured to exist – an English language guide to Finnish guest harbours and some wild anchorages, or 'nature harbours' as they are fond of calling them. Having tried the two large bookshops and the huge chandler, I eventually found this useful, if expensive publication, in the office of the west Mariehamn guest harbour. This last was nearly twenty miles round from east Mariehamn by sea but only half a mile up a tree-lined boulevard by Bertie the Brompt. I also managed to procure an Åland courtesy flag. I'm not sure about the legality of flying the thing, since clearly Åland isn't actually a country, whatever the locals might aspire to. But it seemed that even most of the Finnish boats flew the rather tacky, multicoloured cross, so we also complied.

It was getting to be dangerously close to mid summer's day. We had heard that the Swedonians go a bit mad then and that it might be hard finding anywhere to moor. We suspected that the Ålanders might be the same. There were signs in the harbour at Mariehamn. Families were arriving at their boats loaded down with beer and picnicking materials. For some reason boats were being decked out as trees. Birch branches were being strung about all over the rigging of yachts. We suspected that we were about to be subsumed in some ancient, pagan, Viking rite of summer. We fled Mariehamn.

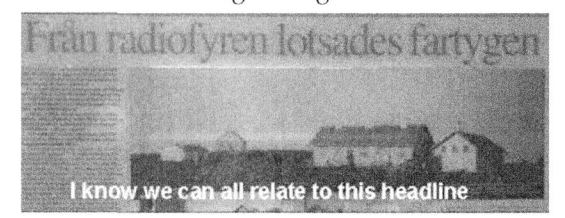

Lumparland

In the morning we motored to the low bridge that opens every hour and lets boats through into the large meteorite crater at the centre of the Åland Islands. Apparently this stretch of water, called Lumparn and about five miles in diameter, is remarkable for having no islands in it. You can actually sail about for a bit without hitting anything. Only in Finland or Sweden would a lack of thousands of rocky islands seem remarkable. Apparently Lumparn was created by a meteorite impact about a billion years ago. We skirted it and headed north through a sheltered, pastoral, riverine environment to take a squint at a medieval castle at, appropriately enough, Kastelholm.

Nautical nutters were out in force. Lots of boats were 'decorated', or ineptly camouflaged, with birch branches. At least two of the passing craft were clearly just houses with outboard motors, which wouldn't have been such an odd sight in a Dutch canal but looked strange in the northern Baltic. The weather was warming up and for once it felt like a real summer's day. Already we had been subjected to climatic moans by Swedes going on about how cold and crap the weather had been and how it's normally thirty degrees in the shade all summer. But today felt like proper summer to us.

We'd hoped for an anchorage, but the head of this bay was occupied by moorings, a guest harbour and a sign saying 'No Anchoring'. The over-eager marina proprietor was hopping about on the shore desperately beckoning us to come in, but we waved cheerily and buggered off again. I don't know if the sign had the weight of law behind it but we couldn't be arsed testing it out. We motorsailed towards Bomarsund, where we had been assured by the old Rustler mannies that a good harbour and loads of fascinating history awaited. Of course it was fascinating because it was British history. An event of the Crimean War involving a British ship, I believe. We weren't that bothered and were looking for an alternative. So when a small yacht ahead of us suddenly disappeared into a wide, shallow bay sheltered from the northerly wind we followed. We carefully dodged the rocks in the bay. The other yacht anchored in front of a house a couple of hundred yards away on the shore. A motor boat came out and took the crew ashore. Clearly they were visiting someone for Midsummer night.

We continued to the next bay and for the first time that summer the actual proper anchor came out and we anchored by the bow – not the stern – in three metres of water. It was a pleasant, open bay and a nice quiet anchorage, but much more like a British one than a Scandinavian. Your average Swede or Finn would have suffered from agoraphobia anchored as we were, over a hundred yards from the shore in a shallowing sea. For most of them one yard is too far away from the nearest rock. We swung to anchor on a pleasant, warm evening and I rowed ashore to explore along the rocks.

The Imray 'Baltic Sea' pilot book says of Finland "The owners of Islands guard their privacy jealously and landing is seldom allowed". Seldom has such a load of bollocks been allowed to be published. The Finns are proud of what their guest harbour guide calls "Everyman Access Legislation", which is similar to, but much older than, the Scottish access legislation. It guarantees rights of access everywhere that's not within a hundred yards or so of a house or on farmland. Since most of the coast – including islands – is unfarmed and uninhabited, this is typically preposterous advice from the largely useless Imray publication.

The leader of the Åland racing fleet looking majestic under full sail

In the morning we set out in the gathering dreich to skirt Lumparland. After Monster, Troll Hat and the canal elves I was looking forward to the Lumparland peninsula at the south west end of the main Åland island. We stayed close to the shore along the north and east coasts in the hope of spotting some of

Lumparland's famously elusive inhabitants. I peered through the mist with damp binoculars but, try as I might, I didn't see a single little orange face or green barnet. Perhaps the little chaps only come out when the weather's nice.

We sailed in fairly miserable weather down main shipping channels that looked like narrow backwaters between islands. Periodically a huge cruise liner would hove into view up the narrow channel, pass us and disappear into the distance. It would leave behind the disturbing image of its terrified, sickly, pallid inmates, their faces pressed to the glass in desperate mute appeal as they were transported off to god knows what hell-hole.

One of the summer's silliest sailing boats

Eventually we approached the island of Kökar. Its main harbour is so well sheltered up narrow convoluted channels that we had to take an almost spiral route into the middle of the island. The pilotage was a wee bit more difficult than many places, but the course was marked by white painted leading lines on rocks, which you'd only hit if you'd really not been paying attention. At the slightly rotting quay we moored between piles – joining three or four other boats – and were stung for the summer's joint highest mooring fee by a superannuated teddy boy. The harbour master was in his forties but unaccountably dressed as a 1950s ted. He charged us thirty Euros for the rickety berth. The Finns are of course the only Scandians who have abandoned their Norks and Kronks and what have you and gone over to the Euro. This fee seemed particularly outrageous when he explained that the showers had no hot water and didn't offer a commensurate discount.

But the village of Karlby, where we were moored, was suitably aesthetic and the surrounding countryside, though bleak away from the immediate environs of the village, was attractive. It was like being moored in a village duck pond a hundred yards from Berneray.

The day wasn't getting any nicer and by the evening it was cold and pissing down. Since I was minging and in dire need of a shower I later braved the cold water. I was shivering under the tap when a horrid, angry old man – I think he was the harbour's night shift – came in and started shouting at me in Finnish. My protestations that I didn't understand Finnish – and let's face it who does, even the Finns struggle a bit – fell on uncomprehending ears. He flung open the windows to let in an icy blast and seemed to be trying to tell me, through the media of shouting and gesticulating, that the water was cold. I explained that I knew it was cold, because I was in it, and closed the windows. He shouted some more, explained that the water was cold, and opened them again. This angry performance went on for some time until eventually I died of hypothermia. His odd behaviour may be partly explained by the Finns' apparent deep antipathy to the simple shower and love affair with the repellent sauna, about which more later.

My discussions with the teddy boy – or teddy geriatric – had strayed onto the subject of national independence. Discovering we were from Scotland he said "We here in Åland are following your struggle with interest, because we also are desperate for independence". Now I'm all for supporting the underdog so I listened to what he had to say about Åland. At the moment they have a degree of autonomy but what he wanted was independence as a 'micro-state'. With a population of about twenty eight thousand it would be a small country, but he cited islands around Britain such as Jersey, Guernsey and the Isle of Man as examples of a successful model. Åland had always been a rich part of Finland, but with autonomy they could attract richer and richer people and become very rich.

Right… now I understood. This was not a case of the plucky, oppressed underdog breaking free from under the jackboot of imperialism. This was rich people not wanting to pay their taxes. They were attracted to the Channel Islands because there people get to use all the universities, hospitals, research, industry and, if necessary, army of the UK, without having to pay for any of it or work to maintain it. He wanted a tax haven for the Baltic super-rich.

I rapidly began to lose enthusiasm for his cause. I pointed out that, with a population of 5.2 million, Scotland was not in a position to have an economy based solely on being a tax haven. In fact Scotland has a population almost exactly the same as that of Finland. In 1917 Finland, population 5.3 million, declared itself independent from Russia, population at the time about 130 million. Was this, I suggested, not a better parallel with Scotland, population 5.2 million, seeking independence from England, population about 55 million? Independence for the Åland islands, with a population almost exactly the same as Elgin, is far more like Orkney seeking independence from Scotland. He was unimpressed. He was sick of paying those nasty Finnish taxes.

Using the proper anchor for once

Popular in the Summer

The next day dawned rather brighter and we sailed off, once we had negotiated the intricate Kökar channels, dead down wind in a force three. I was still getting used to the Finnish way of marking channels. They tended to favour cardinal buoys over lateral ones, making the lines of channels just a little less obvious to follow. A peculiarity of the Finnish cardinals is that they do not have the usual, triangular topmarks. You just have to read which cardinal it is from their colour. At first this seemed a daft omission. But most of the cardinals are tall, narrow, smooth. plastic cylinders. They are about the same width as a topmark would be. It's often difficult to tell the shape of a topmark from a distance. They can appear just as black smears at the top of the buoy. The bottom section of the buoy, of course, is often obscured, either by waves or by weed growth and crap from the sea. If the topmark on a cardinal looks like just a black section of the buoy itself, and you can't tell the colour of the bottom section, the whole system is thrown into confusion. A south cardinal looks like a north or an east, a west cardinal also looks like an east. So missing out the top marks was not actually a bad wheeze, and you soon get used to it.

We were heading for an apparently popular 'nature harbour' detailed in the hugely overproduced Finnish harbour guide. This massive tome looked promising at first, until you realised that its size was a function of the cardboard it was printed on, the huge font and massively blown up chartlets. It was a cross between a pilot book and 'My First Alphabet Book'. Björkö was an island, we were told, with a perfectly sheltered bay in the middle of it. The bay was between three and six metres deep and there were places to tie to the rocks all round, giving protection from any wind direction. This was handy as we had just heard a 'near gale' warning for the area on the VHF. Easterly winds were expected to get up to sixteen metres a second – about thirty two knots – during tomorrow. We were therefore looking for somewhere nice and secure to hole up for the day.

We sailed up to Björkö and motored into the long, narrow loch up its middle. At first sight it looked promising. The harbour was indeed sheltered. A couple of boats were in – a German Westerly and an old wooden motorboat – but they were both tied to a rock on the western shore, with stern anchors to the east. Clearly, if there was going to be an easterly gale, then sitting with your bow literally a foot from a rocky lee shore was a bad idea. We motored around looking for a mooring on the east side. Unfortunately the whole east side was either sheer cliffs with nothing to tie to or shoal rocks with nowhere to get ashore. The entire bay was between twelve and eighteen metres deep. None of it was between three and six metres except just off the rock where the two boats were tied. It was too deep to allow sufficient scope in such a narrow bay to lie just to the anchor. We chucked the anchor over the stern and, with the help of the scantily clad elderly German couple on the next boat, tied to the same rock as them in the meantime. For some time after that I had difficulty sleeping. I couldn't get the nightmarish image of the paunchy old German bloke, dressed only in speedos, bending over to tie our warp to a ring in the rock, out of my mind.

Björkö

Björkö before the gale

I mentioned to the Germen that we had expected this anchorage to be busy. It was billed as one of the most popular in the islands, yet there were only two boats in. The German wifey replied "It is very popular in the summer. In the season there will be a hundred boats here". It was June the twenty fourth. Two days after mid summer. But it was not yet, apparently, summer. We found this categorisation of the seasons to be endemic in Finland. "Summer" lasts from the second week in July until mid August and that's it.

I mentioned to the Germen that a near gale was expected. At first they seemed unconcerned by this information, but half an hour later they pulled up their anchor and buggered off, shouting something about a secure harbour somewhere else. Bloody typical. Within an hour however three other Finnish boats had arrived and tied up next to us. It was probably going to be fine. I spoke to the skipper of a large Halberg and those of the two smaller boats. Each of them was confident that the lee shore rock mooring would be fine in the expected blow. This was a fantastic spot and they'd been here in all sorts of bad conditions.

We relaxed a little and went for a walk along the nature trail that skirted the island. On the island's outside edge we came across two more yachts tied casually to rocks in remote spots. One of them, a large Bavaria, was just tied alongside a cliff as though it was a harbour wall. There was quite a fetch to the east of him. I marvelled at the casual confidence of your Scandinavians. Tying confidently to all sorts of rocks even when gales are expected. I was obviously worrying too much. It was a lovely evening with a fine sunset. We settled down for the night. We were a little discomfited by the thick, pea souper fog that descended around midnight. Nobody ever said they had thick fog in the Baltic. I thought we'd left that behind in the east of Scotland.

We were woken early in the morning by the sound of motors and clinking anchors. The three yachts whose skippers had said the mooring would be fine in a gale were all hurriedly buggering off. They each shouted unintelligible stuff about the coming storm and the need to get into another, unspecified harbour. Shit. We were left with only the motorboat and its monoglottal Finnish occupants. As the wind increased they also hauled up their anchor and tried anchoring on the weather side of the bay. More shit. We hauled up the anchor and tried to get it to set in about fifteen metres on what appeared to be rock in the middle of the bay. I was just considering tying to the poo pump when the anchor held on the third attempt and we nervously awaited the gale.

Yes, the poo pump. In many anchorages in Finland there is a brand new, gleaming, square aluminium floating platform in the middle of the bay. They are in the most remote island locations and seem to be quite a new feature. They are the poo pumping stations where you pump out your holding tanks. I believe every boat in Finland is now supposed to have a holding tank. The Baltic is, after all, a shallow, stagnant sea entirely filled in the summer with boats with pooing crew. I decided however that it was politic not to enquire too deeply into the ways in which we might be breaking the law.

A Bavaria tied to a cliff at Björkö

The wind did indeed get up to over thirty knots from the east from around eleven a.m. until two p.m. As we sailed about violently on the anchor the cliff-tying Bavaria from the previous night also turned up in the bay. Obviously their lee shore rock wasn't proving too comfortable. They tried unsuccessfully to set an anchor for about an hour. In the end I think they just motored around in the harbour until the gale went away. After two the wind began to subside a bit and veer round to the south east. We were grateful that the gallic stuff just showed up fairly briefly during the day. Sitting out a gale in these circumstances overnight would be a very different kettle of fish. We had intended to stay another night on Björkö . We were a tad disillusioned with the place however and I felt I'd had my eyes opened to the reality of apparently easy, confident, devil may care Baltic mooring. We decided to press on east. In the event Björkö was practically the only place I found in the Baltic where the mooring opportunities were less than near-perfect. Nowhere else all summer was so British in its awkwardness. It just didn't conform to the rules of the Baltic Standard Mooring.

At four p.m. we headed off. For three miles or so we battered against wind and waves under main and motor. Then we turned east onto a beat. The twenty knot breeze slowly went round to the south as we turned a little north and had a fast reach at hull speed for twenty miles or so. It would have been the perfect sail were it not fairly cold and damp and did we not have half a knot of tide consistently against us in the non-tidal Baltic. The great thing was that, a couple of hours after it had been blowing thirty knots, there was virtually no swell except at the odd place where there was a gap in the sheltering Skaergaard

As we approached our destination one possible reason for the half-knot tide appeared. We were used to being, if not the only boat out sailing, one of the few. This should have been especially the case on a damp afternoon after a near gale.

But on the horizon a sail appeared and grew closer. Then another. Then three more. Soon the horizon in front of us was a mass of sails as over a hundred boats sailed towards us. It was Monday. At the weekend Helsinki had emptied westwards and was now sweeping towards us. Perhaps the combined force of a hundred boats pushing forward had created the tide. That's possible isn't it? OK maybe not.

We sailed into a bay on the large island of Rosala and picked up a stern mooring in its friendly guest harbour, which was rapidly filling up. Talking of filling up, we topped up with diesel in Rosala. The lad who operated the pump spoke, like all of Scandia, excellent English. The old manny who owned the place didn't however and the lad performed translation duties. I realised that he was speaking Swedish to his granddad, as opposed to impossibly difficult and obscure Finnish. I quizzed him. Even though we were now out of Swedish speaking Åland it seemed that many of the islands in the Finnish Archie spoke Swedish in preference to Finnish. It struck me that this was a potentially difficult problem for the Finns. It is not difficult to ensure that, for example, all Welsh speaking people also speak English as a second language. They need to if they want to study anything to a reasonably high level, for example. Keeping an element of national cohesion through the English language is not difficult. But ensuring that everyone in Finland speaks Finnish is a problem. If your first language is Swedish why the hell would you learn a language which nobody else in the world speaks, with practically nothing published in it, which is famously impossible and bears no relation to any other European language? They seem to get by without apparent deep-seated inter-linguistic hatred though.

Wester Hailes

There were even more yachts pushing west the next day as we beat east into a gentle south easterly. I lost count at around a hundred and fifty. One of them I recognised. It was a dark brown wooden hull with the grain, unusually, running vertically from deck to waterline. It was the cold formed construction of the boat belonging to my chum, the septuagenarian nutter who I had followed out of Delfzijl and over the bar at Borkum, over a thousand miles before. I diverted a bit to say hello They were heading in the opposite direction to us after an anticlockwise tour of the Gulf of Finland. Either he thought the meeting unremarkable or he didn't recognise me, because he pressed on defiantly as if we were pirates threatening to board him. As before I couldn't avoid the impression that I had been lucky, in following the old loony's lead over the Borkum Bar, not to come to grief.

The day was mostly sunny but later the breeze got up to an unforecast eighteen knots and it clouded over. In contrast to Mariehamn the town of Hanko was universally praised by pilot book and Rough Planet alike as a lovely town. We took a stern buoy in one of the two busy guest harbours. In contrast to Mariehamn the town of Hanko was, by and large, a bit of a dump. The area immediately around the marinas was nice enough and there was a sandy beach some way from town which sort of qualified it as a resort. The town was, however, basically a large container port, of the kind that provide vital transport links, a bloody awful bleak, industrial environment and two jobs. In a stroke of planning genius, doubtless inspired by British new towns and estates of the 1960s, the town was rent in twain by utterly impassable roads for the constant container truck traffic to the port. Finding a way across the barriers to the other half of town required some athleticism. About eight tracks of weed-entangled railway sidings provided another lovely landmark cutting through the middle of town. For the first time in Scandinavia I saw empty, boarded up shops and supermarkets with bars on the windows. Presumably to prevent their local customers, sitting pissed on the pavement outside, from looting them. It was a sort of Scandian sink estate. A Finnish Cumbernauld or Wester Hailes.

For some reason, this depressing wasteland was dotted with tourists. Knots of them cycled around, stopping occasionally in front of a chain link fence or a pool of puke to peer at identical, standard tourist maps of the town. What the hell were they doing there? Why would anyone voluntarily spend their summer holiday touring the streets of Hanko? I decided that they were probably anthropological tourists from the future. They had come back through a wormhole to see what a shit-hole looked like in the early twenty first century. Probably they were only virtually there and imagined that I couldn't see them.

Osprey at Alisaari

Back on board I got chatting to a couple of blokes on the boat next door who were from near Helsinki. Like every other adult in Finland who isn't a pilot they worked for Nokia. I mentioned the large number of Swedish speakers I'd seen. They pointed out that this was only a feature of the western fringe of islands. The large majority of the Finnish population spoke Finnish as their first language. In fact there was currently a heated debate about the status of Swedish as the country's second language. Many people, especially from the east, wanted Russian to come more to the fore in schools, on the basis that Russia was very important to the Finnish economy. But there seemed still to be a deep antipathy towards Russia and Russians amongst many Finns. Here it manifested itself as a resentment of all the Russian Mafiosi who, apparently, drove their gin palace motor yachts around Finland driving the prices up. Though I'm sure they exist I have to say that the only Russian yachts I saw in the Baltic were decidedly scruffy, shoestring, Heath Robinson affairs which did not look remotely like the property of billionaire gangland bosses.

Whatever the town's other qualities it was quite cosmopolitan in the marinas of Hanko. There were several German boats, two Russians, a Latvian and, suspiciously, an Australian. At least there was a small speedboat sporting an Australian flag. There was no chance at all that this bloody thing had come all the way from Oz and I concluded that it was a Finnish hire boat that some ignoramus had hoisted his own flag on.

The blokes on the next boat also recommended a very sheltered mooring up some reedy channels thirty five miles nearer to Helsinki, so in the morning that was where we headed. With a force three dead behind us we had recourse to the motor at times, as we sailed and motorsailed across some fairly open water, then down increasingly defined, narrow and sheltered channels towards the Barösund. The scuttler across this sound was a chain ferry. This is a particularly fiendish form of scuttler which can garrotte a boat from a hundred metres or so with its vicious, trailing wires.

As we neared our destination rain squalls caught up with us and gave us a gusty and wet last mile or so. The more exposed quay in the main channel had three foreign boats on it, but we put our faith in the local knowledge of the guys on the boat in Hanko. We skirted a reedy island, passing three quarters of the way round it. We were faced with what looked like an impenetrable shore of tall reeds. The chart plotter just showed green land with no way through at all. The chart on the laptop actually showed woodland right across where the channel should be. But we were expecting this and picked our way round to the narrow, shallow channel through them. We emerged from a winding, muddy, riverine channel as narrow, pastoral and unlike a marine environment as any we'd seen, in the guest harbour of Elisaari. This was a long, rickety wooden staging built out over the water for a couple of hundred yards around the bay, with a wobbly pontoon for the deeper moorings. We picked up one of the few remaining stern buoys next to the pontoon and hopped ashore in what was probably the most sheltered duck pond Zoph has ever been in. A piece of water more unlike your idea of a harsh, northern sea it would be difficult to imagine.

The only conceivable thing that could rock the boat in this most sheltered of harbours was the wash of another boat. It was a through route for shallow draught motor boats and of course a few of their drivers were too dim-witted to appreciate that they were disturbing about fifty people as they passed. Later in the evening the peace was shattered properly however by the arrival of an offshore lifeboat. With lights flashing it surged into the harbour, sending masts waving back and forth wildly. It zoomed up to one plastic caravan of a yacht and stopped. The yacht was just peacefully tied up to the quay. Long and urgent exchanges then began between the lifeboat crew and the crew of the thirty six foot yacht, and on the VHF and phone between the lifeboat crew and god knows what higher authority. Eventually the lifeboat crew, in full wet gear, life jackets and crash helmets, tied the yacht alongside and zoomed off with it in tow. I had evidently just witnessed a dramatic sea rescue. But what possible reason could there be for rescuing a yacht from a peaceful, secure, sheltered berth? None of the Finnish onlookers had an answer. The only light I can shed on the issue is that the yacht was a Bavaria. The normal rules of seamanship and sailing do not apply to Bavarias.

Elisaari

The Scandians do a good lin ein exceptionally sleek sailing boats

Anna was due to fly home from Helsinki in three days time and we were now within striking distance of the Finnish capital, so we decided to stay in this idyllic spot for an extra day. We had, after all, travelled to a different port every day for the last twenty two days, covering 560 miles. We were due a day off. We wandered around the large, treed island. It was a nature reserve with a disused agricultural estate, three or four houses, a cafe, a camp site, the guest harbour and about four hundred saunas on it. We walked the extensive nature trail, with its information signs equally in Finnish and Swedish.

Each of the saunas was in a log cabin strategically placed around the shore, so that its occupants could leap straight into the cold sea from it. You could, apparently, book time in them. The Finns really are crazy for this unhealthy and frightening pursuit. Everywhere has a sauna. Often to the exclusion of everything else. It's not uncommon to find a marina that has several saunas, but no shower. A tall ship available for hire by parties in Helsinki advertised the length, beam and tonnage of the ship, the number of passengers it was licensed to carry and the number of saunas on board. But what is really not right about the phenomenon is the family sauna. Children of all ages, including teenagers, happily trot off to have a sauna with their Mum and Dad. Cast your mind back to when you were a teenager. Imagine you are just chatting to your mates outside when your Mum appears and calls out loud "come and have a nude bath with your Mum and Dad". Deeply, deeply wrong on so many levels and guaranteed to warp young minds. Yet the Finns don't seem to mind even this indignity.

It was interesting to see the way these small, summer islands without scheduled ferry services worked. The café proprietor occasionally, in an open motor boat, crossed the fifty yard channel to the adjoining island, which was connected to the mainland by chain ferry. He reappeared with plastic bags full of food. Just after midnight a large, lumbering workboat slowly entered the channel. It looked almost too wide to squeeze down it, but manoeuvred its way to the shore next to a pontoon. It lifted a pontoon with its fixed crane, moved it a few inches and replaced it. Job done, it slowly manoeuvred its way out down the channel again. On June the twenty eighth they were just putting the finishing touches to the demountable marina for the start of the season.

Thick forest covers most of southern Finland

The Prison Ships

On a beautifully calm, sunny morning, with only a few little Simpsons clouds in the sky, we left Elisaari and motored off towards Helsinki. Griff Rhys Jones admits to having struck a rock, very hard, in the eastern approaches to the Barösund. Now I'm pretty good at finding rocks to hit. If there's a rock there and you want to ram it, I'm your man. But even I couldn't find any rocks in the reedy, silted waters just east of Elisaari.

By mid morning a force three from the south had filled in a little and we were able to sail. The gentle breeze veered behind us however and the day was spent in furling and unfurling the jib as we alternated between sailing and motorsailing. It was a sunny Friday and as we approached Helsinki the world was out on the water. There were more speedboats than we'd seen elsewhere in Finland, but also the usual mix of sailing boats. From large chunky cruisers to racy day boats to classic old yachts.

The prison ships were ranged up in Helsinki harbour. We heard a posh English voice on one prison ship calling another. "Anusol, Anusol, Anusol, this is European Prince, over". "European Prince, this is Anusol, over". We couldn't believe it. Was the bloody thing really called 'Anusol'? We heard it again. "Anusol, this is European Prince". Surely not. It couldn't be. I searched the AIS for a ship with that name. Eventually we decided that it was probably the prison ship 'Aidasol' which was being hailed. As we drew closer I realise it was the ship I had photographed in the Skagerrak with the world's worst taste paint job. A pair of huge Mick Jagger lips painted across the bow to add insult to the injury of the suppositorial name.

We wandered about choosing a suitable marina. The poshest snailing club, on a small island near the centre, seemed subject to a tremendous amount of wash from all the traffic, not least the trip-round-the-bay tourist boats. Oddly there were larger waves in the inner harbour that day than in the middle of the Baltic. We repaired to the east harbour and the HMVK marina, the 'Helsingin Moottorivenekerhon Kotisivuille'. No, I've no idea what it means either, but it was a marina belonging to a club. Here the worst excesses of the touro trip boats were more muted and we were still in easy reach of all the sights of the capital.

The bright lights of Helsinki were a hundred yards away so we wandered off to take a look at them. It was a pleasant city that mostly felt like western Europe but also showed signs of eastern roots. I'm sure this is lacking historical accuracy, but it felt like a city of various periods and those periods include the Tsarist Russian, the Soviet and the modern, post independence. There were, perhaps, even signs of the wartime German influence. Maybe its most striking feature was how much of life takes place outside in the summer. At sixty degrees north it felt a bit like a Mediterranean city. Not only was everyone sitting outside at cafes, but some of the cafes appeared not to have an inside. They were merely kiosks with outside tables. The whole world was sitting about in parks, chatting, boozing and picnicking like crazy. And perhaps that's the key to it. They were absorbing the outside like crazy because they'd not got long in which to do it.

The British have become resigned to being an indoor species. If you suggest that a favourite pub would benefit from some tables outside someone will say "Oh what the hell's the point? It'll only rain". In the UK outdoor pursuits are a marginal, nerdy interest and the term 'rambler' is used as an insult – like 'anorak'. The Scandians – and perhaps the Finns in particular – embrace the outdoors like an ethos – a moral imperative. Perhaps it's still linked to healthy, pagan, Viking philosophies, in contrast to our pallid, musty, etiolated view of life. I'm used to seeing Scandians throw themselves into an outdoor lifestyle in the sticks, but it was interesting to see that your metropolitan Finn had very much the same attitude. So I suspect the love affair with the outdoors is a short lived, manic attempt to absorb as much of life as possible in a few brief summer months.

But many of the people were different to those we'd seen in more rural communities. The city itself was scrubbed and Scandinavian, but a lot of the youth were much more grungy and feral. There were fewer tall, bronzed efforts with flowing blond locks and more pale youths with matted dreadlocks and the arse falling out of their breeks. There was a bit of a punky frisson about the place, albeit quite a safe, sanitised one.

More depressingly, Helsinki was home to large numbers of a group of people largely forgotten by society. They inhabit a cruel, heartless netherworld and most of us choose to ignore their suffering rather than face up to the dreadful reality. Their existence is a damning indictment of a modern, post industrial society which we like to think of as 'civilized'. But no truly civilized society could allow such a situation to continue unchecked. Thousands of them wandered in slowly shifting herds around the centre of Helsinki, their blank faces and dull eyes offering no clues to the torments they must be suffering. As they wandered about they were systematically robbed and exploited by unscrupulous Finns. They are, of course, the occupants of the prison hulks which we still use, shamefully, to get rid of society's flotsam and jetsam – the elderly, infirm and particularly stupid rich.

Every year many thousands of particularly unimaginative old and ill people are systematically herded onto hundreds of these prison ships. They have all their money taken from them, are locked in windowless cells below the waterline and transported at twenty knots around the Baltic, the Mediterranean or the Caribbean. Unwanted by anyone, they are shunted between the dockland areas of many major cities. Here they are allowed, briefly, to leave their prisons, but are made to queue up for hours to get off the ship. Then they are driven in coaches to seamy underworld locations where they have more of their money extorted from them by unscrupulous Mafiosi in exchange for shit souvenirs. Herded back onto the ships they are literally frisked to prevent them bringing aboard any booze or foodstuffs, forced to eat a MacDonald's in a two thousand seater canteen, charged fifteen quid for a gin and tonic then sent back to their cells. The ship then motors to the industrial docklands of another major city and the process is repeated. It is one of western society's greatest causes for shame that this process, so reminiscent of the days of transportation to Australia, still goes on today.

We were getting lazy. We'd only made one passage since our last day off, but again we didn't go anywhere the following day. There were two reasons for this. Not only was Anna flying home on July the first, but June the thirtieth was my birthday… Mind your own business… No of course I wasn't sixty! Since we weren't literally pushing the boat out we decided to do so metaphorically, with a meal in a restaurant. This was in fact the first time I'd eaten out since Den Helder on May the fourth. Sweden and Finland were not quite as expensive as

Norway, but an extended period in either would soon break the bank if you ate in restaurants all the time. The great thing about Scandinavia, though, is that you don't really miss eating out. The Scandians don't really have much of a restaurant culture. To have visited, say, Ireland and not been able to afford to go into pubs would have been tragic. I'd have felt like I was missing out on an essential part of the experience. But everyone in Scandinavia ties their boat to a rock and has a barbeque. If you do the same you're participating fully in the culture. So in an ostensibly expensive country you can live quite cheaply if you go to a supermarket and spend thirty quid or so on the cheapest staples every three days or so.

As long as you bring your own booze. The Swedes and the Finns are funny about booze. They like it. They like it a lot. But they don't like selling it. In Swedish supermarkets there's three strengths of beer. There's three and a half percent beer, which is weak, but still beer. There's two and a quarter percent beer, which is borderline soft drink and there's zero percent beer, which isn't worth mentioning. For anything stronger you go to a state owned shop called a 'Systembolaget', where all prices and products are standardised. It's a similar story in Finland where the State booze shops are called, handily, 'Alko'. I just did a quick Göøglë for the 'Alko' organisation and found that you can download from their website a full set of GPS waypoints for every single shop in Finland where you can buy booze. The data is available in about ten different formats for different map and chart devices. The Finns are fond of both their booze and their chartplotters

If you don't want to be fleeced in state owned booze emporia you can take the Zoph option. Who needs the stress and worry of finding out about foreigners' booze buying traditions. Zoph left Port Ed with 560 cans and a hundred bottles of beer, thirty bottles of wine and about twenty litres of spirits. I was taking no chances. Another commodity that I had run out of and was not expecting to find in Finland was that staple food and nectar of the gods, Patak's Chilli Pickle. Wandering the backstreets of Helsinki I came across a small Asian food shop run by a Sikh bloke who had a small stock of the good stuff. I relieved him of most of it. Unlike other, wimpy, mealy-mouthed, ersatz, amateur chilli sauces, with their promises of searing heat, which are in reality tomato ketchup which has been shown a picture of a chilli, Patak's chilli pickle is just made completely of chillies. I chatted to the Sikh chap about life in Helsinki and the Asian community, such as it was. He reckoned there were about a thousand Indians living in the city. Helsinki certainly felt like much more of a mono-cultural, indigenous city than most major British cities, but here at least there was some evidence of something other than a universal monotone of white Finnishness. And the restaurant meal? Yes, very nice thank you, though it did involve taking out a mortgage for two courses.

A Peeling

Back aboard Zoph I noticed another boat in the packed marina. It was largely unremarkable but somehow, out of the many thousands of boats I'd seen so far that summer, this one seemed strangely familiar. It was a standard thirty six foot plastic cruiser-racer of seventies or eighties design. The only slightly unusual thing abut it was that it was painted red. It was a Danish flagged boat called 'Wasa' and hailed, according to the sign on the transom, from a place called Horsens. I mentioned to Anna that it seemed familiar. She pointed out that this was scarcely surprising. We'd seen thousands of boats. Many of them were cruising in the same direction as us and it would be odd if we didn't see some of them several times. But no. This was different. I felt as though I'd seen Wasa somewhere else, a long way away and quite a long time ago.

I racked by brains to plumb the very deepest depths of my knowledge. As you can imagine this didn't take long. I fired up the laptop and started dredging back through whatever old photographs of Zoph's cruises hadn't been deleted and were still on it. This took a lot longer. I trawled through thousands of pointlessly kept, duplicated, out of focus digital holiday snaps. Finally I found something, just the suggestion of a bit of red topsides peeking out from behind a dot of another boat in a photo of the view across a bay.

I saw a couple of mannies boarding Wasa and wandered over. A chap with an impressive handlebar moustache was in the cockpit. "Good evening" I said, "did you enjoy your trip to the Isle of Man". In an extremely gratifying double take he said "Yes thank y…w w whaaat!" "The Isle of Man" I repeated. "Did you enjoy your stay in Peel, where you arrived at five p.m. on July the fourteenth 2011?" He was properly, pleasingly dumbfounded by this most unexpected connection with exactly the opposite end of Europe. He was even shaking slightly as he called his chum into the cockpit and offered me a beer. We reminisced for a while about the Isle of Man and the Irish Sea and what a pain in the arse tides were. There are a lot of apparent coincidences when you are cruising and statistically it would be odd if there weren't. It's actually quite a small world of people doing much the same things and going to much the same places, but I thought that seeing the boat from Peel at exactly the opposite end of Europe and having a photo of it was a properly appealing coincidence.

In the morning I sent Anna packing on the bus to the airport and thought about heading off east. My goal was the Russian border. I didn't have a visa for Russia so didn't intend to enter the country, except perhaps by sneaking over the border a few yards just to say I'd been. It's not difficult to get a visa, but you do need to apply in advance and pay money and so on. A standard goal for people cruising up the Gulf of Finland is to get as far as Petersgrad, or St.

Leninsburg as it used to be called. This involves not only a visa but an eighty miles passage down shallowing, muddy and increasingly industrial channels to the drab outskirts of a large industrial city. I'm sure it's a great place to visit, but you can get there on a cheap weekend deal from Edinburgh so I wasn't that desperate. I was more interested in seeing the places you can't get to without your own boat.

Another option was to pass through Russian waters off the east of Finland, travelling through Russia by the Saimaa Canal and back into the massive network of inland waterways that makes up the Finnish lakes. The only route into this apparently lovely world was through Russia and though it didn't require a visa, it did require paperwork and permissions to have been filled out several weeks in advance. I had therefore decided that the Russian border would do for me. I could then turn round and potter through Finland's million lovely islands, with perhaps a side order of Estonia just to be able to say I'd been to one of these Baltic states.

But for the moment everything was on hold. Helsinki was suffering from a phenomenon which, I was assured by local sailors, didn't happen in the Baltic, thick fog. With that annoying absolute, confident certainty with which so many old yachting blokes are able to be completely wrong, the local pipe-puffing sage on the landing stage told me that fog never, ever lasts for more than an hour or two. It would burn off over the course of the morning. Just before eleven a.m. his prognosis seemed to be confirmed as the fog thinned. I motored off across the bay, though ominously the ships' foghorns were still blaring intermittently.

I headed down the narrow back roads eastwards out of Helsinki. As soon as I emerged into the more open sea I was, of course, plunged into the middle of both a thick fog bank and a huge racing fleet of classic wooden yachts. Were it not for the fact that the latter kept looming at me out of the thick white fog and it was all I could do to avoid the buggers, it would doubtless have been an impressive sight. About a hundred classic yachts, of two different classes, tacked about in the rocky bay. I didn't bother with the sails until I was well clear of the ghostly fleet in the fog, just to leave no doubt as to who had right of way. But then the sails went up, the engine went off, the fog finally lifted and I had a pleasant down wind sail. Once again the channels were more and more landlocked and shallow the further I went, until I was sailing between shallow, reed clad shores in the sun.

There were still plenty of boats about but a lot less traffic east of Helsinki than there had been to the west. The Finnish Navy was also more in evidence. On a couple of occasions I was passed by a speeding naval shooty-ship. The way the Finnish Navy camouflage their ships says a lot about the waters in which they operate. Instead of painting them grey they daub them with green, brown and black splodges, the way tanks and army trucks are traditionally decorated.

Finnish coastal waters are so astonishingly spattered with forested islands of all sizes that the Navy actually disguise their ships as trees.

The night's mooring had been recommended by the helpful, chatty wifey who ran the marina in Helsinki. Bockhamn was one of the hollowed out islands that seem to be ubiquitous in Scandinavia and to exist nowhere else. It's hard to resist the idea that some bugger has designed a harbour when the middle of a small island is filled by a perfectly round pool, about a hundred yards across and uniformly three metres deep all over. Especially when the entrance is two boat widths wide and two metres deep and the bottom hardly shelves towards the edges at all. Instead a ring of solid, natural rock like a concrete quay, sticks straight out of the water so that you can step right onto it from the boat. And when the entire twenty foot high island is covered in a forest of pines that acts to break the wind completely. The only sign of human activity is the composting bog in a little hut that has invariably been provided for yachties. You could sit out a hurricane in these perfect environments in total security. And, what is more, they are entirely free. I promised myself that, on the way back, I would seek out more of these free anchorages and eschew the marinas. I'm sorry to go on so boringly about how perfect these Baltic anchorages are, but they are. Bockhamn seemed to be a little known example. A couple of locals I'd spoken to had never heard of it and there were only three other boats in the roomy harbour. It was certainly well hidden. As you approached the narrow entrance it was hard to believe that there was a way through for a boat and there was no sign of any boats until I was right inside the round pool.

Helsinki

Prison hulks at Helsinki

Some early morning rain had just about finished and the sky seemed to be brightening as I left the next morning. A nice south westerly was blowing up at between twelve and twenty knots and I looked forward to a pleasant summer sail. It was, very definitely. not to be. A bank of very thick fog rolled in from the sea. From a distance, of course, it looked very nice, glistening white in the sun. Suddenly we were enveloped in a damp, dull, cloying fog much thicker than the day before. It stayed thick all day and, like an east coast haar, the wind continued to blow a good force five. I reminded myself at intervals through the day that, according to the sages on the pontoons, they just didn't get persistent fog in these parts.

A GPS and a chartplotter are, of course, pretty handy things in a fog, but amongst the rock-strewn waters of the Baltic they are essential. In fact it's difficult to imagine how people survived in a fog in the days before their invention. In most parts of the world it was possible to navigate out of the shipping lanes and, when close quarters navigation was impossible, stand out to sea until the fog lifted. Admittedly on the east of Scotland this might mean being at sea for an extra fortnight, but it was a survival strategy. Off the coast of Finland it's entirely different. You are permanently surrounded by a jumbled mass of rocks and small rocky islands. Most channels are well enough marked, but not lit. The margin for error in finding the right path between the rocks can be less than ten metres. In these conditions it's not good enough to be pretty decent at dead reckoning.

When the fog cleared I could see the fleet

Later I asked a couple of old salts what people used to do in a fog before the days of satellite navigation. Apparently there were two strategies. One was just to stop where you were and put out an anchor. Most of the sea is shallow enough for this and the waters are mainly sheltered enough to be able to lie to an anchor even in the 'open' sea. The other was to hit a rock and sink. This latter strategy had, apparently, been followed by many seafarers of old.

I was heading for the island of Kaunissaari and wondering if this was a good idea. The small harbour was reputed to be sheltered, but in a south westerly the entrance was difficult and the offshore reefs meant that you had to follow closely a series of small, unlit cardinal and lateral buoys just off a lee shore. With the help of the chartplotter I picked my way from buoy to buoy. The visibility was no more than a hundred metres. I would approach the position where a buoy was supposed to be and begin to panic as I couldn't see the bugger anywhere. But when they were a bit under a hundred yards away the buoys generally appeared.

We picked our way towards the narrow entrance. The last bit was a slightly adrenalin-filled downwind surf and a sharp turn into the tiny harbour. I could only dimly see the nearby marks and hoped I'd read the topmarkless cardinals correctly. We were pretty much in the harbour before I could see its rocky walls. We picked up a stern buoy as the breeze continued to increase to a force six. The waters in the harbour were perfectly sheltered, but the harbour walls were low and here the wind whistled dramatically in the rigging as it blew more and more fog down on us. As always the weather sounded more dramatic and severe in the harbour than anywhere else. There's always one boat with clanking halyards and one with an in-mast furling main, or some such folly. that acts like a massive, howling wind instrument.

Your typical Finnish fishmonger's shop

There were quite a number of boats lurking in the harbour of the pleasantly sandy island waiting for the fog to lift and I was invited aboard the Beneteau next door for a late lunch. Like almost everyone in Finland they were friendly and interested in where I'd come from, giving the lie to their national stereotype as dour buggers who are obsessed with their personal space. I told my Benetoidal chums that I was intending to turn around at the Russian border and not press on either to St. Len's or the Finnish inland lakes. They told me that they had heard rumours that you no longer needed advance permission to pass through Russia – and the Saimaa Canal – into the Finish lake system. They thought that the Finnish Government had entered into a new agreement, just that summer, that allowed boats to pass through Russia without any advance paperwork. Bugger. I had made up my mind what I was going to do, but now was thrown once more into confusion. Should I just turn round at the border, or carry on through Russia to the lake system.

I pondered the knotty problem as I wandered the island by Brompton. Back aboard I spoke to my neighbours on the other side in a Jeanneau. They were amongst the several people I met in Finland who had bought their boats in the south of England when the exchange rates were favourable. Most were slightly disappointed by the condition of their purchases. The problem is that a ten year old boat from Britain is about five times older than a ten year old boat from Finland. For a start our boats are in the water for about three times as long each year as Finnish boats. They are often on relatively exposed moorings and even our marinas are much more exposed than Finnish millponds. I found describing to a Finn the sorts of conditions you might expect at Port Edgar in a north easterly gale more or less impossible. I have routinely seen conditions in Zoph's home port in which anyone brave enough to go onto the pontoons has to progress on all fours to avoid being thrown off into the sea. Dock lines snap under the strain of the mammoth surge. Visitors can sometimes scarcely believe that this is a marina where people leave boats unattended. In Kaunissaari, with about twenty two knots of breeze and a flat calm harbour, my chums on the Beneteau said that it was nice to be safe and secure in harbour, listening to "the storm" going on outside. They don't get exposed to a lot of proper weather.

But also, crucially, our waters have salt in them. Try this experiment. Buy a packet of peanuts. Get a close friend to suck one of the peanuts for five seconds, then drop it into a pint of tap water. Drink the water. That's how salty the Gulf of Finland it. It's virtually fresh, if manky stuff. So nothing corrodes on a Finnish boat. By contrast ours are rusting, flaking hulks. When you add to all this the fact that the Scandians are absolutely obsessive in their constant cleaning, scrubbing and polishing, I'm not sure that importing a boat from the UK is a good idea

Everybody was open mouthed in amazement that we continued to be in the grip of a fog. They couldn't believe that it was foggy and yet windy. It seemed blindingly obvious to me. It was just a haar. The southerly blowing off an increasingly warm continent was picking up loads of moisture, then cooling across the relatively cold sea and condensing out to make fog. It just made me feel at home, but not, I must say, in a good way. I sat and waited for the bloody thing to clear and allow me a squint at Russia. In the early evening it did so and in the pale setting sun I peered across due south at the oddly named island of Gogland, which belongs to Russia. I was able to see Russia! I was immediately corrected by angry Finns who said that Gogland used to belong to Finland and was, by rights, Finnish territory.

Another yacht appeared and started negotiating the cardinal buoys into the harbour. People seemed terribly concerned for their safety in the lee shore entrance in a choppy sea. Did they know what they were doing? But the visibility was perfect. Nobody had shown the slightest concern for me when I'd navigated the same route and couldn't see my hand in front of my face. Out of sight, out of mind.

No 'U' Turns

I still had not the foggiest idea whether I was going to Russia or not the next morning as I headed off east, towards the border. My plan was to check out what the rules now were for crossing the Russian frontier, by first heading to the customs entry point on the Finnish island of Haapassaari, some fifteen miles away. I negotiated the still rolly sea around the closely packed cardinals and across the reef, this time in full sun. What looked from most angles like a random scattering of buoys were quite worryingly close together and near the rocks. Perhaps I had been lucky to get into the harbour in the pea souper the previous day. The wind was still blowing a nice sixteen to eighteen knots from the south west and I had a really good sail in the warm sun across waters relatively uncluttered by rocks. It wasn't exactly a straight line course but it wasn't the corkscrew track between lumps of rock that I was used to.

It was a pleasant fast reach for once and I sailed at six knots right into the bay in front of Haapassaari island. I tied up against the customs quay next to a rather racy looking, German forty footer with a crew of about eight. They had just returned from St. Pete's and the uniformed customs lad was down below, presumably checking out the boat for smuggled matryoshka dolls, or perhaps a series of identical but smaller yachts hidden inside the large one. I chatted to the crew while I waited. The next time I would see this boat was three weeks later when I helped to rescue them from certain death... well, a mildly embarrassing running aground actually, on an island off the coast of Sweden.

When he'd finished anally probing the German boat I asked the border squaddie whether it was true that it was now possible to pass through Russia without a visa or paperwork in advance. He didn't know – rather oddly I thought – but immediately got on the mobile phone to another border post, further east on the island of Santio, to ask them. They confirmed that the rules had indeed now changed. All I had to do was turn up at Santio and they would process me and send me off into Russia. Bugger. I had been sort of hoping that this would prove an insurmountable barrier and that I would have to turn round and start heading back. I sort of needed someone to put a barrier up and make the decision for me, so that I didn't just have to do a 'U' turn. For no good reason, at some more or less random point. I thanked him and cast off again.

Just to take a look at what was purported to be a particularly narrow channel to a particularly sheltered harbour, I nipped along the south coast of Haapassaari and squeezed down the ludicrously narrow channel, into the surreally sheltered natural harbour which filled the centre of the island. There were rocks within five metres on either side in the channel, but it was well marked and its entrance even had a handy wee island to the south to provide perfect shelter in almost any conceivable set of conditions. Once again it was difficult to believe that it was a product of natural forces. Tied to a rickety wooden stage in the stupidly sheltered harbour were my Danish chums from the Isle of Man aboard Wasa. They were just preparing for an overnight passage to St. Len's Burg. After a brief chat I gingerly picked Zoph's way out of the harbour, lined with red painted ex-fishermen's houses, which now kept in the family as summer retreats. The proud artisan days of yore, when Haapassaari was one of Finland's largest producers of the letter 'A', were now long gone. Outside I set sail again and headed north east for Santio, some twenty miles away.

I still hadn't decided whether I was going to Russia or not even as I sailed, now on a slow broad reach, towards the border. I'd discussed it on the phone with Anna and she had said that I was welcome to go through to the inland lakes for another week or two, in a tone of voice which meant "don't you bloody dare go any further"

Kaunissaari's cardinal buoys were confusing enough even when I could see them

. On the one hand there was a whole new country – practically a new continent – to explore. On the other hand I was now over a thousand miles from Port Ed as the crow flies. And that's nautical miles, not your puny earth miles. Zooming out on the chartplotter it looked a hell of a long way home. I'd come over thirty degrees east of Edinburgh, to the longitude of Turkey. They are somewhat meaningless statistics, but if I went twice as far again I would be further east than anywhere in India. Just in terms of easting I was already more than a quarter of the way to Australia. That's not too bad for a wee summer cruise in a twenty seven footer, a lot of it solo.

Also the season here was short. The Finns all had their boats lifted out by the end of August and in September the Göta Canal more or less closed down. I might want to go back that way. It would take me a couple of days to get through to the town of Lappeenranta, on the lakes. Then a few days cruising around, then two days back again. I was probably adding about ten days to the journey. If I turned round now I would be able to explore the fantastic Archies of Finland, Åland, Stockholm and all down the east coast of Sweden at my leisure, tying to rocks in limpid pools on deserted islands as I went.

But finding these buggers in a pea souper was tricky

Passport control at Haapsaari

I decided I should definitely turn round at the border. I sailed on. On the other hand it was still early July. I had plenty of time and the Finnish lakes were reputedly lovely. Another week or so wouldn't matter. With about five miles to go I decided that I definitely was going to press on through Russia. By now there was no other traffic on the water. The relatively few yachts in this far eastern part of Finland had petered out to none at all as I approached the border.

It's always a problem on a cruise, deciding where to turn round. When I went to northern Norway I turned round at a more or less random point just north of the Lofoten Islands. Everyone said "But why didn't you go on to Tromsø?" If I had gone as far as Tromsø everyone would have said "But surely you should have gone as far as the North Cape". From the North Cape I would have been exhorted to carry on to Russia. And so on. If I turned round now I knew that everyone would want to know why I didn't go on to St. Len's or the Finnish lakes. But then why stop there? Why not head through the Russian canal system up to the White Sea? Or head south through the inland waterways to the Black Sea. If you do a 'U' turn anywhere people will tell you, with the massive certainty of someone sitting cosily in a pub at home who doesn't have to make the decision, that you've turned at the wrong place.

The Danish yacht 'Wasa'. From Peel to Haapsaari

Haapasaari

There are only two rational solutions to this problem. Either you ignore everyone else and just turn on your heel at some random or symbolic point that suits you, or every time you go on a summer holiday on the boat you have to circumnavigate the world. You even have this problem if you go for a Sunday stroll up a track. At some point you have to turn round and go back. I'm always looking for a suitable gap where there's no one looking before I do this. You feel quite eccentric, marching determinedly on, then suddenly just doing an about-face and marching in the opposite direction.

As I was thinking all this I was, all too rapidly, approaching the frontier island of Santio. This was an island inhabited only by the border guards, with a harbour sheltered by a couple of adjacent islands. I sailed past the border post, leaving it to port and snapped some rather uninspiring pictures of the Russian islands to starboard and ahead. As is always the case at such borders, there was nothing at all dramatic about the difference between the two countries. The border now came from the sea on Zoph's starboard quarter and snaked off northwards, between islands so close together you could, if it wasn't that it would have been considered an act of war. throw a stone from one to the other.

Russia

I was now just a couple of hundred yards from Russia. I didn't want to risk crossing the border without the proper permissions as I'd heard bad things about being boarded by the Russian Navy. Now I really had to decide. I had come 1741.6 miles and was now over a thousand miles from home as the crow flies and Zoph very definitely doesn't sail. I was at 60°27.133' North, 27°42.602 West. Only as far north as Sullom Voe in Shetland, but just over thirty degrees east of Zoph's berth under the Forth Bridge. I was now at the longitude of Turkey. The same distance east again would put me at the longitude of Pakistan. If I could carry on for twice as far as I had been I would be north of Calcutta. To stretch the literal interpretation of my easting to breaking point, I was over a quarter of the way to Australia. That was enough for a summer cruise in a twenty seven footer, wasn't it? Especially when a lot of it had been done solo. I put the helm hard over to starboard, gybed and hardened up on a beat to start the long, slow trek home.

I had only gone about a mile when there was a flurry of activity from Santio. Two uniformed blokes with schemy haircuts like american soldiers leapt aboard a large military RIB and zoomed towards me. As is the custom with Customs they described almost a full circle around Zoph at a considerable distance before screeching to a halt beside her. Where, they wanted to know, had I come from and where, moreover, did I think I was going? I think they were a tad confused and that someone was due a telling off. They were obviously supposed to be watching the border but had presumably been dozing off when they suddenly saw a small yacht, which had apparently entered Finland illegally from Russia, heading west. On the other hand they had been phoned by their mate from Haapassaari and knew that they could expect a British yacht to come from the west. I explained that I had just turned round at the border having decided not to go through Russia. "But why don't you want to go through Russia?" they demanded. All the

Passport control at Santio

published information says that the border between Finland and Russia is a heavily guarded and difficult one. You are told that visas are a must and trying to cross the border without the requisite paperwork will land you in jail for years. Here were the Finnish border guards practically pleading with me to bugger off into Russia. I must confess I was tempted. But I said "no, thank you". They shook their heads in mute frustration and zoomed off back to their base, their day's excitement over.

I turned Zoph back on course, adjusted the main sheet and settled down over the tiller to start my seven week journey westwards.

Bloody Subscriber Identity Module

A potential problem with this journey immediately became apparent as the gentle, following summer breeze and friendly ripples turned into a chilly headwind and a short, steep chop. Most of the trip back would be directly into the prevailing wind. I knew this would be the case, of course, and that it would not be a serious problem amongst the closely packed, sheltering islands of the north and west Baltic coasts. But the prospect of battering into a chop all the way home was nevertheless uninviting.

Although we were now in High Summer and the waters were reputed to be packed with holidaying Finns, I saw very little traffic this close to the Russian border. A single large ketch overtook me, coming from Russia, as I headed west for ten miles to spend the night on the island of Koursalo. The English language Big Boys Book of Finnish Anchorages, published by the Sea Scouts, dedicated a whole double-page spread to the jetty here, which turned out to be a small deserted pier for the occasional small ferry, complete with timetable posted on the wee shelter provided for passengers. An old bloke and his grandson were fishing off the pier as I arrived. When I asked if it was OK to tie up there they disappeared wordlessly into the woods like a couple of startled hobbits. With no other boats about I tied up alongside the pier in one point four metres of water and went for a wander.

There were no roads on the two square mile island, which was dotted with holiday cottages. These ranged from the humblest of sheds to four and five bedroomed houses of the kind the seven dwarves might have holidayed in if they had been overpaid graphic designers. With no sewerage on the island the gardens each contained the composting bogs which are the most common things in Finland after boats and trees.

I wandered with difficulty between the largely deserted houses. The only tracks on the island were swathes of shorter grass, cut from the undergrowth quite recently by a bloke with a strimmer. But each track ended at a house. When I tried navigating off piste I soon became lost in the dense forest. Not for the first time I thought that the Finns, along with the Swedes, must be the world's least fit outdoor freaks. They live and breathe the healthy air of the countryside, but are more or less house and boat-bound by the thick vegetation that crowds in on them on all sides. There they sit, revelling in the healthy outdoor lifestyle, whilst they stuff themselves with high cholesterol barbeque-matter and alcohol.

Not for me this unhealthy lifestyle. I went back to Zoph and began the serious daily task of depleting the stock of beer cans. I did a rough stock-take. I reckoned I was down to the last two hundred and fifty cans or so. Calculating roughly how many more days I had to spend in Scandinavia, I realised that this situation could be serious. This got me thinking about my route home. Having skirted the north coast of the Gulf of Finland on the way out, it might be interesting to travel along the south coast on the way back. This would mean getting a look at the Baltic States of Estonia, Latvia and Lithuania, the Russian enclave of Kalingrad, then Poland and Germany. This southern coast is however very different to the Scandinavian side. There is no sheltering fringe of islands. Instead there are long, monotonous stretches of shallow, sandy coast with few ports. I would need to head west, then south west, into the prevailing wind, along a coast where it would be necessary to do several long passages, including perhaps a couple of overnight ones. The latter part would be off a lee shore. On the other hand it would also not be exactly monotonous to explore the coasts of Finland and Sweden again. They are so rammed with rocky islands and perfect anchorages that I felt I had only scratched the surface on the way out. Surely it would be better to stay to the north side.

A pleasant, interesting and less ugly alternative to the prison ships

The Finns dislike their sprogs so much they always tow them at least twenty yards behind the boat

On the other hand, the beer was much, much cheaper in Estonia. It was, as the young people apparently say, a 'knob rainer'. I would nip across the Gulf of Finland, at least for a visit to Tallinn, the capital of Estonia. That way I could say I'd visited one of the Baltic States and also stock up with beer.

Unfortunately, I had to go back to Helsinki first. My means of communication with home, my mobile phone, had packed up about ten days before. It seemed that the bloody SIM card was, somehow, terminally broken. The massive multinational company Vodaphoney had refused point blank to send a new SIM to anywhere in Finland. Not even to their main office in Helsinki. The huge international leviathan could only dispatch stuff within Britain. It was up to tiny, sub-national me to deal with the international carriage. After a long email exchange and on the brink of a seizure due to their infuriating communication policy, I had given up. The thing that came closest to sending me into an apoplectic fit was the format they used for their emails. Clearly this had been designed by a sadistic practical joker. They would say "Thank you for your enquiry. No, we cannot do what you ask or indeed anything else to help you. I hope this has been useful to you. Please let me know if I can be of any more help". Anyway, the long and short of it was that Anna was sending a new 'SIM' to the sailing club marina in Helsinki, where they had kindly agreed to hold mail for me. Hence my trip to Estonia would need to be postponed until I had been back there.

I sent texts to a number of people bragging that I had reached the Russian border. Gordon, who had joined me for the North Sea crossing, replied saying "Why did you stop there?" I thought again about the border guards' near insistence that I sail on into Russia. To compound things further, Anna told me that the Saimaa Canal website mentioned that some yachts make the transit and that "You may see yachts from as far away as the southern Baltic". How bleedin' annoying! We could have been such an exotic rarity and it was only a day trip away. As usual massive regret, amounting almost to a gut-wrenching guilt, engulfed me at the thought that I should have carried on. Hopefully I'll never have to make a decision that has properly serious negative consequences for anyone. I get to feel regret after deciding to have an egg butty for breakfast instead of a bacon one, so I don't know how I'd cope with that.

My pondering on routes was interrupted by a spectacular sunset over a mirror-calm bay. I spent possibly the best evening of the cruise to date contemplating serene nature and photographing the sunset for, amongst other things, the cover of this book. As the pink and orange flush in the sky moved slowly round to the north, I sat enjoying the view from my own private pier on an ostensibly deserted island, congratulating myself on having at least made it as far as Russia.

I needn't have worried about contrary winds for the moment, as the next day dawned bright, warm and sunny with bugger-all breeze and a mirror-like sea. After a while a very gentle easterly blew up and we made slow progress under full sail. But it soon went round to the west and died completely. We pressed on under motor with the main up, though it wasn't achieving anything. Some entertainment was provided by a large Swiss motorboat of about fifty feet. They had an AIS transmitter and I watched them on the chartplotter heading up dead ends, round small islands, stopping and starting and turning in ever decreasing circles for no apparent reason. Evidently they were just going slow and mucking about. Perhaps trying to catch one of the three remaining fish in the Baltic.

For some odd reason they had called their craft 'Rolling Swiss'. Doubtless they thought this a cool, romantic sort of name, redolent of the aimless wanderers in hippy 'road movies'. An alpine equivalent of a rolling stone. In fact, of course, it made me think only of a rolled up jam sponge. Though a much faster boat than Zoph they were clearly in no hurry and I was to come across Swiss Roll on a number of occasions in the coming days.

Another gin palace overtook me, this time at about twenty knots and throwing up a large, antisocial bow wave. I was surprised to see that this monstrosity was British flagged. But it was a relatively small one with more the look of a thing used for sport fishing than long journeys, so I suspect it was Finnish based. Paradoxically, you don't find boats going properly long distances at twenty knots.

As I headed further west the yacht traffic increased a little. It was becoming properly hot now and the Finns were starting to go into full-on summer mode. A number of boats were towing dinghies a long way behind into which they had put their sprogs. This excellent arrangement seems to be a Scandian speciality. Just bung all your recalcitrant sprogs into the Avon Redcrest on a fifty metre line. Then you can motor along enjoying your snooze and your G&T to the full. Put some music on and you can't even hear their moans, or the screams as one of them falls overboard and is left behind. Perfect.

The hot weather hadn't changed the preferred nautical attire. Most people still had, of course, bare feet, but they still sported thick woolly bobble hats. A very odd arrangement presumably occasioned by a temperature imbalance caused by excessive saunaing. Nearly all the sprogs in Finland wore woolly hats at all times, even when they were running around madly and it was twenty eight in the shade. Very strange.

After forty five or so very pleasant, summery miles I nipped into the almost landlocked loch at Lillfjärden. This was another anchorage with a double page spread in the Finnish Big Boys Book of Buoys. My first attempt to find the advertised public mooring buoys came a cropper. Near the entrance to the loch was a series of glossy red stern buoys off a spick and span pontoon with an array of leccy connections. I was – reasonably politely but firmly – informed by a wifey on the only boat on the huge pontoon that this was a private club mooring, so bugger off.

Nearby was a rickety old pontoon with four half-sunk old stern buoys and, fifty yards away on land, a picnic place and the ubiquitous composting bog. There were no other boats and I had my pick of the buoys in this pleasant spot, with thick reeds stretching out from the heavily forested shore.

Soon I was joined by another boat. It was a Finnish Jeanneau intriguingly called 'Ecosse Spirit' crewed by a fireman, his Janice Battersby doppelganger wife and their two children. It transpired that the boat had been bought from a Scouse bloke in Conwy, but had been named by a Scottish bloke who had originally kept her, unaccountably, on Lake Windermere. Very strange. I mentioned casually to the fireman that I was surprised at how quiet everywhere still was. He sort of agreed, but explained that the season hadn't really started yet. It was July 4th. He was gratifyingly amazed that someone so young looking and fresh faced as me could possibly be retired. But then he was married to someone who looked exactly like Janice Battersby, so perhaps his eyesight wasn't that great.

I asked the fireman about property values on these islands. Did they often change hands or were all the holiday 'huts' in the family for generations? He supposed that a decent house with a view and a piece of sheltered seafront might fetch around €400,000.

The butter was migrating into the bilge again. After the brief heatwave in May it had reverted to being a solid block. I didn't exactly need an ice pick to chip bits of it off, but it was definitely a solid. Now the temperature was back up to proper summer and it was once again in its liquid state. It didn't even solidify properly in the bilge, as the sea temperature in the sheltered anchorages was now up to twenty degrees. This was the magic temperature the Scandians had been looking for to begin their nautical cavorting. When picking out an anchorage your average Scandian pays much more attention to the thermometer, which comes as part of the hull transducer, than he does to, for example, the weather forecast. His main concern is to find water of lounging temperature.

As well as the stern buoys off the pontoon there were also a couple of conventional mooring buoys a bit further offshore. A motorboat turned up and picked up one of these at the stern. They couldn't be arsed walking it forward to the bow so swung all night to a mooring tied to the stern quarter with a piece of string. Your crusty old RYA trained British skipper would have a hairy fit.

I spent a pleasant evening marred only slightly by the distant, deep growl of an internal combustion engine. Some twat had evidently fled to the quiet of the countryside, then felt the need to run a generator all night. There is nowhere on the planet free from this noise. Paradoxically the further from centres of population you go and the quieter the ambient noise gets, the louder and more intrusive the motor of the individual anti social bastard sounds.

In the morning I was treated to more gentle easterlies and hot sun as I headed further west under full sail. The true breeze peaked at twelve knots but was frustratingly fickle. At times Zoph sailed along nicely, goose winged. At other times the sails hung like net curtains and I had to fire up the motor. The traffic was increasing exponentially as I headed west and got nearer and nearer to Helsinki. The boats without far to go persisted with sailing. One or two flew spinnakers. The rest of us had a go at sailing, but gave up from time to time and motored across the flat calm sea.

This time I took the back route into Helsinki. This involved passing

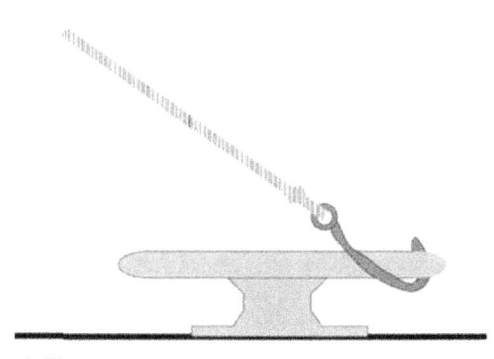

A Finnish approach to mooring using a cleat

through a lifting road bridge which was supposed to operate every half hour at quarter to and quarter past the hour. I joined a stream of vessels of all kinds heading pell-mell for the bridge. They all drew ahead of slow old Zoph. But the bridge opened as we approached, about ten minutes earlier than scheduled. Zoph just squeezed through and the bridge slammed shut before the next boat could get through. A wee stroke of luck. I filled up with diesel at the sailing club marina, then picked up the same pontoon mooring I'd left five days before.

There were two other British boats in the Marina. One of them, a small and scruffy Westerly Centaur was, predictably, permanently based in the Baltic. The other, a posh, French built, aluminium Allures 45, was the only boat I saw in four months that summer which had come from the UK and was intending to return to the UK in the same year. They were from Brighton Marina – so they must have had money – and were heading for St. Petersburg before returning to Brighton. Other than them, it is remarkable how entirely uniform the rest of the British flagged fleet was. I didn't see that many, but all the rest of the twenty five or thirty British flagged boats I saw throughout the Baltic, Germany and the Netherlands were based abroad.

The bloody SIM card hadn't arrived yet and I had to wait for the thing to appear. It didn't come in the post the following morning and I had just about resigned myself to waiting another day and was heading off into the town when the marina girlie appeared waving a small envelope. With the new Vodaphoney chip fitted into my phone I cast off at one p.m. and headed west.

A Side Order of East Land

It's only about fifty miles across the water from Helsinki to Tallinn, but a one p.m. start was clearly far too late for a wimpy day sailor, so I just headed eighteen miles or so west along the coast to the wee island of Stora Bredskar. I wasn't that disappointed to be too late to make the crossing, since there was a south easterly force five to six blowing, which would have made a fifty mile journey south across open sea rather unpleasant. So I picked my way down the usual convoluted channels between islands, sailing fast in the warm sun, mostly on a broad reach.

Stora Bredskar was billed in the Finnish harbours guide as being a cornucopia of perfect places to tie up, around a series of sheltered bays. In reality there were few places to nose into the steep cliffs and nowhere that looked very secure, with strong easterlies forecast. I found a deserted pontoon with a series of stern buoys for public use. Though it was exposed to the east I managed to sneak behind the pontoon into the shallows, getting at least some shelter from the floating barrier.

I had just decided that we were secure enough, albeit on a lee shore, when I heard a gale warning on the VHF. Winds in excess of sixteen metres a second were expected from the east overnight. Sixteen metres a second – about thirty one knots – counts as a gale in wimpy old Scandia. There was a half mile fetch from the east and we were moored about three metres from a lee shore. Deciding that this might be decidedly dodgy I cast off and went looking for somewhere better.

Three boats were tied to rocks on the other side of the shallow, rocky bay, their sterns attached to buoys. A fourth buoy lay unused. They were facing directly east onto an island shore. The island was only two cables across but provided perfect shelter in a small bay behind tall trees. From the signs on the shore, though I couldn't exactly understand them, it was clear that this was a set of moorings belonging to a private club of the type that had evicted me before. I headed into the shallows and hailed an elderly couple, who were disporting themselves on rocks. I asked if it was OK to moor there. They didn't reply – they were that rare breed of Scandian, the non-English speaker – but beckoned me onwards. They pointed out a route that avoided the rocks and took my lines. Sorted. I congratulated myself on finding the perfect mooring for the night and the coming gale, I thanked them, finished tying up securely and went below to make dinner.

From the window in the galley I saw my chums approaching the crews of the other two boats. A long conversation ensued between the three couples, with much waving of hands and pointing at Zoph. Things seemed to be getting quite animated. Finally a couple broke away from the group and walked determinedly along the shore towards me. They stopped next to Zoph and called 'Hello!' Bollocks. I was clearly about to be evicted. I toyed with the idea of pretending not to have heard them, but in the end, with a heavy heart, went into the cockpit.

"Hello" the old bloke said. "This is a private club". Damn it! I knew it. I prepared myself for a plea to their better nature, but with a feeling of inevitability. "You are very welcome to stay here. Welcome", he continued. It was with some relief that I heard that he was a Vancouver enthusiast, who had been surprised and pleased to see a Vanc. enter the bay, as it gave him a chance to blag his way aboard and take a look at her. I invited them aboard and fed them a beer. He explained that, whilst club moorings on islands like these are private, only the snootiest ones will send you packing if the place isn't full. since there's an element of sharing and visits between different clubs.

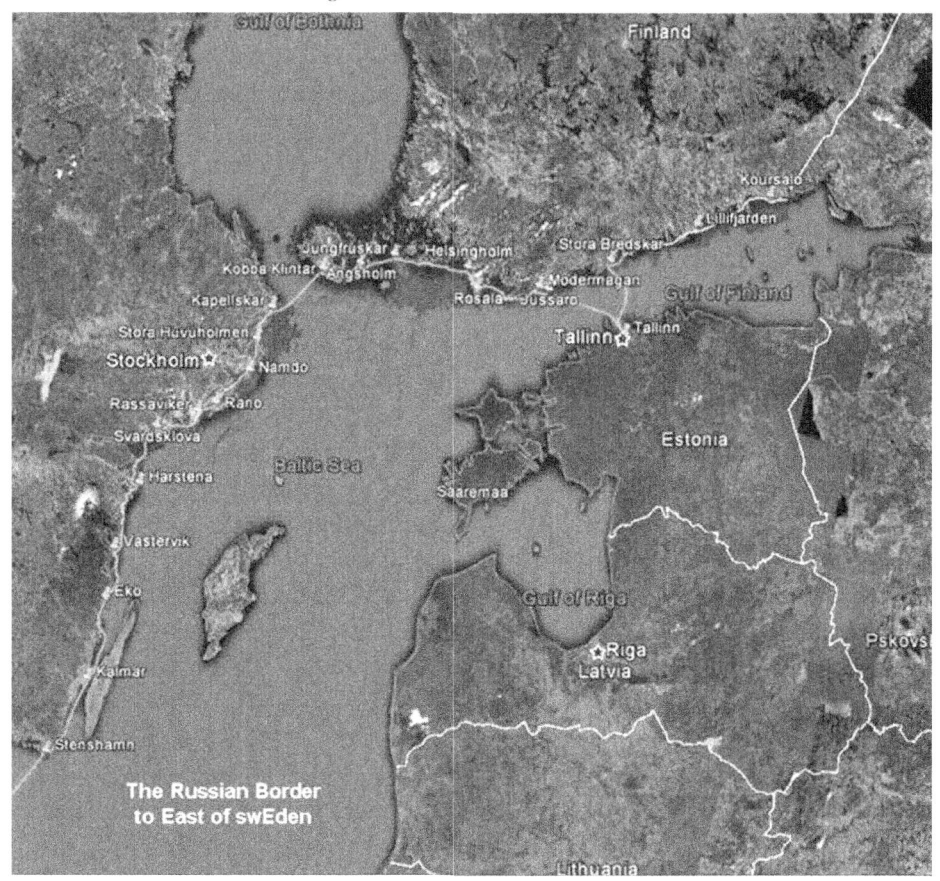

The Russian Border to East of swEden

Later, after a complete exploration of the pleasant island, which took a full ten minutes, I went aboard his wee long-keeler, not too dissimilar to Zoph. Most of these sailors are coastal potterers, not serious passage makers. My new chum was a case in point. He proudly showed me his new, very basic VHF. He was pleased with himself as this was the first time he'd owned a radio. He was a retired electronic engineer who had been sailing and owned a yacht all his adult life, but had never felt the need for a radio aboard. The RYA, I thought, would not approve. We exchanged email addresses and parted firm friends.

Back aboard I mused on the Finnish character. Before I arrived in Finlandia I had a stereotypical view of its denizens as a shirty, private, potentially unfriendly crew. This was reinforced by the nonsense about privacy published in the Baltic Pilot published by Imray. I was reminded of the Finnish 'joke' I had been told the only other time I'd visited Finland, for an academic conference in 1991. It went like this. A Finnish bloke lives by himself in a hut in the forest. He has no neighbours and knows of no-one else. One day he finds an empty fag packet on the banks of the river that runs past his house. Clearly it has washed downstream. So he prepares for a long journey. He hikes up the river . For days he sees nothing. But eventually, after walking for many days, he sees smoke curling above the trees. Guided by it he finally reaches the door of a hut, similar to his own, in which one bloke lives. He enters the hut and shoots him dead.

Now I appreciate that this 'joke' isn't actually funny. But I had been persuaded that it accurately represented the Finnish psyche. Nothing could be further from the truth. For the most part they were startlingly friendly and gratifyingly interested in where I had come from and how I had got there.

The wind of the small gale whistled in the rigging all night as I steeled myself for the coming crossing to Estonia. East Land at last.

After a couple of days of sun, cloud was building as I left the next morning. The gale hadn't really lived up to its billing and all that was left of it was a force four from the east south east. Following the directions of my Vanc.-fancying chum I picked my way south through the rocks of the sheltering reef. Here there was no pink or black line on the chart and I was off piste, but managed to reach the open sea without embarrassing myself or sinking. The breeze was due to continue from the south east, perhaps moving a little more south, so I headed due south and whenever possible tried to push a little bit further east. This would allow me to bear away to the west a little, as I approached East Land, and would hopefully prevent me getting headed. There always seems to be some reason not just to go in a straight line from A to B.

But in the event the wind soon dropped for an hour or so. After I'd motorsailed for a bit, it came back as a nice force three from due east. I bore away a little to the west and had a fine efficient sail, on a beam reach and a near flat sea. Apart from dodging some shipping heading between Russia and the rest of the world, the only thing to mar the trip was the rather ominous looking clouds that began to build up in the afternoon, bringing with them an unforecast bit of westerly breeze. It wasn't much of a breeze, but I'm always unreasonably paranoid about weather that doesn't do what it's supposed to. My paranoia knows no bounds. On this passage I saw a couple of white flecks in the air as the ominous clouds were building. I immediately assumed these stray seagull feathers were the start of a freak snowstorm. It was about twenty six degrees in the shade.

As usual I enjoyed that part of the trip from fifty percent to seventy five percent through the passage. For the first half I'm always worrying about what conditions I can expect. After that I relax. This time I was so relaxed I kept falling asleep. I yawned my way across much of the Gulf of Finland – the Yawning Gulf, as it isn't known. For the last quarter I'm always worrying about where the hell I will stay that night. Unlike Finland, Estonia was said to have a dire shortage of places for yachts. Boating of all kinds has recently taken off and demand is far outstripping supply. The one large, out of town marina at Tallinn was rumoured to be permanently full and all the books said that the main harbour had no facilities for yachts. But I had heard that there was a new visitor facility in this harbour and it was to this that I pinned my hopes for a mooring.

High, towering black clouds were building ominously as the Finnish flag was struck and the one for East Land, which I had not recognised in Rendsburg, was raised. I followed three or four boats converging on Tallinn from various directions. A fifty foot ketch, motorsailing fast, overtook me. Then I passed it as it stopped and described a series of small circles as they struggled with their jib furler. They passed me again sans jib. Then I passed them again as they drifted about trying to get the staysail down. Eventually they overtook me again. Then I passed them for the final time as they struggled personfully with the mainsail in-mast furling system. From miles away I could see the recalcitrant main flapping about as they sought in vain to get rid of the thing. It confirmed my suspicion that the concept of a furling main is only useful as the name of a minor character in a period drama. As in, for example "Forsooth, sirrah, do I espy that gay blade The Honourable Sir Reginald Fortingbrass-Furlingmain?" Amongst the mass of vessels beginning to appear on the AIS in Tallinn harbour was a fishing boat. She seemed to be high and dry, about a quarter of a mile from the sea, in a shipyard on the outskirts of town. She was called 'Nessie'. Therein, no doubt, lies a story.

The fantastic Baltic Sea Pilot says that the approach to the general area of Tallinn is easy because there's a TV mast and a convent which can be seen from a long way away. But it doesn't bother mentioning where they are, what they look like or indeed what they actually lead you to. Reading it is like asking for directions from a five year old. "You just keep going until you get to my Granny's house!" Instead of giving directions for getting into the harbour, the 2010 edition of the Imray pilot devotes a paragraph to explaining how to find the room in a Tallinn hotel that has a fax machine. Yes, a fax machine. Remember them? An elderly, retired Finnish sailor to whom I mentioned this said "Fax machines... yes... my Father told me about them".

The new visitors' facility is buried in behind the ferry port so I needed to call up the harbour on the VHF for permission to enter. This was the first time I'd used the radio in anger since the Dutch Coastguard debacle, more than two months earlier. I entered the harbour and was shepherded to a very sheltered spot on the half full, brand spanking new pontoon complex, by a young lad on a BMX bike. The only thing wrong with the mooring was that Zoph had her arse pointing straight at an open air disco, at which the good denizens of Tallinn partied until the wee hours.

On the positive side the hyper swish pontoons all had cleats. Yes, real cleats! Gorgeous, smooth, moulded, cast alloy truncated 'T' shapes bolted onto the decking. You could just hop off the boat and wind a couple of turns of a warp around their lovely, sensuous curves. This may seem unremarkable and I may appear to be salivating in an unseemly way at a mundane artefact. But in wee-metal-ring obsessed Scandinavia the normal cleat is as rare as hens' teeth. Everybody finds the wee metal ring extremely difficult to use for mooring. Finns and Swedes agrees that cleats would be much better. But no cleats at all exist in Scandinavia. It was amusing to see some of the Finns' attempts to use these lovely items to tie their boats to. Wedded as they are to the wee metal ring – of the sort traditionally attached to the nose of a bull – they desperately seek a means of clipping their tiny short lines to the cleat with a hook, with hilarious and potentially disastrous quinsequonces.

I was still admiring the gleaming cleats bolted to the new brown wood when BMX Boy said "You will need to check in at the office with your Technical Passport". "My What?" "Your boat's Technical Passport". I explained that I hadn't the foggiest idea what he was talking about, that I had never heard of a

'Technical Passport' and that there is no requirement for a British boat even to be registered as anything at all, never mind being issued with a passport. With furrowed brow he muttered that this might present a serious problem.

Later I wandered up to the hyper-swish new office, through the serious security gates with a key code and an intercom. I took Zoph's 'Certificate of British Registry' and insurance document in the hope of diverting attention from the 'Technical Passport'. In the event the official, with his swanky new job extracting money for berths in a swanky new marina, didn't bother asking for anything except money. He seemed preoccupied by an inability to operate the computer system. Technical support was provided by BMX Boy.

This is fairly typical of cruising in northern Europe. It's easy to find scare stories, on the interweb and in the sailing press, about how you need reams of documentation in every port. You will apparently be fined for crossing a shipping lane at an angle, imprisoned for not using an anchor ball and beheaded for carrying red diesel. The horror stories are fuelled by the Daily Mail reading Little Englander's antipathy towards the EU. The reality is that you would be extremely unlucky to experience any problems at all cruising round every country in northern Europe without any documentation, insurance, passport, radio, lights or indeed trousers. If you turn up somewhere, they are most unlikely to turn you away.

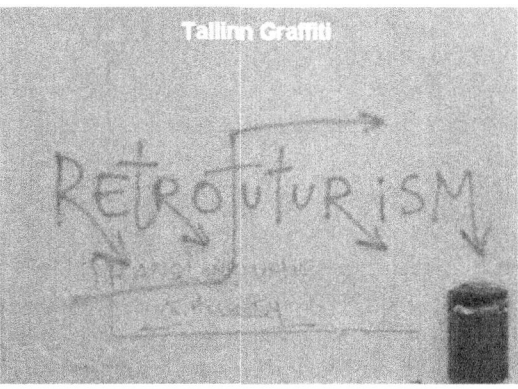

Tallinn

Tallinn Graffiti

Better Out than In

The main point of the posh new marina was as a loading point for Finns to stock up on booze. Unlike the equivalent facility for Norgians in Lerwick, which consists of a bloke called Bert with a Transit van, the dockside at Tallinn is thick with huge warehouse supermarkets stacked to the rafters with cheap beer, wine and spirits. A constant procession of beery Finns trundles trolleys of booze back though the Alcatraz security gates to their overloaded boats. Much of the booze is Finnish. It is delivered by Ferry and freighter from Helsinki to the off licences of Tallinn, where Finns buy it and deliver it back to Helsinki. Clearly a massively inefficient system but driven by a natural desire for tax avoidance. It struck me it would be a lot more efficient if the Finns could go to a booze outlet in Helsinki to load up their trolleys. At the checkout they would be asked if they had a boat and if so how much booze they would normally carry back from Estonia. If they said, for example, twenty crates of beer, they would be allowed to buy twenty crates tax free. This would save everyone an awful lot of trouble. What could possibly go wrong?

There were sound medical reasons for joining the Finns in stocking up with cheapo, fizzy local beer. I can understand that you might not be interested in this, but I have always been wholly incapable of belching. At farting I'm something of a master. Indeed I would not have been cruising in the Baltic had London been holding the Flatulympics that summer, as well as the boring old Olympics. I would have been romping to certain gold. But for most of my life I have never been able to manage even the tiniest apologetic burp. This inability to excrete large buildups of excess gas has been something of a disability in that it restricts me to drinking flat, 'real ale' types of beer. Or, indeed, their ersatz canned equivalents with 'widgets', such as Boddingtons.

Over a period of over thirty years of dedicated beer drinking I had only belched about three times. After enforced consumption of a few pints of fizzy, lager type beer I have very occasionally felt such a build-up of internal pressure that I have become absolutely convinced that I am going to throw up. On these occasions I have hurriedly left the pub and found a fence to lean over. After a minute or two the banks have inevitably burst but, instead of throwing up, I have let out tremendous, hugely prolonged, devastatingly loud belches of world-beating proportions. After which I've felt fine again. On no other occasions have I been able to manage even so much as an oral zephyr. This bizarre condition has meant that I have never been able to consume proper quantities of fizzy beer. Instead I have had to resort to wines and spirits or, since I've had the boat, lug hundreds of gallons of non-fizzy beer around with me.

Then, at the age of fifty two, for no apparent reason, one day I let out a small belch. Over time more followed. Now, for the first time in my life, I am able to burp more or less at will. I can drink near-infinite quantities of fizzy drinks and contentedly emit periodic belches to relieve the pressure, just like the rest of humankind. Like a toddler with a new skill I'm not very mature at using it and am still undergoing social skills training about when and where it is appropriate to burp, but it's a skill of which I am inordinately proud. All of which means that I could now, for the first time in my life, join the parade of Finns trekking backwards and forwards to the cheap booze shop. You may not feel the richer for learning about this miracle healing of mine, but better out than in is what I say.

I followed the rumble of the trundling trolleys and stocked up with a modicum of alcoholic beverage. I was just in time. Just after I'd loaded the booze aboard, the towering clouds loomed darkly over us. There were several bright flashes of lightning closely followed by loud crashes of thunder, then it started pissing down. It proper pissed down. Huge drops of rain bounced off the sea, the pontoons, the boats and the land so that it became difficult to distinguish which was which. The air was so full of water as to blur the distinction between sea and atmosphere. It was a proper, warm summer downpour.

Since I was only intending to stay one night I wanted to take a look around the town, despite the continuing downpour. So I sploshed up the hill in full waterproofs. Soon I was immersed in the steep medieval streets of the old town, amongst knots of bedraggled, wandering touros in flimsy cheapo ponchos crafted of approximately the same material as bin bags. That's one advantage of being nautical. You are well equipped with waterproof gear compared to the poor inmates of the prison ships who didn't bother packing a mac' because it was a summer holiday.

Tallinn was surprisingly vertiginous compared to everywhere else I'd been that summer. It seemed odd that the town behind this shallow, gently shelving, sandy coast should be built atop high rocky cliffs, whilst all the land behind the steep to, rocky shores of Scandinavia was low, shallow and sandy. I only climbed a couple of hundred feet up through the town, but after the flatlands of that summer it seemed like scaling the alps to the viewpoints from the high, commanding walls.

You can see why Tallinn is a draw for culture-and-booze tourists from Finland and further afield. As a relatively new addition to the European Union it was refreshingly cheap, pleasantly scruffy and a little run-down. To a British tourist it had some of the appeal of the Mediterranean town of thirty or more years ago. Here it was still possible to patronise the old and wizened by snapping their photos as they trudged to church dressed in black.

Architecturally the feel was not at all Scandian – no timber houses here – but much more Germanic or central European. I slid around on the steep, cobbled streets, crowded in by overhanging old buildings. One area of the old town was hooching with large bars churning out cheap beer in surreally large glasses. From the bars leaked the raucous cries of the Essex lads, together with their equivalents from the rest of Europe, on their stag dos. The grey, stooped figures of the prison ship inmates shuffled past in the rain in long rows, hurrying back to their cells before the curfew.

I had problems with the economic model in Tallinn. I understand why booze is so much cheaper in Estonia than in Finland – they just tax it a lot less. But why are the restaurants a quarter of the price? There's no massive taxes on food. There's no differential import duties. Both countries are in the EU and both now use the same currency. The Estonian Kroon, or EEK! As it really was known, was recently abandoned in favour of the Euro. (You don't officially have to put an exclamation mark at the end of the EEK! But it really looks like it needs one). Any Estonian restaurateur could quite legally set up a restaurant in Helsinki, import all the food and staff by ferry and, presumably, undercut his rivals by well over fifty percent. But they don't. It's not as if land and property is at such a premium in Finland. Yet the Finns continue to pour across the Gulf of Finland by ferry and yacht for their annual affordable restaurant meal. I don't understand economics.

Back at the maximum security marina I had a go at a shower. Though posh, the marina was suffering a bit from Finnish disease. Though littered with saunas there was only one shower room, which was in a portacabin, labelled male and female. I had a quick look inside. It was indeed just one open changing area and a communal shower for both sexes. Obviously modesty forbade the use of this shameful, Scandinavian arrangement, so I braved the male sauna room and used the adjoining, open, preparatory shower. Half way through my ablutions two fat, pasty Finns came in, stripped off, slapped themselves heartily about the haunches and paunches and sweated off to the sauna, laughing and slapping each other on their naked backs. Having rinsed off the worst of the detritus I fled into the night, leaving them to their strange and disturbing practices.

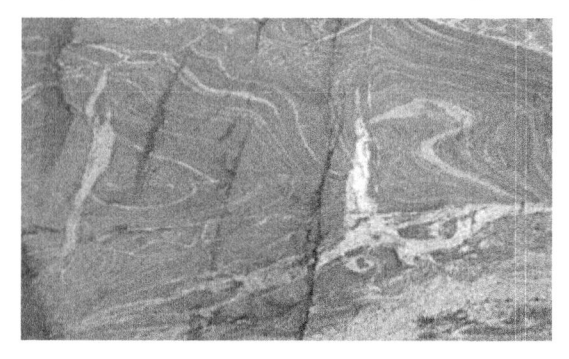

I spoke to a German solo yachtsman who had apparently seen Zoph in Helsinki. He was doing a circumnavigation of the Baltic and now heading home via its south and east coasts. I agreed that this was an appealing route, but pointed out its difficulties. He was now faced with several long passages, including a couple of overnighters. He had one day of settled weather to come, after which the wind was due to come back quite strongly from the west or south west. On the Finnish coast this shouldn't be a problem. On the coast of the southern Baltic States, with their shallow lee shores and bugger all shelter between widely spaced ports, it could mean a lot of long hold-ups.

He told me he was from Berlin. Assuming that the boat wasn't actually kept in Berlin I made the mistake of joking that there couldn't be many yachts in Berlin, given that it was hundreds of miles from the sea. He took a quite Germanic approach to being affronted and explained to me that there were more boats round Berlin than in the whole of the rest of Germany. Tens of thousands of yachts, apparently, sail the inland waterways and lakes of the middle of Germany. Europe is riddled with massive complexes of well used internal waterways, where our small scale maps just show a lot of green stuff. Because we have a lot of coastline in Britain we continue to imagine that we have a close and intimate relationship with boats and the water. But the rest of Europe floats about on a million canals and lakes and fjords and canals, without even asking our permission.

It was quite cosmopolitan in Tallinn harbour. There were even a couple of Oz boats, though they weren't real ones, but bought by Aussies in Europe and sailed locally. That night the loud partying in the disco twenty metres from Zoph carried on until the small hours. Given that I am generally driven mad by unnecessary noise at night I remained remarkably sanguine and relaxed about it. The reason for this is simple. Partying late into a summer Saturday night is not unnecessary noise. It is an entirely necessary activity. I draw the line at karaoke at two a.m. though. Or indeed any karaoke at all at any time. For god's sake will you please frigging well shut up!

The Phone was in the Oven

The following day was warm and muggy, with hazy sun and a gentle south easterly to send me back to Finland. Four other yachts followed Zoph out of Tallinn, but all turned more to the north east, presumably heading back to Helsinki as we turned a little west. After the first hour I saw no more yachts but a fair amount of commercial traffic to dodge, looming out of the haze. I was accompanied on this journey by a million insects of practically every conceivable type. Bees, wasps, flies, ladybirds and butterflies flew past or alighted on Zoph right in the middle of the Gulf of Finland, over twenty miles from land. There were, mercifully, no large tarantulas though.

Doubtless the insects were caught in the updraft of warm air that began to form towering thunder clouds by late morning. There was an ominous inevitability about the onset of thunder and lightning. As always on Zoph the first sign of atmospheric electricity was the anemometer packing up. I don't know if this is a recognised problem with the wireless, Tick Tack system, but since fitting it, every time I've come across lightning the anemometer has refused to transmit any data beforehand and for the duration of the storm. At one p.m. the electrical storm arrived, accompanied by massive downpours bouncing off the sea and taking the visibility down to a few hundred yards. A couple of ships appeared out of the rain surprisingly close, but I was able to keep monitoring them on the AIS.

Or rather, I could keep monitoring them as long, as we weren't struck by lightning, frying the electrics. Being the only thing for miles around with a big metal stick pointing up into the sky is never an enviable position during a thunderstorm. I must say I'm not a fan of it. Given the number of products marketed to yachty types which are described as essential on the grounds of safety, I'm always surprised that we aren't sold more products to conduct lightning, or prevent damage to electrics and computing caused by it.

In the absence of any more specialised technology I put any vaguely sensitive electrical equipment that wasn't screwed down into the oven. In went two laptops, the camera, a hand-held GPS and the phone. I'm assured that this isn't as eccentric as it sounds as the oven is an improvised Faraday cage. Happily nobody rang during this period and I didn't have to say 'Sorry, I didn't hear the phone ring on account of it being in the oven'.

We weren't struck by lightning, the storm passed and in due course Zoph picked her way back through the Finnish rocks to the relative shelter of a pontoon with stern buoys on the island of Jussarö. When I arrived there were sixteen boats ranged around the small pontoon and it looked full. But I was beckoned forward to a space and by the end of the evening the pier was rammed with twenty four boats and was definitely full. One of the newcomers was the Swiss Roll and from their arrival onwards the air was rent with the sound of tiny wavelets, slapping hard under their transom and oddly shaped bow. It must be nigh on impossible to sleep on a lot of modern boats with this common design flaw.

I was approached by another Vanc. enthusiast – the second in Scandinavia – and invited him aboard for a beer. He had an Albin Vega and could only, of course, aspire to the heights of a Vanc. I wandered ashore onto the facility-free island. Aside from a single composting bog the only facility provided was a man to demand money – a rarity in these normally free National Park anchorages. I paid him then asked where I could put rubbish. "Nowhere" he said, going on to explain that there was no water either. Thanks.

I walked round the island on the 'nature trail'. Jussarö had large reserves of iron ore and had been an iron mine until the 1960s. A large part of the island was many metres deep in spoil from these mines and its centre was a surreal, post-apocalyptic film-set ghost town, of knackered industrial buildings and blocks of flats. It seemed an odd choice for a popular National Park island and I wondered why so many boats were here, given that they all had to pay.

I wondered at it even more when the forecast westerly force seven arrived in the evening. All the boats started rolling about fairly dramatically and 'Rolling Swiss' began living up to her name. The pontoon was exposed to a long fetch to the west. Various skippers roamed the pontoon looking concerned. Being used to the routinely extreme conditions at Port Edgar, I wondered what all the fuss was about. The masts weren't even crashing together yet and it was still possible to walk on the pontoon without staggering about or going on all fours.

The strong westerly was forecast to continue the next day, but Jussarö was a little uncomfortable, so in the morning I decided to press on a short distance to a more sheltered anchorage. I was, of course, spoilt for choice, but headed for the perfectly sheltered bay at Modermagan. I battered into a force six for an hour and a half, peeking into a couple of anchorages before settling on Modermagan. I chucked a stern anchor in and tied to a couple of trees next to two other boats. With a low rocky hill covered in thick pine forest a yard ahead of Zoph, it was hard to believe that there was any breeze at all. A quick scramble up the hill confirmed that it was still blowing a good force six. Not a ripple disturbed the flat calm of the lovely bay.

An afternoon and evening in Modermagan would have been pretty much perfect, had it not been marred by the rudest, most ignorant, shirtiest bastards it has ever been my misfortune to run up against in Scandia. It's not always easy to see the underwater rocks on the approach to shore in these anchorages. Nor is it always easy to hop off the bow with a line without ramming a rock. So there is a generally accepted convention that people help each other by taking lines. Everywhere you go, if there is another boat already tied up, someone will hop ashore from and you can throw a line to them. This is not always a blessing, of course, as ham-fisted gits haul the boat onto the rocks or tie a line on the downwind side, but it is a useful and friendly convention.

A small yacht, crewed by Daddy and Mummy, a male teenager and a female teenager, came into the bay while I was wandering about away from the boat. They circled the anchorage, then slowly began nudging into the shore near where I was standing. I wandered over, smiled and waved encouragingly. No acknowledgement. I stood in front of the boat as it came within a yard of me. The glaikit teenaged lad stood on the bow next to me. I said "Hi" and held out a hand to take a line. He looked right through me. There was not the slightest hint of a sign that any of them could see me at all. He jumped from the bow, straight at where I was standing. I leapt out of the way or he would have collided into me. The Dad jumped ashore and walked straight towards me. Again I had to jump out of the way before he walked into me. I began almost semi-seriously to wonder whether I had become invisible. They bustled around trying to make the boat fast. From their garb – they wore everything short of a woggle – and their activities, it was clear that they were of a boy scout persuasion. Daddy spent half an hour futilely trying to hammer a galvanised spike between two rocks to hold a line. Clearly this was a new toy for him as he could have made fast to one of the numerous trees or massive boulders that were strewn on the shore.

I mentioned the behaviour of these twats to the bloke on the next boat to Zoph. He confirmed that it was normal practice to take people's lines for them and couldn't understand their rude behaviour. I suspect that they were a family of accomplished fantasists. Their holidays consisted of an Arthur Ransomesque pretence that they were intrepid explorers and the first to set foot on newly discovered lands. Part of the game was to ignore the existence of the rest of humanity. Very strange.

Abandoned iron ore miners' housing on Jussaro

I spent the evening tracking Hamish the Flying Vegan on the AIS. My chum Hamish the Flying Vegan, who is not really called Hamish, isn't a Vegan and is not capable of unaided flight, had foolishly been persuaded to join a German prison ship with his brood. Astonishingly, he was apparently being shunted around the Baltic in our old acquaintance the Good Ship Anusol. We had been vaguely thinking of meeting up if our paths around the region crossed. But theirs was a whistle-stop tour of the crappest industrial harbours in Scandinavia. Now they were heading from Russia to Stockholm, passing about ten miles offshore.

Zoph's mast just protruded out above her sheltering island and on the chartplotter I could see Anusol, being slowly overtaken by an even more gargantuan block of floating flats. Texting AIS positions was as close as we got to meeting up for a pint that summer. It was so sheltered and quiet that later in the evening I began to worry that the loud report of opening another can of beer would wake everyone on the other boats moored in the bay. One of my brands of Finnish beer from Estonia was called 'Koff', another 'Lapin Kulta', which surely means, for some reason, 'Rabbit Cult'. Around midnight a low, long, sleek wooden yacht sailed into the bay and tied to the rock next to me just before we were enveloped in thick fog. The din of them rolling up their nice crisp white sails for the night echoed deafeningly around the bay.

I was expecting much lighter south westerly conditions the next morning, but was still battering into a force five or six just off the port bow, for the first four hours or so. Starting with a full main I soon reduced it with two reefs and the bit of sail did help us push through the short chop. Despite this I didn't see a single other boat going west with any sail up. And there were a lot of boats. Probably more than I had seen at any time so far that year. A constant stream of vessels of all kinds was streaming west against the wind, with a fair number of serene, smug gits sailing calmly east. Most of the route was nicely sheltered behind islands, of course, but there were places where a larger swell or an unpleasant chop broke through the skaergaard and endampened me. The conditions were not improved by the occasional gin palace that would churn past, semi-planing, with the bow high up in the air and pushing along a wall of white water.

Half way through the journey I passed the peninsula of Hanko and was able to bear away to the north west a bit, unfurl the jib and raise the staysail. With a strung out fleet of holidaying yachties, we sailed on a fine reach at up to six and a half knots and it felt a bit more like a pleasant summer passage. We hardened up to sail into the bay at Rosala, which was predictably busy. At first the pontoon there looked full, but I managed to squeeze diagonally onto a corner of it, between a large Beneteau and a middle sized one. All the buoys were taken, so I deployed the stern anchor on a particularly long line, since the pontoon was to the lee of us and there was still a strong breeze blowing.

Later I realised that I could have been pushier in squeezing between the boats in more shelter, further down the pontoon. That's what later comers did. But my neighbours on the smaller of the Beneteaux were friendly and with a few fenders all that would have happened had the anchor not held was that Zoph would have been pushed sideways onto it. I was invited aboard the smaller

Beneteau for a drink. I congratulated these local Finns on their excellent English. Apparently the wifey had a degree from York University, their daughter was doing a PhD at Cambridge after getting a first degree from the LSE and they had bought their previous boat in Lymington, on the south coast of England, and sailed it back to Finland. For refreshment I was offered both the sublime and the ridiculous. A 56% proof Bowmore single malt, with a bowl of M&Ms on the side. There must surely be some European directive against that.

The Beneteau bloke told me a Finnish joke. It was the same one as I'd been told twenty years previously, about the bloke seeking out and shooting his nearest neighbour. Presumably there is only one Finnish joke. If, as a nation, you are going to have just one National Joke, you should at least try to ensure that it's a funny one.

Back aboard Zoph I saw another boat approaching. It was about a thirty six foot cruiser racer of 1980s vintage, crewed entirely by toddlers. There were about eight folk on board, none of whom, literally, could have been over eighteen. I had seen such crews before and a bloke on the pontoon confirmed that this was probably the Sea Scouts. They approached close to Zoph's diagonal anchorage. I had about forty five metres of chain and warp out in twelve metres of water. The sprogs headed quite fast at Zoph then, with half a boat length to go, flung an anchor over the stern. People took their lines and made them fast. They were blowing down hard onto Zoph in a twenty five knot breeze. They had out no more than twelve metres of anchor warp, in ten metres of water. The anchor was effectively resting directly under the boat, achieving nothing at all. It would not have been possible to make it set at all, even if any of the foetuses on board had felt the inclination. The thirty six footer was just relying on Zoph's anchor holding, as indeed was Zoph. Most of the Finns present seemed to find this a perfectly reasonable arrangement. I didn't. I suggested, politely enough I thought, that they try again. Seemingly terrified they raised the anchor, cast off and retreated to the other end of the pontoon.

The next incompetents to show were aboard a Swedish Ketch. Their attempts to moor were so inappropriate and half-hearted as to be laughable and they too soon gave up and buggered off. It was remarkable to see the Scandians, cool and casual in perfectly calm, sheltered conditions, trying to moor in a bit of breeze and a little chop.

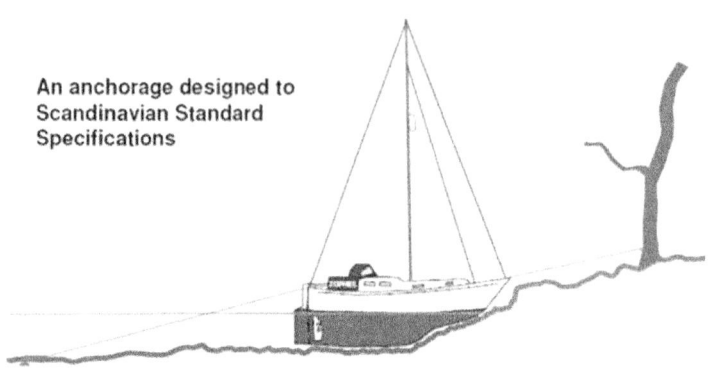

An anchorage designed to Scandinavian Standard Specifications

Terrible Tidal Tales

It was clearly getting busy now and finding a secure spot for the night was becoming the first priority. I worried that this situation was only going to get worse as I approached the more populated area of the Stockholm Archie. I had to get better at finding the elusive, secure wild anchorages. In the meantime I resolved to arrive at my next port of call, the reputedly popular Helsingholm, early enough to secure a space.

I sailed easily north under jib in twelve to eighteen knots of breeze. With the wind on the stern quarter there was enough for sailing out in the open, but we slowed down too much when passing behind the close islands. I checked out three other anchorages on the short, thirteen mile passage. As we hardened up latterly we had a pleasant, faster reach into the sheltered bay on the small island of Helsingholm, which had a cute, low key, privately run set of visitors' moorings.

At first I thought that all the buoys were taken. A number of yachts were circling about as if they couldn't find a space and others had resorted to anchoring close together in the bay. Then I noticed a couple of free spaces close inshore, amongst some small motorboats in the shallowest and most sheltered part of the bay. Though I thought it was probably too shallow, I nudged into one of the spaces and found a perfectly adequate one and a half metres of water. It was so sheltered that the only way I could tell that there was still any wind at sea was by listening to the surf crashing onto the rocks on the other side of the island.

Zoph was the only sailing boat along this bit of the wooden quay. All the others had clustered together in deeper water and larger spaces. Again we were benefitting from the usual advantage of sailing a small boat. I was also beginning to realise that, just because a potential anchorage is empty, it doesn't mean it's necessarily crap or untenable. The fact is that the Scandians all tend to flock together in small knots of boats. Sometimes because they are all pals having a barbeque together. At other times they are just being a bit ovine and clustering together because there's safety in numbers. It's worth remembering that they have a very short season. There's a good chance that a lot of the local 'experts' are nearly as much strangers in an anchorage as you are.

Helsingholm was particularly twee, with a not unpleasant, low key, family holiday sort of atmosphere. Attractions included a wee shop, with home made bread and a sort of amphibious horse, which spent its time wading and swimming across the bay for the amusement of the tourists. OK it wasn't Disneyland or Las Vegas. Come to think of it, it was infinitely preferable to either.

Another attraction was the spectator sport of watching Finns anchoring in limited space. A large yacht called 'Black Pearl', which had been in the same bay as Zoph in Modermagan two days before, arrived and anchored. A Beneteau 44 arrived and dropped about eight metres of anchor warp into the four metre deep bay. They just dropped the anchor then turned off the engine. No attempt was made to set it. Everyone then went below without bothering to wait and see if they were being swept down onto the rocks. A motor boat arrived and flung an anchor over the stern, leaving the boat swinging by the stern overnight. A large Elan arrived, bunged an anchor over the stern on a reel of cloth tape. The line was then carried two thirds of the way forward and loosely tied to a cleat. They didn't bother passing it through the anchor roller. The line just lay over the side. They set the anchor by getting a small sprog to pull feebly at the tape. Boats swung by the bow, the stern and the side with the dodgiest of anchor arrangements, within a very few yards of both each other and a lee shore.

A force seven was forecast for the night, but nobody seemed bothered. Oddly, none of these casual idiots ever seemed to get their comeuppance and actually founder on the rocks. I know what would happen if I tried their approach to anchoring. At the slightest opportunity Sod's Law would dash us against the shore. Several of the anchorers got out dinghies and though some were equipped with outboards, a few rowed. I was once again struck by the fact that, in Finland, everybody rows dinghies backwards. That is, facing the way they are travelling. Perhaps it's to stand a better chance of avoiding the myriad rocks, but it doesn't look very efficient.

A British boat called 'Puffin' came into the bay. They evidently had an altercation with another boat over a mooring as the air was blue with the outraged rantings of a posh English voice berating a Finn for nicking his space. Puffin motored off in disgust. I tried raising them on the VHF to say that there was a good space next to Zoph, but got no answer.

I thoroughly explored the island in about half an hour. Aside from the usual composting bogs and a crappy craft shop there was one house and a series of outbuildings. In one was a scruffy, battered looking petrol driven skidoo affair, which obviously constituted the winter transport to and from the island. In the woods were the usual large poos. On most small Baltic islands there was the odd large, curly poo, lying amongst the moss. They were clearly the droppings of some large beast. I never did establish what species of creature left them, but I fervently hoped that it was a nice benign herbivore, not some monstrous, terrifying predator with huge pointy teeth.

In the early evening a wee sailing yacht did join Zoph on the shallow moorings. An old wooden folk boat sailed up without a motor and inched towards us. I hauled her alongside Zoph and she was made fast. She was crewed by a father and son team. We chatted about the experience of sailing outside the Baltic, which they had never done. Inevitably in such discussions the height of tides comes up in the conversation. The Baltics sit around wide-eyed, with mouths open in wonder as they try to imagine a six metre tide on the Forth. My terrible tidal tales grew from the tides of the west of Scotland, through the Forth, to the thirteen metre range of the Bristol Channel and the eight knot tides though the Pentland Firth. It's like telling tales about magic and dragons to five year olds. We sat on our ripple-free moorings looking down at the unmoving bottom of the sea, four foot six below, as they tried to imagine how devastating it would be it the sea rose by thirteen metres.

I discovered another advantage of these shallow anchorages as I washed down the decks at twilight. The fourth

The Lady Cruiser 9000. A boat, a pimpmobile or a brand of leg shaver?

time I dipped the bucket in the sea the rope came off the handle. (Some idiot can't have tied it on right). It was an expensive, if largely useless, folding bucket and I was pissed off to have lost it overboard. Then I realised that I could practically reach it. The boathook easily grabbed it from the bottom of the sea and brought it back on board. So many things about sailing in the Baltic make it almost surreally easy.

In the morning the crew of the folkboat very kindly gave me a couple of theoretically freshly baked rolls from the island shop for my breakfast. I wouldn't have paid money for the hard, stale items, but I'll not look a gift cob in the gob.

After breakfast I headed off west in a steadily rising southerly that eventually gave me a nice reach. A couple of times the engine had to go on as we passed through particularly narrow, sheltered channels. Otherwise we reached under full sail at over six knots when heading west and just over four knots when heading north west. The sun occasionally struggled out through the thin clouds and we had a pleasant day's sailing. I passed 'Puffin' and approached within a couple of yards to carry out my continuing survey of British boats. Predictably she was, like nearly every other British boat, based in Baltic.

As the day wore on we sailed faster on a finer reach, eventually across quite open water, to the northern Åland island of Jungfruskär. We entered the long, sheltered sound between it and Hamnö, the next-door island. The sound was so narrow at the southern end that it was more or less a landlocked bay. Boats were crowded round the pleasant, free, National Park quay and again I thought at first that there was no room for Zoph. It wouldn't have been a problem, since there was loads of space to anchor, but once again I saw a space against the most sheltered, shallowest part of the pier.

I nudged in past the other boats, keeping a close eye on the depth sounder. In fact there was plenty of depth. I bunged the stern anchor into one point eight metres of water and tied to the pier in two and a half metres, in surreal calm. This was another family holiday spot and hooching with sprogs, staggering about on the land on a warm summer's day under the oppressive weight of woolly hats and huge, day-glow life jackets. As their parents called them back aboard there was the evocative sound of shoes being

A confused aquatic horse on Helsingholm is convinced it's a whale

slapped together to remove the sand. Symbolic of summer and beaches. The only problem was that there was no sand, only large flat rocks, and nobody is allowed to wear shoes on a Finnish boat anyway. So the slapping, though nostalgic, was pointless.

Sailing in Finnish waters is a dangerous business

Jungfruskär

There was more fun with anchoring here. A large, new Halberg Rassy hove into view. The skipper dumped a pile of anchor chain on the bottom, turned everything off and went below. Again there was no attempt at all to set the anchor or even wait to see if the boat drifted off. The Finns must imagine that anchors work by a sort of magic. Perhaps they just trust their muddy bottoms. My limited experience would seem to confirm that everywhere in the Baltic has a European Standard Bottom, designed to exacting standards. Thick, gloopy mud, between two and five metres down, sticks to anchors with tedious reliability. Finns don't worry about what the holding is like because it's always the same. As an aside, quite a high proportion of the anchors were CQR ones. This seems to be the only Scottish product – apart from whisky – which is sold widely throughout the Baltic. Presumably the holding is good enough that people don't care that the CQR is, apparently, not a very good anchor. What they are good for is standing on in order to get on and off the bow of a boat with a wrap-around pulpit. Mine stayed permanently fixed, hanging over the bow as a step, throughout the Baltic trip, hardly ever being used as an actual anchor.

I explored the island, which was about a mile by half a mile. There was considerable evidence of past farming but, in common with many other places in Finland and Sweden, the interpretation boards were quite proud of the fact that no agriculture was now practiced. Simply abandoning farms and allowing the land to become uncultivable seemed to be public policy and trumpeted as positive conservation. All mentions of farming were in the past. On many islands the signs would proudly proclaim not only that there was no longer farming, but that the land had become waterlogged or otherwise too useless even for rough pasture. Perhaps a history of pillaging villages around Europe allows the Scandians to be so dismissive and unconcerned about their apparent abandonment of farming.

Into the Yachts' Graveyard

The next morning I motorsailed into twelve knots of breeze just off the port bow. After a cloudy start the sun came out to accompany my pleasant, splashing progress into a small chop across open water. After ten miles I entered some narrower channels between two of the Åland islands, bore away a bit and sailed serenely along at between three and six knots for a couple of hours. The course was a tortuous one between closely packed tweenery and at times Zoph was pointing to within twenty five degrees of the breeze. Normally she wouldn't sail at that angle, but the sea was so flat between the islands that we still ghosted slowly onwards.

Things were getting busier as I headed both further west and deeper into the holiday season. I was worried that all the best moorings were going to be full by the time I arrived in Sweden. I was also aware that, due to congenital wimpiness and lack of good local information, I was not really getting the authentic Scandian experience, of tying to random rocks, in random bays, on random islands. Everyone said that there were so many wild anchorages that it was impossible to list them all. Everyone said that you could just tie to any rock, wherever you were. But my experience to date was that every time I saw a likely spot there was a house in it, with a private quay. I realised that I was too keen to take my cue from others and that I just needed to gird my loins, take a deep breath, ignore the pink lines on the chart and head off piste, up some of the rock-strewn dead ends.

An actual gun in a hut on Jungfruskär

Sailing down the channels to the north of the island of Finnholm I decided to do so. My first attempt was not a success. I nudged Zoph into a small bay about four boat lengths long and two boat lengths wide. Once the depth went under two metres I cut the speed down to about a twentieth of a knot and went up into the bow to look for rocks. Unfortunately I found some. We ran gently aground about four metres from the shore. The space to turn round was only about as long as Zoph and doing so involved embedding the stern into the mud, but we soon escaped and went looking for a better spot.

There was a shallow, rocky bay between Finnholm and the adjoining island of Angsholm and we gentle picked our way across it, trying to avoid the theoretical submerged rocks on the chartplotter and the real ones in the sea around us, which were in entirely different places. I headed off to the fantastically sheltered weather shore at the far end of the bay. I was expecting a good twenty knots of south westerly overnight. As I tiptoed across the deserted bay I had a paranoid image of people on passing yachts, folk fishing in wee open boats and locals peering out of their holiday homes. All of them would be pointing at Zoph incredulously. "Look at that idiot! What the hell does he think he's doing? Doesn't he know that no yacht has ever survived in there? Nobody goes into the Yachts' Graveyard!" After all there were a load of boats out sailing and looking for anchorages, yet nobody else in here.

My own private loch at Angsholm

But for the moment my insane paranoia seemed misplaced as we drifted slowly in to within a couple of feet of a large flat rock. The depth sounder said there was 1.6 metres of water. Zoph's draft is about 1.4 metres. I tied long lines across the rock to a tree and a large boulder. The technique for this sort of mooring is to try for two lines at about 120 degrees to one another, forming an equilateral triangle with the stern anchor. If there is a wind on the beam you might also take a wide shore line from the stern on the windward side.

I sat in the perfect calm and the sun, worrying about the lines of triangulation, wear and chafe on the lines, the weight of the boulder we were tied to, possible wash from passing boats – of which there were none, the chances of a freak tide happening and the pooey smell of the seaweed on the shore. In fact this sunny, perfectly sheltered spot on my own personal desert island was as close to utter perfection as anyone could hope for. I got quite annoyed with myself for my capacity to worry about the tiniest of minutiae and ruin these memorable experiences, which should live in the memory for many years. For Angsholm was indeed one of these very special places that day.

As everywhere in the northern Baltic there was, of course, no tidal rise or fall at all. It was really impossible to detect so much as an inch of tide. Whilst this was fantastic for mooring, it did have its down side, of which the pooey seaweed smell was symptomatic. With no swirling, washing movement of the sea the marine environment is somewhat dead. Because of the low levels of salinity, relatively few species can thrive in the Baltic, but even those which can are limited by the low nutrient levels of the non-tidal, relatively lifeless sea. Apart from a couple of scabby seals I saw no marine mammals this summer. The population of seabirds is also limited, with cormorants being the main ones in evidence. As in Britain these are scarcely seabirds anyway, nowadays, having fully colonised the fresh water lakes and rivers. In Finland you could see their colonies a mile off. They dotted the white sticks of stands of dead, denuded trees. All the trees on a small island would have been killed by generations of cormorant shit. I suspect they do it deliberately. They are a vindictive species, rendered nasty and crotchety by being the only common species of water bird without waterproof feathers. Apparently that's why they are always standing about spread-eagled, drying themselves. They must feel really hard done to.

Angsholm

Later, a couple of small open boats motored busily through my bay. I realised that, where there appeared to be a dead end, there was in fact a narrow, shallow, reedy channel between islands. A thoroughfare for a few locals. One aluminium, open boat, with a family aboard, came through the narrow channel and sped over the bay. When they reached the middle there was a sudden crunching sound and the boat stopped abruptly. They had just discovered that the rocks weren't where the chart said they were. They reversed off slowly and continued at a somewhat more sedate pace, hopefully at least a bit embarrassed.

I mused that, with my paranoia, I was utterly crap at everything to do with this cruising lark. Everything, that is, except finding uses for a plank. At that I excel. The latest use for Zoph's five foot long B&Q plank was as a gangplank, with one end resting on the low rocky shore and the other suspended a step below the CQR in the bow. It was an eccentric but nonetheless brilliant arrangement.

Minging a bit and in the absence of proper shower facilities I had a Baltic Bath. My method for this involved soaping all over using a bucket of seawater, then leaping into the sea to rinse off. Given the near complete lack of salt in the Baltic and the fact that it was now heating up to twenty degrees or more, this was quite a successful method. I cooked some tatties in Baltic water and had to add more salt.

Sophisticated plank engineering

Zoph is severely lacking sunbathing space so I threw the Avon Redcrest over the side upside down and lay on it for an hour or so. Back on board I dangled a fishing line with a series of fishing hooks in the shallow water, more in hope than expectation. I must get better at tying knots. Like the Ship's Bucket the hooks came undone and I lost the lot. In lieu of fishing I took to contemplating Zoph's back garden. Perfectly formed wooded islands dotted a mirror-calm sea, out of which a dark red moon rose. Fantastic. Evenings like that make it worth travelling thousands of miles at walking pace for.

I reluctantly consulted the Baltic Sea Pilot to check the route for the following day. Nearby, apparently, was a channel that ought to be useful. But a seventeen metre high bridge had been built over it. Presumably the author's boat has an air draft over seventeen metres, because instead of describing this useful channel, or at least saying where it is, he just has a moan about how it has been rendered utterly useless by the bridge. If it's useless, why mention it? If it's not useless, tell us where it is you pillock. You would almost be better off trying to navigate using the current rambling rant than that piece of Imray nonsense.

The next morning I battered to windward against a force five, for just six or seven miles, to the small town of Degerby, where I picked up a stern buoy on a busy pontoon. After a bit of shopping I pondered on whether to press on around the southern tip of the Åland Islands, in open sea against the twenty knot breeze, or just to stay in Degerby for the night. I quizzed the occupants of a Finnish boat, who said that my probable destination, Rodhamn, was getting full by two p.m. these days. I decided to stay put.

Immediately I had done so a Swedish yacht turned up and I helped with their lines. The bloke asked what my plans were and I told him. He started waxing lyrical about a fantastic island called Kobba Klintar, which he swore was the most incredible place in the Baltic and not to be missed. It was also a fantastic staging post just before crossing the Åland sea to Sweden, had a perfectly sheltered harbour and was always almost completely empty. I resolved to press on to this unlikely sounding Nirvana.

After a wet beat to windward for a few miles against a good force five, tacking back and forth across the shipping lanes plied by the prison ships, I followed a couple of other yachts, bearing away around the southern tip of Åland's main island. I reached past busy and overpriced Rodhamn, where we had spent the first night in Finland, and northwest through the islands in search of Nirvana.

Kobba Klintar

Kobba Klintar turned out to be a bleak, treeless rock with the odd clump of heather on it. Entirely reminiscent of one of the bleaker outer Hebrides, it seemed unremarkable, except for the fact that it had a large wooden house and a pyramid on it. The large house was, of course, the inevitable old pilot station. The pyramid was a new museum dedicated to old pilots. These buildings, as well as the tiny, perfectly sheltered, neat harbour, were the only evidence that I was not somewhere near Benbecula.

There was only one other boat in the harbour – a small Finnish yacht with a young family aboard. They told me that a large yacht had tried to approach down the shallow, rocky, exposed channel earlier in the day, but had run into a few rocks and given up. Happily I arrived too late to be made to pay harbour dues. The island was presumably sufficiently bleak to drive its operators away at night.

On a few occasions Scandians had waxed lyrical about the unparalleled attractions of islands which had turned out to be, more or less, bare rocks. To me, used to the windswept landscape of the west of Scotland, the lush, heavily treed, sheltered, calm bays of the Baltic were gorgeous and irresistible. They were so completely unthreatening and user-friendly compared to anything we have at home. Presumably the Scandians were bored with the monotony of forested wonderlands and hankered after a bit of windswept barren rock – a bit of rough, if you will. I began to learn to take their recommendations with a small pinch of salt.

Kobba Klintar was bracing and quite pleasant however. It was also lent a surreal edge by the fact that it was close to the shipping lanes. When I say close I mean about twenty yards. Perched on this untenable rock in the middle of the sea, it was extraordinary to see the huge ferries and prison ships steaming between Mariehamn and Stockholm, all lights blazing and dwarfing the island that they almost grazed against, as they passed at fifteen knots. I listened to the wind whistling in the rigging all night as it whipped over the low, exposed rock.

The ferries and prison ships sail within an inch of Kobba Klintar

Self-Scrambling Eggs

After Kobba Klintar there was nothing else before Sweden. In the morning there was still a good twenty knots of breeze, but happily it was from the east south east. Under full sail we reached off towards Sweden across a choppy, rolly sea with two metre waves. Out on the western fringes I had a head start over everyone else. Most of the other boats on the crossing were coming from Mariehamn and during the day a lot of them passed slow old Zoph, even though she was making five and a half to six knots.

Interest was provided on the passage, which took us well out of sight of land for a while, by trying to work out exactly where all the huge ferries were going and how best to avoid them. This time there was relatively little shipping heading into and out of the Gulf of Bothnia and most of it was, like me, just crossing the Åland Sea. Later a Finnish sailor to whom I mentioned this suggested, in all seriousness, that there wasn't much freight on the Gulf of Bothnia because it was a Sunday. Given that the average passage time for this cross-continental traffic runs to several days this seems unlikely.

More interest was provided by passing yachts. We were overtaken by a Finnish Beneteau with the unlikely name 'Realt Na Mara', which is Irish Gaelic for 'Star of the Sea'. A perfectly good name but an unlikely language for it. For once loads of other yachts seemed to have the same idea as me and I was going with, as opposed to against, the main flow. I passed more time by cooking up a couple of fried eggs for lunch. Or I tried to. With a two metre chop sending us rolling about the only variety of egg it was possible to cook was scrambled, as they squooshed about in the pan, mixing themselves perfectly. I decided to treat this self-scrambling device as a boon rather than an impediment. After all there's not a lot of land based kitchens that can boast a self-scrambling eggs device.

As I closed on the Swedish coast and began running up the shipping channels between the islands we were also overtaken by an arsehole. A dark blue gin palace speed boat came roaring up behind us at about twenty knots. Closer and closer it came until I genuinely began to fear that he'd not seen us and was about to ram us. With plenty of sea room there was no other reason for this behaviour other than simple sadism. When it was about twenty yards away and a collision seemed inevitable it suddenly swerved to port to pass us, throwing up a wall of water which dumped a good few bucket-loads into Zoph's cockpit. He sped off accompanied by my apoplectic, hopping mad insults. If there had been any way of knowing where he was heading I would have seriously considered following him, for several days if necessary, to give the bastard a piece of my mind and possibly a punch on the snoot.

As the afternoon wore on the sky clouded and it began to rain. My timing was pretty good for once, as I was making use of the last of the easterlies to make the crossing, before the breeze went back to the south west the next day. Worried by reports that the Stockholm Archie gets unbearably crowded by mid July I headed to a large, low key marina for small boats near Kapellskär. Surprisingly, it was half empty and I took a 'U' shaped boom mooring on a long pontoon. The marina was run in tandem with a campsite about half a mile away, to which I repaired in the rain on Bertie the Brompt for a shower. On the way I was passed by a car! Yes, an actual road vehicle. I realised that I hadn't seen one of these new fangled contraptions in operation since I was an Tallinn, over a week before.

Returning all scrubbed and shiny I was invited aboard a twenty seven foot German yacht on a nearby pontoon for a drink of Danish aquavit with an elderly couple. She was a severe, very Germanic cauliflower-head, he a cherubic old Mr Kipling character. Or rather, he was like the actor who goes on about Mr Kipling in the adverts. Which of us can say that we know what the actual, mysterious Mr Kipling looks like? I suspect something like Ernst Stavro Blofeld. Anyway it was all very pleasant. It was slightly less pleasant the next morning when I appeared on deck, bleary eyed, to be met by the sight of the septuagenarian German wifey standing around unconcernedly in their cockpit in the buff, mammaries swinging about in the breeze. Very Germanic, as I say.

I had a minor coup in Kapellskär. Attached to an information board at the start of a nature trail I found a pile of free brochures and took one. This was by far the best pilotage information I had found about Sweden to date. It was at least seven hundred times better than the stupid Imray pilot. It was produced by the 'Archipelago Foundation' and gave the location and details of loads of the best anchorages on the prettiest islands in the Stockholm Archie. I had been wondering about heading inland to the city of Stockholm, then south via the sheltered channels and canals. But with a reasonable forecast for the next few days and armed with my new pilotage information, I resolved to island-hop along the outer edge of the Archie and try for a few more wild anchorages. Apart from anything else, the prospect of free berthing was appealing. The previous eight days had cost about twenty five squid in berthing fees and I resolved to drive this exorbitant sum lower.

I headed off in search of desert island paradises. For a while I had to motor-sail to windward, but then was able to sail in the sun, in a breeze that varied from force two to force five. The whole world was out sailing. A

Stora Huvuholmen

sea of sails could be seen down every side channel we passed. I rolled up the jib temporarily to have a squint into an anchorage at Stallbottna. The perfection of the day was slightly marred by running into an unmarked rock on the approach to this anchorage. It was on the chartplotter, but not marked on the ground. I was motoring merrily away when I suddenly saw it on the chart and jammed on the brakes, not quite just in time. But we did graze the rock at two knots instead of six, so no apparent damage was done. Hopefully.

I passed the busy and popular anchorage at Finnhamn, with several jetties crammed with boats lying to stern anchors, but pressed on. Now that I was well on my way back down the Baltic, I had calculated that I no longer needed to put in such long passages every day. This meant I had the leisure to explore these anchorages and could afford low average speeds. I could therefore afford to sail – as opposed to motoring – in a wider range of conditions. And the summer amongst these islands deserved to be experienced slowly.

My free Archie booklet mentioned several anchorages at Stora Huvuholmen and, obsessive as always, I squeezed into the shallowest and tightest. The almost perfectly round pool, about a hundred metres across, was pretty much uniformly three metres deep, except at the ten metre wide entrance, which was one point six metres at its deepest point. About eight inches deeper than Zoph's keel. Three or four motorboats were having a party at one side of the bay, on the lee shore. I tied to a couple of trees on my own private slab of flat rock on the sheltered, weather shore. With the proviso that you needed a keel no more than one point six metres deep, this was probably the most perfect anchorage I found in the whole of this sea, which was stuffed with near perfect anchorages. Over the early evening one or two more small motorboats braved the bar and tied to other rocks, but nobody came near my own private rock. In fact no sailing boats at all attempted the shallow entrance. All the motorboats chose the lee shore to moor against. I was puzzled by this until the sun began to go down and I realised that they had moored so as to remain basking in the sunlight for as long as possible. The wind was a much more minor consideration.

The motorers had a fine old evening of barbequeing and leaping into the warm sea in the hot sun whilst I sat getting pleasantly sozzled and eating Bolognaise Archipelago. That's meatballs in tomato sauce with pasta, by the way. The only down side to the evening was that my diet was getting a bit monotonous. Scandinavia generally is pretty expensive for everything except the berthing of boats. When things are expensive and you are relatively skint, it makes economic sense to buy some food in bulk and I was reliving my student days, scouring the shops I visited, once every three days or so, for bulk-buy bargains. The Scandians seem to take an extreme approach to this. If you buy about ten kilos of something, it's not just cheaper than a hundred grammes of more or less the same stuff per unit weight. It's actually about a quarter of the price for the whole pack. So a couple of small chicken breasts might cost about twelve quid. A whole frozen chicken, on the other hand, would be about a fiver. This was leading to a diet of some monotony. This week I was eating cheap meatballs. For days and days on end. A large bag of them had been a lot cheaper than a small portion of anything else at all. Having no idea how I was supposed to cook Swedish stuff, I was improvising a whole range of international cuisine with me meatballs.

It seems likely that the airports in Sweden and Finland are not hooching, in July, with pasty-faced families queueing morosely to be abused by trolley-dollies on sardine-tin flights to the Costa del Pissup. Why would they suffer so much to go abroad on holiday when twice a year abroad comes to them? In Britain our climate is a gently undulating graph of varying levels of dampness. We more or less get twelve months of autumn. Even if we do get a period of warm summer or crisp, cold, snowy winter, it's entirely unpredictable and not to be relied on. In the Baltic they get Greece for a month or so in the summer and the Alps in winter. A Scottish loch may look a little drabber in winter than summer, but by and large it's the same scene. This anchorage, which was like somewhere in Corfu in July, would be a solid lump of white stuff for several months in the winter. We never experience the levels of change that the folk of the Baltic see in their environment.

So far my wild anchoring using the free Archie book was going well. I resolved to try for more of the same in the next few days. I started the day in shorts and 'T' shirt, sailing in a force two. I finished up in big jumpers, woolly hat and full wet gear, sailing in a force five and pissing down rain. The morning was very pleasant and I raced a Swedish Albin Vega for a while, winning over a period of an hour or so. If I hadn't won, of course, I would not have been racing. The narrow channels were busy with Swedish cruisers. But during the day tall, threatening, black thunder clouds developed. I diverted from Björnö, where I had been heading, towards the anchorage at Nämdö, to try and avoid the inevitable downpour and lightning. I didn't avoid it, of course, and was hit by a strong headwind, ultra-heavy rain and a steep chop. Happily however, I wasn't hit by lightning.

Nämdö was a busy bay with many boats tied to the rocks and quite a number anchored in the three metre deep, large, sheltered bay. There was still plenty of room and I moored against a rock on the weather shore, tying to a rotting tree stump and a boulder. This was a popular spot, with the usual composting bog, on a somewhat larger island, with actual roads. I say roads. There was no tarmac or cars but a small network of flat, gravel paths around the island.

After a meal of Meatball Madras – or Curry Archipelago – marred only by the shrieks from a nearby yacht with at least eight people aboard, I went for a long walk to explore the island. Along the 'road' network was a smattering of well kept, gingerbread houses, but no evidence of motorised transport and all the driveways were just grassy lawns. On the face of it, it looked like just a summer retreat. On the other hand there was an apparently operational school and a church. I still don't know whether this was a seasonal, summer island, or if it has a year-round population. Was this the haunt of urban graphic designers and bankers, playing at a rural idyll, or a proper island population? This corner of the outer Hebrides was exactly twenty miles as the crow flies from the centre of the capital city of Sweden.

There were interpretive signs telling me about the history of the island. They proudly pointed out that there was now no useful agriculture. Apparently it had all been good arable land until the 1940s, but had become waterlogged and was now no use even as rough pasture. What has happened to the climate and rural economics of this archipelago that has, so recently, entirely destroyed its agriculture? There is a feeling on some of these islands that they have only just had their 'Clearances'. The highlands of Scotland suffered this depopulation two hundred years ago. Sweden seems to be getting it now, encouraged by eco-aware Government acting in loco the evil aristocratic landlords.

Heroically Unsticking a German

My daily journeys were shorter now and the next day I had a very gentle sail for twelve miles, then a motorsail for about another twelve or fourteen. We passed down yet more channels which were hooching with yachts out sailing and motorboats heading purposefully to the next barbeque spot, or drifting about fishing in the fish-free sea.

Rano was another recommendation of the Archie brochure. It was busy and not quite as handy as the previous two anchorages, in terms of rocks to tie to. By obsessively exploring exactly how shallow Zoph's draft was, however, I managed to find a place where I could hop ashore with the help of my patented gangplank. This time I used the plank as a bridge from the shore to a small offlying rock. With Zoph's draft of one point four metres, the depth sounder registered one point two metres of water. We had a full minus point two metres under the keel. Zoph was so obsessively tucked into the sheltered shallows that I suspect I was looked on as something of an eccentric by people on other boats.

A popular, fun summer pastime amongst the islands is stapling passing strangers to a wooden cross and setting fire to them

Again I went for a wander along the winding gravel tracks of the quite large island. Again there was an assortment of fairy tale houses. This time there was also a campsite with one tent on it. Or rather one encampment. An old gent was watering all the plants around his sprawling tent suburb. A large central tent was adjoined by several others, each with several rooms. There were various outhouse tents within a makeshift fence. The whole ensemble was like one of Soweto's larger suburbs. Clearly the bloke had set up camp for the entire summer. Presumably taking advantage of the laws about free wild camping to live for nothing for the entire summer. At the other end of the island I was surprised to find a general store with attached pontoon selling diesel, a café serving beer and a sort of outside restaurant. I could hear this last long before I saw it and it sounded quite a lot like a large gannet colony. A hubbub of voices rang from the fifty or sixty Swedes, who sat ranged either side of several long dining tables, outside on the grass. God knows how a restaurant like this stays in business, operating for about three days a year.

A German stuck in the mud in Rano

Nynashamn

As I waited for my Szechuan Archipelago to cook, I watched other boats entering the bay. A scruffy Lithuanian yacht moored to the rock next to Zoph and its three hairy hippy occupants leapt into the sea and proceeded to snorkel round the bay. The next boat in was one I recognised. It was the big, red, racy German yacht I'd seen in Haapassaari, the day I reached the Russian border. She was still mob handed, but I suspect with a different crew to the one that had coming back from St Len's. The yacht approached a spot on the shore near the Lithuanians and ran rapidly and firmly aground, about seven or eight yards out. They jammed the engine into reverse, opened the throttle and promptly broke the gearbox, so that the engine would no longer work in reverse. They were firmly jammed on the bottom in what I would have thought was quite deep water. I asked one of the crew how deep their keel was. Apparently they had a draft of two point four metres. I have no idea why a German would choose to have a boat with a two point four metre draft, since the deepest the sea gets, in any German waters, is about three metres.

This was just what the assembled crews of the twenty or thirty boats in the bay needed. It provided both entertainment and an excuse to demonstrate their superior knowledge of boats and how to float them. The Lithuanians, in particular, revelled in the opportunity to break out their extensive range of anchors, long warps, block and tackle gismos and the like. Lots of people offered advice of varying quality from the shore. My own advice – that when they did finally free the boat and get to a repair yard, they should get about a metre sawn off the keel – was not well received.

After various unsuccessful attempts to dislodge the keel from the mud, eventually a long anchor line was strung from the starboard quarter of the wide flat stern of the German racer. It was taken by dinghy to a well dug in anchor, thirty yards or so out into the bay. The crew of about eight and several onlookers were directed to sit on the port side of the German yacht. The boom was pulled over to port and a couple of folk hung on it. The effect of this was to heel the boat considerably to port. Then the anchor warp was wrapped round the starboard primary winch and the skipper winched in like billy-o. This, of course, had the effect of turning the wide sterned boat, so that the winch was on a straight line between the anchor and the centre of resistance, the sharp, pointy keel. It also, of course, pulled her back over to starboard. The more he winched the more the boat levelled off and was just pushed straight downwards into the mud.

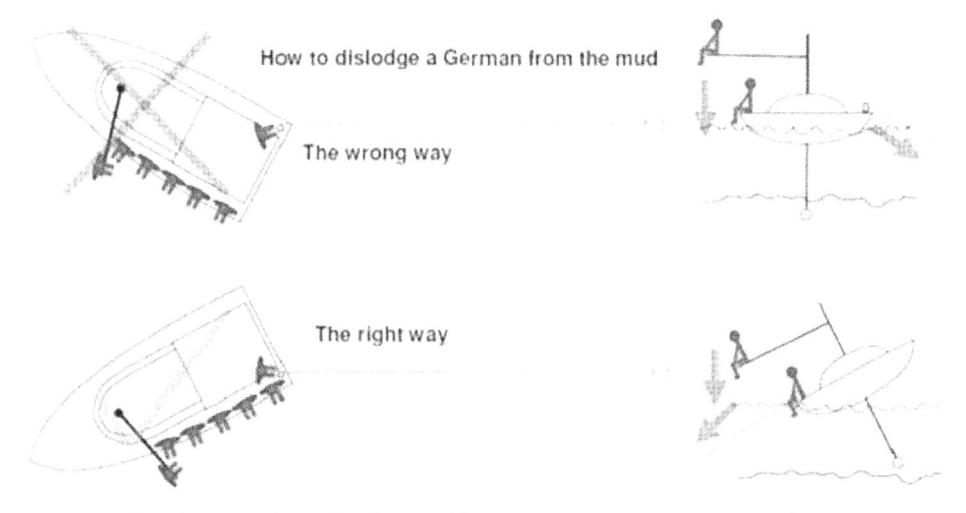

How to dislodge a German from the mud

The wrong way

The right way

Enter Professor Edge, the String Theory expert. So many people were trying to offer advice – and my previous suggestion had been deemed so flippant by many – that I had difficulty making myself heard. But eventually the skipper got the message. If he simply transferred the anchor warp to the port side and winched from there, the boat would swivel round, the action of the winch would reinforce the heeling moment of the dangling crew and the keel might float free. From a number of options the skipper chose mine and it worked like a charm, within a few seconds the boat was floating free. The German skipper was generous with both thanks and beer to the Lithuanians and others, who had provided much of the brawn, but seemed not fully to recognise the high value of the brain power, which had effectively secured his release from the mud.

It was probably a fair illustration of national differences through history. I was able to visualise what would happen to something if you pulled on a bit of string. But that primitive sort of knowledge was the summit of British engineering that day. The Scandinavians and Germen then applied themselves to the minutiae of the operation of a new Volvo gearbox, which as far as I was concerned was just a magic box possessed by a demon. What is sailing, after all, if not a hankering for a golden age when string was the ultimate technology, and he who could master string could master the universe? My primitive technological knowledge didn't stop me being smug though. That night Zoph was both the only boat small enough and shallow enough to moor close in amongst the reeds, and the only boat to have crossed the North Sea in a force six.

There was a Danish boat anchored just offshore with a particularly noisy, partying crew and tacky, garish regalia, including a large inflatable palm tree on the deck. Their cockpit chatter continued long after other people had given up and gone to bed. I could practically hear tocks clicking across the water on the other boats. The Danes also flew what appeared to be a saltire from the port spreaders. I was therefore not surprised to hear a Scottish voice ringing out across the water in a slightly drunken argument. In the morning, after I hauled up the anchor, I pottered over to where they were breakfasting to confirm my suspicions. Unfortunately my diagnosis of the accent was poor and I accused the Scottish bloke, who was a Weegie, of being from Inverness. This was the only Saltire and the only Scottish person I saw on another boat all summer.

Back through the world's narrowest channel

Grungy Black Punk Dreadlocked Russian Hippy Fascists

I sailed slowly in the sun past Nynäshamn and into the fantastically sheltered waters beyond, where we had stayed on the Sölon Staff Association mooring in June. I passed a British yacht called 'Badger' and sailed close enough to ask them if they had come from the UK this year. As always they confirmed that they were, in fact, permanently based in the Baltic.

My free Archie booklet showed a whole pile of enticing moorings round here so, though I had only gone about fifteen miles, I started to choose a suitable one. After passing again through what must genuinely be the narrowest, most treed, least maritime looking channel in all the seas in all the world, I made for the shallow, reedy loch at Rassaviker. The channel into the loch was supposed to have a least depth of one and a half metres, but there were plenty of boats using it and in fact I don't think the depth went below two metres. On the way I poked around into a few of the other surreally calm, sheltered spots, where Swedes barbequed from a wide variety of boats.

Again I tied to a rock, this time in quite a busy spot near some motorboats. After a swim and a bath in the twenty two degree sea and while I waited for my Bourguignon de Archipelago to cook, I took a wander ashore. This time I was tied to a mainland rock and thought I ought to be able to take a decent sized walk, perhaps finding an actual road and a settlement. But beyond the few tracks along the coastal rocks made by barbequeing boaters, there was just a tangled mass of undergrowth, punctuated by swamp and knackered fences.

Nevertheless, alone amongst the contented boat-bound, I pressed through the scratchy undergrowth and tried to follow dodgy, overgrown paths. Like elsewhere it appeared that the Swedes had now more or less abandoned attempts at agriculture in favour of just leaving everything alone. I finally found a rough track across a bit of swamp, on which a few toy, aesthetically pleasing goats were grazing. I was pressing on down it when a couple of youths hove into view. They were a black girl and a white lad, both of about eighteen. They both wore faded, baggy, ripped khaki gear, scuffed Doc. Martens and tight beany hats – in the muggy heat – from beneath which matted dreadlocks poked. Both were surprisingly comprehensively pierced, throughout their ears, noses, lips and various other bits of their faces. They were accompanied by a large, gently growling, deeply threatening Rottweiler, on an inadequate looking bit of string.

The girl said something in Swedish and when I obviously didn't understand repeated in English, "Can we help you? Where are you going? You know that this is private land?" Slightly stunned I forbore telling her it was none of her business where I was going and that the right to walk on private land was enshrined in law. Instead I said that I was looking for the road. They wanted to know why I was looking for a road. Eventually the girl, looking me up and down critically said "I think I trust you and will allow you to walk through the farm". She dispatched her Russian boyfriend to show me the way past the farm buildings. Here the only evidence of livestock were a single chicken and a Vietnamese pot-bellied pig, both of which the Russian lad pointed out proudly. I thanked him and said I would walk that way later, after my meatballs. Had it really come to this? Was I now so elderly, eccentric, dissolute and scruffy that my movements were being monitored and controlled by dreadlocked, dog-on-a-string, teenaged refugees from a grunge band, who couldn't get a gig selling the Big Issue? A pair of pubescent, pierced, punks had become the establishment and I was the non-conformist, determined to flaunt their fascist rules!

After dinner I retraced my steps and was again accosted, this time by a wee tubby Asian lady, again accompanied by a Rottweiler the size of a polar bear. Though very bubbly and chatty she also wanted to know what I thought I was doing on her land. But eventually – and as if she was doing me a huge favour – she deigned to let me walk to the road. So much for the famous Swedish attachment to the right to roam.

Rassaviker

I finally found the road and had a long and bracing walk, fuming slightly that I had been forced to justify the desire to go for an evening stroll. After a while I passed pastures which looked a little better tended and more like an actual, real farm. I even saw a couple of cars. The first for four days. On my way back a couple of hours later, there was a hippy standing at the gate to the toy farm. A faint aroma of dope rose from him as he leaned lazily on a gatepost, eyes half shut with laid back satisfaction. It would flatter him to say that he reminded me of the character played by Donald Sutherland in 'Kelly's Heroes'. He also started quizzing me about where I was going. News seemed to have travelled fast and he knew all about me. I had been described by the Asian wifey, his wife. This was his farm, but he would be leaving it next month to go to the Edinburgh Festival. He went every year apparently He liked the place, the food, the beer, the whisky, the festival and, for some reason, the people. Eventually he also deigned to let me pass, with the air of someone who had just carried out a fantastically generous deed.

Clearly this was a hobby farm, belonging to a dissolute meeja type from Stockholm. Possibly someone from the telly or the music industry, who employed various groupies to look after his toy animals. What was perhaps oddest about this experience was that I had to justify the desire to go for an evening stroll, as if it was a really odd and eccentric thing to do. It was not until I was well on my way back to Zoph and they were well out of earshot that I felt my outraged nonconformity bubbling to the surface. How dare these hippy fascists question my every movement and scrutinise my motivations, just for going for an evening stroll? Could they not tell that they had become the establishment that they, doubtless, reviled? It was like finding myself in the middle of some nightmare alternative episode of The Archers, with the landowning gentry of middle class middle England unaccountably replaced by Swedish hippies. Being properly repressed and middle class, of course, I didn't actually say any of this out loud. But being policed by the hippies – that's a first for me.

An innovative arse-to-arse anchoring technique

Svardsklova

One of Zoph's neighbours was a large, chunky and quite elderly local motorboat and I chatted to the skipper. I asked him about anchorages further south but he was unable to give me any information. Here, about twenty five miles from his home base in Stockholm, was the furthest he'd ever been. He'd come this far because the sea temperature was two and a half degrees warmer than in an anchorage a mile nearer to his home port. He explained that, though his heavy block of flats was just about capable of planing and could do twenty knots, he couldn't afford the huge quantities of fuel needed to go more than a very few miles.

As so often I was reminded of the tortoise and the hare. Zoph is in some respects a sort of harey tortoise. She's twitchy and always wanting to be on the move, but travels slowly. She's nearly always travelled much further than all the hares that surround her.

It was a lovely sunny day as I motorsailed in the calm, managing only forty minutes or so of unassisted sailing on a beam reach. We passed through more convoluted channels past astonishing tweenery. At one point we sailed through a narrow channel on one side of which, overhanging the sea on a low rock, was a large restaurant. Half of Sweden had moored alongside, stepped ashore and were now eating lunch in the sun a yard from their boats.

After twenty five miles or so, as I was passing near the harbour at Broken, where we had stayed in June, I noticed a small, uncharted marina with a guest harbour sign and decided to nip in there for the night. A friendly German bloke hopped off the only boat in the marina to take my lines. This was a fifty or sixty foot long, chunky, workmanlike steel speedboat which looked more like a pilot boat or a ferry than a yacht. He explained that it was an ex police boat from the Elbe at Hamburg.

Svärdsklova was a brand spanking new facility, with boom mooring on a wide concrete pontoon, complete with leccy, water and proper showers and bogs. It was attached to a restaurant and holiday chalet complex and presumably built to encourage folk to eat in the restaurant. It was a Friday night, smack in the middle of the holiday season, yet the German and Zoph were the only boats in. I suspected that this might be because of an exorbitant pricing policy, but the German bloke thought otherwise. He had stayed there for several days before and nobody had ever asked for any money. "Just wait" he said. "It's Friday night and within a couple of hours this marina will be absolutely full".

Sure enough, within a couple of hours, the marina was completely empty. A couple of dinghies arrived and disgorged passengers, but then left. A scruffy, half sunk motorboat, which looked like it had been grafted together from the bow of one boat and the stern of another, arrived. I hopped off Zoph and took their bow lines for them. The couple of wifeys in the bow smiled nicely in thanks, then just got off the boat and wandered away. I was left holding the only lines securing them to the pontoon and fending off the bow. The blokes in the stern ignored me and didn't bother tying on any stern lines. They made absolutely no attempt to attach their boat to anything. In the end I tied the bow lines to rings and left the boat banging hard into the pontoon. They did absolutely nothing to prevent this or to secure their boat. Very odd. After a couple of hours they left.

Only one other yacht turned up all evening. It seemed that the marina was so new that nobody yet knew of its existence. Despite my congenital paranoia, which was telling me that there's no such thing as a free marina and there must be something wrong with it – perhaps a tsunami was forecast or something – it was both perfectly pleasant and perfectly free. Even the leccy appeared to be free.

As I waited for my meatballs in peanut sauce – 'Satay Archipelago' – to cook, I fell to talking with the couple of lads on the one local yacht which did join us that night. I mentioned that we had moored at nearby Broken and asked if it was a private club, where we shouldn't have been. I said I had got the distinct impression that we weren't really welcome. He laughed and said that it was interesting that we had got that impression. It was, he said, open to everyone. It was just that club members didn't have to pay. He had been going there several times every year with his Dad since he was five. Yet every time he went he was made to feel like an unwelcome outsider. It seemed that Broken, though seemingly idyllic, was occupied by a load of shirty, cliquey bastards who didn't welcome outsiders. Perhaps it was an inevitable consequence of the name. If it was an American film and the heroes ended up in a town called 'Broken' you would be left in little doubt that they were about to be eaten by the inbred, mutant occupants.

The lads on the next boat were steel workers from nearby Oxelösund. They said that their great ambition in life was to sail in the west of Scotland. In particular they fancied the annual 'Whisky Cruise' of distilleries. I came across a number of people in Scandinavia who had heard of this slightly obscure event. Happily they illustrated their liking for whisky by breaking out a bottle of Laphroaig and feeding some of it to me.

In the morning I realised that the marina wasn't entirely free, as I went into the wee bakery shop attached to the restaurant and paid a fiver for a pint of milk and a small loaf. Fresh bread from tiny, overpriced bakeries seems to be endemic throughout Scandia, even on some of the smallest, virtually uninhabited islands. Folk are crazy for fresh bread for their breakfasts and prepared to pay, apparently, practically anything for it. It seems to be a way of pretending that these temporary, summer haunts are proper, old fashioned village communities.

Goulash Archipelago

The next day dawned somewhat overcast and dreich. An unexpected north westerly force three, however, meant I could sail all the way to Arkösund at five knots on a reach and three knots, goose winged, downwind. After Arkösund the wind dropped, the amount of yacht traffic on passage up the narrow channels increased and the sky cleared. I started the day in the west of Scotland in October and ended it in the Mediterranean in July. The amount of yacht traffic I passed was probably swelled by the fact that now, just south of the Stockholm Archie, the channels were more linear than they had been amongst the more widely distributed islands further north. Here there was little choice but to sail up and down the coast behind the islands.

The Stockholm Archie is just thick with islands. This is how many islands there are. Imagine, if you will, that you have a hangover. You stagger out of bed far too late and fall downstairs. Bleary eyed you pull an almost full, family sized box of Rice Crispies out of the cupboard. In your confused state you try to open it whilst holding the box upside down. The bottom opens and the whole lot falls out, spreading to cover practically the whole kitchen floor in crunchy cereal. You stare down at the mess. You are looking at a satellite image of the Stockholm Archie. Being in a right state and in your attempts not to crunch them into the floor you fall flat on your face. From an inch away you can see that the Rice Crispies, which appeared identical from a distance, are all in fact subtly different. Each one has a different shape and pattern of holes. That's the islands of the Baltic.

I was now leaving the Stockholm Archie and entering the Östgöta Archie. I had sailed off the end of my free archipelago booklet and, reluctantly, I opened the Imray Baltic Sea Pilot to see what it had to say. I was heading for the Island of Harstena, which had been recommended by an old manny in Sodashopping, in the Gøta Canal, as a gem of tweenery.

Not bins but post boxes for all the houses within a couple of miles

The sage pilot is unequivocal in its advice on approaching this archie. On no account, it says, should you ever rely on electronic means of navigation. Instead, it says, you should always carry a supply of stick-on coloured paper arrows. These should be affixed to a paper chart at intervals to remind you where you are. Honestly. It literally says that. I should point out that the book was published in 2010, not 1970. Now of course we can all agree that you shouldn't rely only on a GPS to tell you where you are. Where the sea is littered with a million islands it is important to do the normal sort of pilotage to confirm your location. Often the channels are so narrow, and you need to approach rocks so closely, that even modern GPS would not be accurate enough. But what the pilot book means, is that you should only use paper charts, with paper arrows stuck all over them. Not only would this technique be prohibitively expensive, it would also make you a laughing stock in the eyes of every Scandian navigator. For god's sake use a bloody chartplotter and some sensible eyeballing and ignore this idiotic advice.

It's often claimed by British sailors that we shouldn't rely too much on chartplotter navigation because the Americans might just turn off the satellites at any time out of spite, or because they are at war with someone. Old buffers, pissed off at youths who haven't had to learn all the traditional techniques, are always claiming this. And they have a point. Americans are a very spiteful people and nearly always attacking someone. I'm all for not relying on their technology. But really, what are the chances of the world's GPS system going down? And if it does, won't the consequences be much greater than just a few yachts getting a bit lost? Won't a thousand aeroplanes come crashing out of the sky? Won't the shipping fleets of the world, hurtling around our oceans on autopilot, keep bumping into things? And anyway, even most of the old buffers who don't have chartplotters still rely on GPS, to plot where they are on paper charts these days, don't they? I'm all for self-reliance, but I can't help feeling that the argument against technological reliance is part sense, but mostly simple Luddism. I'm aware that many may draw the line at my own strategy for dealing with the failure of all navigation aids, which is to follow another boat in the hope that it knows where it's going.

The invaluable pilot book then goes on to say that you should never go into any anchorage which isn't detailed in a pilot book and never, ever, navigate outside the marked channels. On the very next page, without giving any details of how to get there, it recommends that you visit Harstena. There

A free range tractor and its newborn cub

are no marked channels to the island of Harstena. It's a popular and busy place and people get there by picking their way between the various islands, literally miles away from the nearest channel of any sort. It would be literally impossible to get to the anchorage recommended by the pilot book if you navigated using the principles it recommends.

Its advice on dealing with commercial shipping is also breathtakingly useless and naïve. It simply says that you should always give way to all commercial vessels and that ferries, in particular, always have right of way, at all times. It goes on to point out that some fast ferries appear as if from nowhere very quickly, leaving you no time to get out of their way, and that some channels are too narrow for two vessels to pass each other. On the one hand it tells you never to leave the channels. On the other hand it tells you always to avoid all commercial traffic, all of which, of course, navigates in the marked channels.

Let's just analyse this idea that you should always act as the give way vessel when you see a ferry. Let's say you're not in a restricted channel, but just motoring along at sea, when you see a dirty great hydrofoil ferry going about thirty knots just ahead of your port beam. You reckon you're on something like a collision course. You've read the advice in Imray's Baltic Sea Pilot and decide to take avoiding action. There's no way you can outrun the ferry, so you stop the boat. Meanwhile the ferry skipper, who is well used to dodging thousands of slow yachts, has seen you and his radar says he's on a collision course. Being a professional he knows the rules, so makes a course alteration to starboard to pass behind you. But of course you've now stopped. The subsequent enquiry finds that you were entirely at fault since you were the stand on vessel, but didn't stand on. You produce your waterlogged copy of the Baltic Sea Pilot in your defence.

Perhaps you survive that encounter and later are navigating up a narrow channel beating under sail. You aren't able to sail directly up the channel and are tracking from its starboard side to its port side on starboard tack. At the moment you are roughly in the middle. Suddenly a fast ferry appears behind you, closing fast. It looks like it's passing just slightly ahead of you, but you can't be sure. You want to adhere strictly to the rules in your bible, the Baltic Sea Pilot. So you tack immediately by turning hard to starboard. The ferry's doing over twenty knots and has little time to react. But its crew are past masters at avoiding yachts. Seeing you sailing ahead they make the proper course alteration to starboard to pass behind you. Imagine their surprise when you tack suicidally. Happily you are unable to attend the subsequent hearing, due to having drowned.

I navigated, like the rest of the population, out of the marked channels, using electronic navigation aids, to Harstena. The sheltered anchorage bay was designed to the normal high natural standards, and though it was quite busy, I soon found a suitably perfectly sheltered spot to moor Zoph. I tied her to two standard pine trees, a foot from a standard specification rock, in a standard, Scandinavian specification, perfect anchorage.

Harstena plasters hitherto unimagined layers of almost painful tweeth onto the normally fantastically twee tweenery of the Swedish summer island. As so often, the motorboats in particular were crowded together in little knots of barbequeing partiers, leaving plenty of spaces for the likes of us.

Unlike other islands there was a well trodden path taken by most of the crews in the anchorage to the other side of the island. It wasn't much of a path, being wet and boggy, but the delights of the other coast attracted the usually supine summer Swedes. A mile away I found an inlet narrower and more perfectly sheltered even than anywhere I'd seen to date. Around it were clustered some of the most obscenely perfect holiday cottages imaginable, a bakery, a fish shop, a packed restaurant and a marina. This had stern buoy moorings onto a long, rickety wooden stage built along the steep-to rocks. For the first time I think it was fair to say that this marina was genuinely full. It appeared to attract the more flashy, aggressive looking speedboats, for whose crews, I imagine, leccy and ablutions were a higher priority than wilderness and quiet.

I had a look in the poorly stocked shop, which seemed mostly to sell smoked eels. The annoying old Gerwoman in front of me in the queue insisted on examining every single smoked eel in the shop, in detail, before selecting a small piece of one of them. This tiny island summer village was getting so crowded that I began to feel a bit hassled – as though I was caught up in a manic crowd at the January sales. I realised how unused I was becoming to normal human society, where personal space is at more of a premium than on a solo cruise of the Baltic.

Harstena

This is actual sea. Honestly

Here I had, more even than anywhere else in Sweden and Finland, a sense of the unreal, fleeting nature of summer and of life on these islands. The little pretend community, laid out around a neatly clipped lawn, felt like a temporary film set for an extravaganza about hobbits. The museum, dedicated to fish, was open for two months a year. The timetable for the tourist ferries showed that they operated for only one month. The Scandians are like Mayflies in the summer, except it's July. So I suppose the Scandians are like Julyflies in the summer. They live bright, active, sunny lives, flitting about outside for just the shortest of periods, then crawl off into a corner.

It was cool for July. The bloke on the next boat announced with some disgust that the warmest place in Sweden had only been twenty one degrees. The sea, however, was warm enough for a dip, as I waited for my Hungarian style meatball stew to cook. I was finally celebrating the end of the large bag of meatballs with this nourishing Goulash Archipelago. I can't help thinking that I've heard of that dish before. Perhaps it's not completely original. Wasn't there a book called something like that?

Even though Zoph was moored against a weather shore in under two metres of water I had, in my usual obsessive way, put out rather a lot of anchor warp astern. Later in the evening a small Swedish yacht appeared, with a young couple aboard, and moored to a nearby rock. She lay at about forty five degrees to Zoph's anchor line and I suspected that her anchor warp might cross over Zoph's. When I pointed this out to the bloke he was fairly incredulous. We were so far apart that the anchors couldn't possibly be tangled. I wasn't so sure. When I left before eight the next morning he was fairly pissed off to find that his anchor was indeed laid over my warp, which extended a full twenty metres beyond his. His initial breezy willingness to let out more and more warp, so that I could recover mine, became a little chillier as he had to let out more and more. Why the hell did I have out about thirty metres of warp, in two metres of calm sea, was his unspoken but not unreasonable question.

I left so early because I was expecting a bit of adverse weather. After some pretty benign conditions for the previous week the wind was due to increase from the south west during the afternoon. There was then a south westerly gale forecast for the following day. It would be a good opportunity to stay put for the day and take a rest, preferably somewhere with showers and shops.

I motored with the main up the four miles back to the marked channel, then all day, for forty miles, down the increasingly intricate lanes. More and more boats appeared during the day as the breeze increased, mostly heading north and taking advantage of the forecast south westerly. I passed a large, British flagged ketch, with no visible name. One large, racy French boat kept tacking along the channels, under conditions where Zoph would have made too slow progress. Distressingly, she nearly kept up with a Zoph, who was under motor. Sometimes, on these flat, sheltered seas and in not much breeze, I do envy those with racier, less robust boats. Clearly I wasn't the only person who navigated by the pink lines on the chartplotter which showed the routes. I watched a yacht with AIS as it religiously followed every inch of the winding pink line on the chart, even where the channel was wide enough to cut corners, it didn't deviate by a millimetre from the prescribed line across the sea.

When the wind did increase to a force four or five it came from slightly east of south and we had a decent sail. It became a little choppy for the last eight miles or so, across increasingly open water. We were slowly approaching the end of the land of the archie and would, in a couple of days, enter the shallow, sandy, exposed shores of the southern Baltic.

The Last Rock of the Year

The pleasant town of Västervik has a couple of marinas in the centre. One is a large, overpriced commercial one, the other a club with a few spaces for visitors. It also has, a mile or two out of town, another club marina which welcomes guests and which is much better sheltered from strong southerlies. I chose this latter, at Westerviks Segelsällskap, for a two night sojourn. There was a series of long pontoons with boom moorings and three or four spaces still empty for visitors. The bloke who came round wanting money for the berthing was very friendly and the price very reasonable, but I still somehow resented paying for berthing. I had, after all, with the help of my free Archie brochure, paid precisely nothing for berthing for the past week. In fact I had paid about twenty five quid in total for berthing in over a fortnight, since Tallinn.

Apart from parting with money, another thing I wasn't used to was civilisation and Västervik was a decent sized town with a range of shops, pubs, cafes, banks and even traffic. I navigated the streets on my Brompt, nervously and unsafely. The little town with its population of twenty thousand felt like a vast, frightening metropolis. The Baltic Pilot, of course, characterises Västervik as a very ordinary, industrial town. This is sort of true in as much as the main industry, in the summer at least, is tourism. The whole place was rammed with them. Their most interesting manifestation was in the huge, institutional campsite near the marina where Zoph was. This occupied a stretch of coast and a series of islands connected by rustic bridges. At its gated entrance was a huge queue of traffic to get in and a large complex of service and entertainment buildings. The campsite was filled with holidaying Swedish families, barbequeing and leaping in and out of the sea. I suppose it was the traditional Swedish version of the old fashioned British holiday camp. It was a Scandian Butlins. With two major differences. It was still used by ordinary people for their holidays and it was really very pleasant.

Harstena

Harstena

Everyone leaving Västervik

The next day I wandered around the overpriced marina near the town centre. It was run by the same company as the one in Arkösund which had established a near monopoly there. As far as I could tell, the company, 'Promarina', seems to have a policy of trying to buy up marinas and create local monopolies, enabling them to double prices at a stroke. Here they were asking about twice what I was paying just around the corner. Happily they have not managed to establish a monopoly in Västervik and at the peak of the season their pontoons were half empty. It's also encouraging that the Swedish Cruising Association were outraged enough about their pricing policy to complain and mount a campaign against them. In Britain we would just shrug our shoulders and say "well, what can you do?"

It was blowing up to thirty knots and the larger boats in particular, a few racy examples of which were secured to the outer, lee side of the pontoons, were suffering a bit in the chop. There were two British boats in the marina, a large ketch and a Halberg Rassy. Both were based in the Baltic and the chatty Halbergians almost had me persuaded that their practice, of leaving the boat over winter in the German Baltic, was a sensible one. Until, that is, they described the 'ex-pat' group of elderly southern English who made up such a vibrant community there. The thought of being part of an English 'ex-pat' community, importing marmite, tea and baked beans and complaining about the Germans, sent a cold shiver of horror up my spine.

In Västervik I had a major coup on the information front. I found a decent pilot book. Stupidly, I had not bought any of the pilots written by Swedes before the trip, on the grounds that I didn't know where I was going and each of them only covered a relatively small part of the trip. Like most pilot books they were also rather expensive. I had been wrong. I was stuck with annoyingly useless British publications which were made the more annoying by telling me, periodically, to refer to Swedish books I didn't have. I knew that there were English language versions of two pilots, 'Arholma to Landsort and Gotland', covering the Swedish Archie, and 'Landsort to Skanör', covering the area to the south, which I was now crossing. Though it was extremely unlikely that I would find the English language versions, I resolved that I would buy the Swedish edition of the latter, if I could find it. I was hugely pleased when I found a copy in one of Västervik's two bookshops. I was delirious when, under it, I found the English language version. It turned out to be a genuinely useful guide to all the wee rocky anchorages which I had been wanting to explore. My greatest regret was that I'd not bought both books before.

Västervik

Back aboard Zoph there was no sign if the near gale blowing outside, from her secure berth, fifty metres from a weather shore. People lay around sunbathing in their cockpits in the warm afternoon sunshine, complaining bitterly about the dreadful weather we were having that was keeping them in port. I tried to explain what dreadful summer weather on the west of Scotland was like, but I don't think they believed me. That evening I was somewhat disturbed, long into the night, by seriously poor oompah music. Two very staid and respectable geriatric septuagenarian couples, on the German boat next door, started ramping up the dreadful drinking songs as the night wore on and more schnapps went down their necks. My musical tastes are fairly catholic, but there can be no musical form more execrable than the German drinking song, apart perhaps, from modern jazz and anything that Simon Cowell has had a hand in. These elderly yachting hooligans were giving it laldie until the wee small hours, as they joined in enthusiastically with the dreadful songs on the CD.

You will have gathered that there are literally thousands of islands off the coast of Sweden. Nearly all of them have something to recommend them. Most have fantastic anchorages and sheltered sailing waters. The only island on the whole of the coast of Sweden on which it is impossible to land by yacht is called Blå Jungfrun. It is one of the myriad islands south of Västervik and one of the thousands south of the Stockholm Archie. It is a lump of rock not dissimilar in some ways to Ailsa Craig on the Clyde. All around it is deep sea, the bottom of which is entirely strewn with boulders. There is nowhere to anchor off it for more than a fleeting visit in a flat calm. The only island off the coast south of Västervik which is mentioned at all by the Baltic Sea pilot is Blå Jungfrun. Honestly. They only bother to mention the one island which is completely useless to their readers just to say that there's only a daytime anchorage. The best advice to cruising yachties wanting to visit the island is to take an organised boat trip from the mainland. None of the thousands of other small islands, for a hundred and forty miles of coast, from the south east corner of Sweden up as far as Harstena, gets any mention at all. It would be interesting to get an insight into the thought processes of the writers of these guides. Certainly the Baltic Sea Pilot beggars belief. Actually it does more than that. Not content with beggaring it, it stops belief's benefits, has it arrested for loitering, confiscates the money in its hat and has its dog put down. Naturally, I ignored bleak Blå Jungfrun as I sailed past after a day's rest in Västervik.

I left late as the breeze, still strong overnight, was due to fall during the day. We sailed close hauled down still convoluted, complex channels to the next destination, which I had picked from the cornucopia of goodies in my new, excellent, Swedish-published pilot. I had picked this anchorage purely for its name and when I got there, I have to say, it did exactly what it said on the tin. Snuggösund was yet another perfectly sheltered – indeed snug – rock to tie to, with a few motorboats from the local Figeholms Båtklubb having a barbie and enjoying the sunshine. The Swedes seem to be terribly fond of bats, for some reason, and practically every village has a Bat Club of some sort. I assume they spend their summers pipistrelle spotting and protecting the habitat of these charming flying mammals.

I had only sailed about fifteen miles and there was still a nice sailing breeze, so it was with some regret that I turned my back on Snuggösund and carried on southwards. As soon as I'd decided to carry on, of course, the wind headed us and we had to motorsail down some increasingly twisting and winding channels.

A long, narrow Swedish yacht sailed past at some speed. It was about fifty feet long and seven feet wide and called, appropriately 'So Long'. There's quite a lot of these sleek, old fashionedly racy looking craft on this coast. They are a product both of the sailing conditions and marina pricing policy. With low freeboards and large sail areas they would not be the best choice for a North Sea passage, but in these fantastically sheltered waters they are ideal for ghosting at speed across a calm sea. All Scandinavian, German and Dutch marinas charge for annual berthing by the square metre, not the linear metre. In the UK if you own a long, sleek fifteen metre by two metre classic yacht, with a bowsprit and two cramped bunks, you will pay the same for berthing as the bloke next door who sails a brand new, fifty foot Beneteau Mussolini, with eight berths, a jacuzzi and a snooker room. In the Baltic, quite apart from the fact that all berthing is generally cheaper, you will pay half as much for the narrow beamed boat, because it only has half the beam. This must, surely, have influenced yacht design and the types of boats people want to own.

We nipped offshore, past a large nuclear power station, then into practically the last small island anchorage in the eastern Swedish archipelagos, at Ekö. The new pilot book, written by yer acsheral Swedes, was a fantastic help, with chartlets showing more detail than the largest scale charts and, unlike nearly all British pilots, descriptions which gave places a positive slant and made you actually want to visit them. The British ones seem to be so concerned to point out the appalling dangers of everywhere that every time you open them you want to give up sailing and buy a caravan. Why do we navigate using information provided by people who have only passed through an area once or twice? Why don't old fishermen take to writing yachting pilots? Especially in the Baltic, in the absence of fish to catch.

Ironically, having reached the southern extent of the Swedish archies. this was almost certainly the last rock I would tie to this year. There were very few good wild anchorages further south and forty five quid was a big steep for pilotage information on only one anchorage. The southern Baltic is a much more open, sandy coast. Even where there are islands they tend not to be well enough designed for you just to tie your boat to a rock. I resolved to return to this coast, to get my money's worth out of the book.

Ekö was designed to the usual, high anchorage standards, with a few Swedish boats dotted around the various rocks. I tied up next to a Swedish family on a small yacht and, fifty yards away, the smallest cruising boat I had come across that year. Floating in the shallows, in a six inch deep puddle, and tied to a twig on the shore with a piece of string, was a faded and slightly battered one man canvas canoe.

A German cruising yacht smaller than Zoph

As I wandered about nearby I came across her skipper's camp, in a clearing in the rather swampy forest. He was a fairly elderly, grey-bearded German bloke, cruising up the coast having brought his craft over from Germany by ferry, on top of his car. Whilst for me the Skaergaard was running out, he had come northwards behind islands, hugging the coast where no yachts could pass. His tales of ablutions, acquiring food, charging batteries and getting weather forecasts in a canoe made me appreciate how spoilt I was, with my bog and galley and eighty amp-hour battery.

It was another perfectly calm, quiet night, with Zoph so still she might have been set in concrete. The peace was interrupted only by the hacking cough of a girl on a boat about a quarter of a mile away, the ticking of clocks on other boats and the buzzing of a few insects. I was aware that I would probably not find anywhere quite as quiet and perfect as this last rock of the year.

Ekö

Assimilation into the Hive of the Borg

The next day's passage was an uneventful, but quite long one. After a lot of indecision Anna had finally bought a ticket for a flight to Copenhagen on July 30th. I had somewhere I needed to be in six days time and it was almost two hundred and fifty miles away. My passages were going to have to get longer again. After initially picking my way out of the intricate rocky channels, I entered open water, with bugger all pilotage to do. For most of the day there was virtually no wind and I motored south, over a perfectly flat sea. Although there's no Skaergaard here as such, this bit of the Baltic is well protected by the island of Őland. The strait between the mainland and this long, narrow island narrows, from about thirteen miles in the north, to a couple of miles near Kalmar, where I was heading.

The day was lent a frisson of fear and excitement, however, by the main town on Őland, which I passed halfway though the day. We are indebted to Star Trek for alerting us to the dreadful dangers presented by the cyber-race the Borg. I can't be sure that Borgholm is actually the headquarters of the Borg Hive on earth, but with a name like that I was taking no chances and gave it a wide berth.

A wee breeze started up in the afternoon, but only enough to provide a bit of cooling on this warm summer's day. Eventually I motored under the huge, three and a half mile long bridge just north of Kalmar, linking Őland to the mainland. I had feared that the guest harbour in the relatively large town of Kalmar would be full, but there was plenty of room for visiting boats. There was no room for other species of tourist however. In the large, swish tourist information office, I overheard someone being told that there were no hotel or B&B rooms, of any description, available in the town that night, because the weather was nice. Why people visit a more or less random town because the weather's nice I don't know. I fleetingly considered renting out Zoph's two spare berths to the highest bidder, but thought better of it.

Kalmar was the most proper, big town since Tallinn. There were a lot more stone buildings than elsewhere and a sense of proper, pompous Euro-history – of kings and barons and castles and sieges and

A posh hotel on the way to Kalmar

stuff. There were even proper eccentrics. One pissed bloke, sitting outside a pub, insisted that I do him the great favour of taking his photograph. He was possibly making a point about it being the people who make up the heart of a town, not just the old buildings I was snapping. Or perhaps he was just a nutter.

After the peace of the rocks I found the noises of a town intrusive. Even this far north in Europe, nobody can design a simple building in a city without installing a dirty great air conditioner to keep it cool at night. Even when the ambient temperature is the same as, or below, room temperature and everybody's gone home and left the building empty, they leave the bloody thing on. But as well as the ubiquitous hum of the air con there was another noise. Wherever I went there was a loud, high pitched whining sound, which went right through me. Probably in much the same was as those ultra high whistles annoy dogs. A wifey on the only British flagged boat in town – a new Halberg Rassy – told me this was emanating from a dodgy pump in the university's marine experimental facility. Some idiot in planning had allowed them to build it in the town centre. I was hankering after my limpid pools in the wilderness. Needless to say, of course, the British Halberg was based in the Baltic.

The next day, In perfect summer weather, I joined a small procession of yachts heading southwards, to the open water south of Öland. All morning the sea was so calm and the summer air so drowsy and hazy, that it was only possible to tell where the horizon was by the odd dot of a boat floating on it. As I pressed on, the landscape, already devoid of wee rocky islands, grew flatter. Here the shores are shallow and sandy, though still, of course, devoid of the catastrophic tides that make so many low, flat, British coastlines into wastelands. A wee breeze started again in the afternoon and I tried sailing. Once again it was mildly frustrating that Zoph really had to motorsail to make significant progress, whilst a few of the flightier yachts were still able to sail at up to four knots. But most folk, like us, motored.

I checked out the anchorage at Öppenskär, detailed by my new pilot. In fact I followed a German ketch called 'Friborn' which had AIS, as I watched her on the chartplotter, circling in a bay, then coming to a halt. But Öppenskär didn't look much cop in the predicted easterlies, so I carried on, on a winding course to the small visitors' harbour a Stenshamn. After the relatively featureless coast I had passed, I was back in the land of the archipelago. The landscape didn't look as different to the archies further north as I had been expecting, but these islands hadn't been designed by Slartibartfast and didn't each provide a perfectly sheltered rock to tie to. In the much flatter and sandier landscape, more buoyage was needed, to pick my way through the channels to the island harbour.

Kalmar Castle

Kalmar

I picked up a boom mooring in the fairly busy harbour. Yachts were already rafting up on the harbour walls but, as so often, Zoph was able to fit into a wee, narrow, shallow space, which most yachts wouldn't go near. Stenshamn was a pleasant place, with a shop which sold only tourist crap – no food or anything – a couple of composting bogs and, of course, a sauna. No showers, just a sauna. Most of the boats were small and seemed to be local ones. The majority of the longer distance cruising boats appeared to have headed for the larger and apparently fascinating port of Karlskrona, which I ducked mostly to save two or three hours on passage. Stopping on the wee island of Stenshamn, where I could wander about ashore but still be right out at sea, on this exposed corner of Sweden, so that I could see where the weather was coming from, turned out to be quite a good move.

Leaving Kalmar

The bridge to Oland

The forecast was for a force four or five from the south east the following day. This was perfect for sailing the sixty miles or so to Simrishamn, right across the wide sweep of bay that makes up the south east bit of Sweden. So I woke early and expectantly. Sure enough a good sailing breeze was coming from the south east. But there was also a thick fog.

Locals were bemused. Apparently it was almost unheard of to get fog in the summer. But they assured me that it couldn't possibly continue for long. After all how could it remain foggy in a good breeze? They were confident that it would lift soon. "No, you never get fog in a south easterly" said one wise old ancient mariner confidently. I was not so sure. Again the conditions looked to me precisely like those we get on the west side of the North Sea in the spring.

An easterly was bringing warm air swirling up from further south in continental Europe. The hot air, heavy with moisture, hit the relatively cool air over the Baltic as it headed north and west. The moisture condensed out as a thick haar. This could go on, I thought, for weeks. Bollocks.

Svardsklova

Why a Baltic summer cruise is more pleasant than a North Sea crossing

All day the thick fog remained. Occasionally it thinned a bit and the locals got their craft ready, expectantly, but then it thickened again. In the afternoon a few boats headed out in convoy, following one of their number which had radar. The ferry arrived from the mainland a couple of times, but by and large everything stopped. People phoned their mates on boats in other harbours along the coast. Everywhere it was the same story of a pea-souper obliterating everything. In the afternoon a yacht arrived from the small, outlying, offshore island of Utklippan. Apparently everyone had been stuck there in the haar. When it cleared briefly, a few had made a run for it. But very soon the fog had closed in again. The folk I spoke to had a miserable time, trying to find their way to the buoyed channel into this harbour. I decided that I was going nowhere that day.

I explored the island by Brompt. Previously pastoral it was now, of course, primarily a summer holiday island with all the old fishermen's houses turned into holiday cottages. As so often, the interpretive signs said that the island used to be arable land until the mid twentieth century, but now couldn't be farmed. Why? What disastrous event has happened to make the land so crap now? There was a pleasant holiday atmosphere, marred only by the fact that, in the damp mist, everyone knew that it was gorgeous summer weather only twenty or thirty metres above their heads. As usual the local boaty crew were not your posh yachties, just ordinary, working class families, all of which, in Scandinavia, have a boat of some description.

A big, rather scruffy, racy sort of catamaran turned up and managed to squeeze alongside the harbour wall. Between its narrow hulls was a large net and a long 'wing' of fibreglass, on which a cabin was mounted. Underneath this 'wing', facing downwards, four feet from the surface of the sea, was the boat's name, 'Isis'. Call me superstitious but I'm not sure I want to go to sea in a boat whose skipper feels the need to paint her name underneath the hull.

I observed some of the more unusual harbour residents. There were two blond girls of about eighteen wandering about, from one of the nearby speedboats. They appeared to be identical twins. But whilst one of them was of a fairly ordinary – even aspirational – reasonably thin shape, the other was a painfully skinny bag of bones. It seemed likely, to me, that she was anorexic. Now it's a well known cliché that anorexics look at themselves in the mirror and, however skinny they get, see an overweight person. If you are an anorexic identical twin, presumably, when you look at your normally shaped doppelganger, you see something that approximates to Jabba the Hutt. If you think you look fat, they must look absolutely gargantuan. Just a thought. I can't claim anorexia as one of my areas of expertise.

It was July 27th and Anna told me that it was the day of the Olympic opening ceremony. I shuddered to think of the level of inappropriate jingoism that the media would be descending to, in the next couple of weeks, as a bloke from Birmingham won a cycling race that only three people in the world had ever taken part in, involving going as slowly as possible round and round a track in a silly hat. As usual, a few Brits would share in the medals that only posh people from rich countries could afford to take part in. Shooting, horse riding, rowing in boats with different numbers of crew and sailing obscure types of dinghy, that nobody has ever heard of. Meanwhile the athletes of Africa would all compete against each other for one running medal.

If you can have four different gold medals for swimming exactly the same distance, in slightly different ways, why can you not have four gold medals for running ten thousand metres, in slightly different ways? If you can win eight different gold medals for rowing a mile in a scull, a pair, a double scull, a coxed pair, a four scull, a coxless four, a coxed four and an eight, why can you not win eight different gold medals for running a mile in different types of shoes? Or with very tight 'Y' fronts on, or something? But no, that would allow the folk from poor countries to win more medals and ruin the comfortable club for the posh.

Svardsklova in the fog

Of course this time it was worse than usual. Otherwise reasonably sane people I knew were celebrating having been able to shell out huge piles of their hard-earned, for tickets to see the early heats of the Women's Underwater Synchronised Shot-Putt, or the Light Welterweight Mini-Golf. How pleased I was to be missing it all. I was going to miss every single, nationalistic second of Britain's last, dying act, as a significant force in the world. "Look at us! We used to be important you know".

The weather was due to be cloudier and cooler the next day, but an easterly was still forecast, so before eight a.m. with no sign of fog, I headed out to sea. Plenty of others in the little harbour had the same sort of idea, but all the rest, as usual, headed off in the opposite direction, as I sailed south west, under full sail, across a rolly sea with about a five or six foot chop. Initially we headed dead downwind in a force four to five, but soon the wind veered to the south-south east. Zoph picked up her skirts and bowled along on a reach at over six knots.

I wasn't entirely sure which country I was going to. My basic plan was to head for Simrishamn in Sweden, but the Danish island of Bornholm was about twenty five miles from Simrishamn, to the south. Both were about equidistant from where I was. If the easterly strengthened, Simrishamn would be on a shallow, shelving lee shore. At Bornholm, on the other hand, I could nip round the northern end to the small port of Hammerhavn. Exposed to the west, its entrance would be completely sheltered from easterlies. For the moment I headed on a compromise course, which would allow me to make a decision later, depending what the wind did. As usual I couldn't just go somewhere in a straight line, but had to have a justification for a more eccentric, curved course.

As we sailed on I noticed that one of the telltales on the jib seemed to have got stuck, so that it looked like it was always streaming nice and horizontally. What a brilliant marketing idea, I thought. Telltales which you just stuck permanently, all along their length, to the sail. Then they would always be streaming nicely and you wouldn't have to bother with all that tedious sail trim. I crossed the course of two ships, which I looked at on the AIS. One was going to Beirut, the other to Hull. One to a burned out, war torn hellhole of a place, whose inhabitants had suffered more than any people should ever be made to suffer, over the past decades of conflict, the other to Beirut.

As the day wore on the wind began to die and I altered course slightly to head for mainland Swedish Simrishamn. I got just close enough to Bornholm to get a telegram from Vodafone saying "Welcome to Denmark", then we were off to Sweden again. As we got closer a couple of other boats appeared. One was the German Ketch 'Friborn' that I'd followed into an anchorage two days before. A couple more appeared. They were big yachts going much faster than Zoph and seemingly heading on beyond Simrishamn, round the southern tip of the mainland.

As we got within about seven miles of Simrishamn, in a falling south easterly of less than ten knots I saw the sails flapping wildly on the couple of boats ahead of me. In less than a minute the wind had whipped up to nearly thirty knots from the west south west. This was one of those horrible, unforecast winds that, though not so dreadful in themselves, make you a little nervous of trusting forecasts. I tucked in a couple of reefs, rolled

Svardsklova

in a bit of jib and hardened up, beating to Simrishamn, which was now on a weather shore. Friborn, meanwhile, seemed to be struggling with their furling main. The boats that had been heading further west seemed to change their minds and everyone now started heading to Simrishamn.

When I arrived, the very large and quite swish marina was fairly full, but as the larger yachts were eying each other up and deciding who to raft on, we found a decent sized berth on – get this – a proper pontoon, with cleats! After a while I went and chatted to the crew of Friborn, a German couple, he of Chinese origin. They confirmed that they had been stuck for two nights on the anchorage where I had seen them, because of the relentless fog.

The unforecast wind whistled through the rigging for hours. One boat was particularly annoying. As is so often the case, it was a small, racy day-sailing boat that had a wire halyard clanging against the mast repeatedly. The whole rigging acted as a massive un-musical instrument, as the cacophonous clanging rang around the marina. People with wee, racy, round-the-cans boats, of course, rarely spend the night aboard,, so don't realise just how frigging annoying this can be for other marina users. Eventually I decided that I'd had enough. Ignoring local convention and etiquette I marched round to the offending boat, several long pontoons away, boarded it and secured the offending halyard away from the mast, with a bit of dangling string. Phew, the relief. I worried slightly, as I made my way back to Zoph, that I may have broken some Swedish taboo and be set upon by the locals. In the short walk back I was congratulated, by no fewer than three people on the boats I passed, for taking this unilateral, guerrilla action. Nobody else had dared, but everyone else wanted to go and shut up the bloody racket. A rather anal lot, the Swedes.

Buoyed up by this observation, I carried out some further anthropological research. As I've mentioned, this marina had proper, nice, sturdy pontoons. Two boats shared a large 'U' shaped space, in the normal manner of 'proper' marinas in the UK. The finger pontoons weren't of the dodgy, wobbly variety. They were proper, rock solid platforms. From Zoph's cockpit I observed people on the boats in the busy marina. I watched at least fifty people getting off their

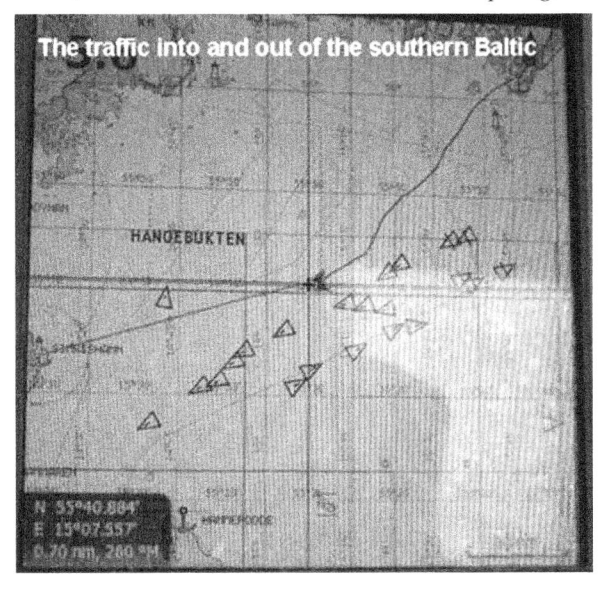

The traffic into and out of the southern Baltic

boats. Not one, single, solitary individual got off the side of the boat onto the pontoon. Every single one climbed out of the cockpit, made their difficult way along the side decks, past all the usual obstructions there, crossed the foredeck, vaulted over the pulpit and climbed down to the pontoon over the bow. Every one of them. The same applied to everyone returning to their boats. It was quite extraordinary. Climbing over the bow of your boat would be seen as a near certifiable activity in Britain. Here not a single person even considered the possibility that the side of the boat might make a suitable entry and exit point. Habit is a strange thing.

A stupid looking thing on the way into Copenhagen

This is a huge lump of Morvern, which is being ripped apart to line the rapacious pockets of a bloated aristo

Sand castles on the quay in Copenhagen

More sand castles seen from the water

Welsh Sweden

The next morning there was quite a procession of boats leaving, before nine, to head south and west. I counted twenty eight sailing boats. Most of them were serious looking, quite large cruising boats, dwarfing Zoph, and over half of them were now foreign, mostly German or Danish. But she felt quite at home amongst her much larger kin. Zophiel is something of a Yorkshire terrier of a boat. Dogs have this weird species recognition thing. A Chihuahua easily and immediately recognises an Irish wolfhound as a creature of the same species. It also doesn't seem to appreciate just how much smaller it is and how the wolfhound could kill it just by inhaling it through its nostrils. It doesn't associate with – say – a rat, which is much more its own size. Zoph is a proper cruising boat and associates with other proper cruising boats. She doesn't hang around with the wee motorboats, day sailers and local boats of her own size. She doesn't seem to appreciate just how tiny and insignificant she is beside a sixty foot cruising ketch. After all they are both in the same game

The forecast was back in charge and the gentle breeze came from the north east. Again we had the annoying sort of conditions which allowed the faster, larger boats to sail, whilst Zoph couldn't do more than about three knots and had to motorsail – our destination was almost fifty miles away. I turned the engine off and sailed for periods as we turned more to the west, but whenever the wind fell a bit the engine went on again. The breeze never went round to the north west as forecast and the whole procession had a pleasant enough, but uneventful passage.

A Swedish flagged, forty foot Princess gin palace overtook us at some speed. She had written on her stern 'Spionkop, Liverpool'. There, no doubt, hangs a tale. About halfway through the passage we crossed the shipping lanes for fast ferries to Bornholm, which zoomed to and fro every half hour or so. They were emanating from the town of Ystad, a couple of miles away to starboard. Ystad must, surely, be a Welsh town, mustn't it? It has to be a Welsh word. In fact I just looked it up on Göögle and it's the Welsh for 'Estate'. As in a rural, landed estate, as opposed to a housing estate. Presumably this is the Welsh part of Sweden, founded hundreds of years ago by immigrants from Cardiff.

That evening I arrived at the marina in Gislovs Lage, which is really just a suburb of the larger Trelleborg. The latter is rumoured, unusually for a Scandian town, to have no facilities for yachts. The marina was getting to be full, but most of the day's procession of boats had gone elsewhere – god knows where – and I found a large space for Zoph. There were two British flagged boats in port. I chatted to the occupants of one – a Southerly. Predictably they had been based in the Baltic for seven years and spoke enthusiastically about the 'ex-pat' community. The other was a scruffy, chunky, dirty, knackered looking Nauticat with no mast and no sign of any rigging. I suspect that the lack of a mast was not just a temporary condition, but that it wandered the Baltic deliberately mastless.

The only minor problem with this peaceful and pleasant enough marina, was that the entire place stank to high heaven of shit. This seems to be an endemic condition on this coast. The south westerlies blow tonnes and tonnes of seaweed onto the tideless shore, where it rots, and smells quite a lot like poo. There was a fair chance that I did as well. I had gone fairly feral over the past month. This happens to me during long periods sailing solo. I spend days and days, entirely away from civilisation and don't bother too much about personal grooming or hygiene. When I finally get to a town, I am surprised to find that people recoiling from me and small children screaming and running away at my approach. Then I catch sight of myself in a shop window. A tatty-headed, bedraggled neanderthal tramp stares back at me, feet poking out of holes in his shoes, flies undone and a week's worth of breakfast matted into his tangled beard and filthy, salt-encrusted clothing.

I was meeting the other half in Copenhagen tomorrow, so Standards were going to have to improve. Just in case the smell of shit wasn't the seaweed's fault, I took the opportunity to wash all my clothes, for the first time for about two months. Bur would I wash my clothes first, or have a couple of beers first? It was a chicken and egg situation. It was a chicken and egg situation in the sense that it was blindingly obvious that the beers came first. I've never really understood that apparent conundrum. Of course the egg came first. At some point in evolution a bird similar to a chicken – let's call it a proto-chicken – made that last little mutation and the last little evolutionary step, to the point where it could be confidently described as a chicken. A proto-chicken laid an egg, out of which hatched a chicken. It doesn't matter at what point you want to describe the final transformation into a chicken. All previous generations had been hatching out of eggs since they were invertebrates. So if anyone ever asks you, the answer's the egg. After a couple of beers I managed to wash and dry huge, minging mountains of washing, by beavering on well into the night.

At eight the next morning I headed out bright, early, scrubbed and shining, for the allegedly wonderful, wonderful Copenhagen. I was followed on the mirror-flat sea by a wee racy Beneteau, with a grumpy looking crew of three, who refused to respond to my cheery wave. There is a shortcut round the bottom left hand corner of Sweden, consisting of the Falsterbo Canal. This is a one mile long, straight channel through a suburban landscape, that allows you to cut the corner, behind the Skanör Peninsula. There is an opening bridge, which runs to a timetable. I was a wee bit early arriving, so progressed under motor as slowly as possible down the canal, timing my approach so that I didn't have to circle. The wee Beneteau screamed past me under motor, then whipped manically round and round in circles for ten minutes. The bridge opened, we motored through and, immediately on the other side, I raised the main, shook out both jibs and reached slowly up the narrow channel away from the shallow, sandy coast towards Copenhagen. We passed a couple of boats, moored at the western exit to the canal, which had been in the procession the previous day. At least one seemed to have been following us for many days.

As we approached closer to Copenhagen, the shipping lanes got busier. A gentle breeze from the south slowly veered south west quite timeously, allowing Zoph to sail on a reach all the way. Though the weather was calm and benign, giving us a pleasant sail, there were apocalyptic signs about. Huge thunderclouds were building to the west and there was an inevitability about the way they seemed to be bearing down on us. With a couple of miles to go and the wind increasing from the west I got rid of all sail, to avoid having to do so in the inevitable, pissing down rain.

Though Copenhagen is a very maritime city, with a long sea front and it's possible to sail right into the heart of it, it's surprising how little the sea is evident from it. Most of the bits that front onto the sea are extremely unappealing, industrial areas. At the heart of the city is a waterway that looks like a canal, but is in fact a narrow bit of the sea. There is no wide, sweeping sea front to walk along. In the industrial port, I passed a massive lump of Scotland. I had last seen the huge bulk carrier 'Yeoman Bridge' heading up the Sound of Mull. Its job is to transport the large mountain at Glensanda, near Oban, to mainland Europe, to be used as roadstone. Six million tonnes of granite a year are removed from the mountain. This provides jobs for two local people but, more importantly, lines the pockets of the local landed gentry. They use the money for a spot of Marie Antoinette toy farming and running overpriced, empty, hobby restaurants. I had a moan about this in last year's tome, "A Gigantic Whinge on the Celtic Fringe", when I visited Glensanda.

Jammed into a tiny space in Chistianshavn, Copenhagen

Sure enough, as I turned the corner to enter the channels into the city, there were huge flashes of lightning, crashes of thunder and the heavens opened in a downpour of quite spectacular proportions. I almost said 'biblical proportions' but it was just water, not frogs or anything. Sopping wet, I poked Zoph into a few of the mooring options. I was expecting Copenhagen to be busy and soon began upgrading 'busy' to 'full'. It did look genuinely difficult to find a berth.

I poked into the apparently famous Nyhavn in the city centre, but it seemed to be restricted to posh, classic old wooden craft. I wondered about pointing out to someone that Zoph had actually been featured, sort of, in Classic Boat magazine, but I don't think I'd have been taken seriously and anyway, there was nobody to tell this to. As I was leaving Nyhavn to rejoin the main channel a large, fast ferry was passing down the channel. It was crossing from my starboard side so I stopped Zoph to let it past. But as I did so it suddenly turned violently to port to enter the narrow, short Nyhavn. As Zoph sat static, hard against the starboard side of the short cut, it turned to power straight towards her. At the last moment it jammed on the brakes and screamed to a halt, sending a wall of water crashing onto Zoph's bow. To add, literally, insult to injury, the driver of this monstrosity then started gesticulating at me and shaking his head. It was clear what he thought of idiot yachties who got in his way. Bloody hell I was furious. After about five minutes in Copenhagen, I treated the city to a stream of bile and invective which would have shocked Frankie Boyle. What the fuck did he expect me to do? I'm not a fucking mind reader. Was I supposed to sacrifice Zoph by ramming her into the quay, so that his sodding bus didn't have to slow down or deviate for an instant? Bastard. On the side of the ferry was the logo 'Arriva'. Well that explains it. The bloody thing was being driven by a train driver.

I explored the full length of Copenhagen's most historic, built up central canal mooring area, Cristianshavn. This narrow canal was made the narrower by the hundreds of boats packed into it. Other boats were searching for a mooring as well and Scandian friendliness had been replaced by a scowly competitiveness. People on boats I approached, with a view to rafting up, either waved me away or pretended not to see me. In the pissing down rain I was beginning to lose patience. In the end I decided to moor alongside a motorsailer, in the smallest, tightest dead-end spur, off the main Cristianshavn canal. I was just preparing fenders and lines to forcibly board the reluctant boat, when I noticed a narrow mooring, between piles, on the other side of the wee dead end. I sized it up. The thin, knackered tree trunk piles were only about four metres from the quay. Usually you look for spaces which are at least as long as the boat, preferably a couple of metres longer. They were also very close together. Eyeing them up I guessed that they might, just, be wider than Zoph.

I slowly edged forward and jammed Zoph between the piles. She just fitted. I tied a couple of lines to the quay then thought about fenders. Zoph's beam is eight foot eight inches. The distance between the piles was nine foot two inches. There was no room for fenders. But Zoph has a bit of tumblehome. That is, her topsides are narrower at the top than they are further down. I found my two smallest, crappiest fenders, one two inches in diameter, the other three inches. I pushed them between the piles and Zoph. Because of the tumblehome I was able to stand on them and wedge them into place. Although I did stick on a couple of lines, these were entirely redundant. For four nights – the longest I'd stayed anywhere that summer – Zoph remained literally wedged between tree trunks amongst the historic buildings, in one of Copenhagen's pleasantest, tweest central areas.

And that was the end of Zoph's cruising – and my solo cruise – for July 2012. In travelling from Helsinki to the Russian border and back as far as Copenhagen, we had gone nine hundred and eleven and a half miles, in twenty eight passages, with two days off. Not up to the record breaking standards of May, but almost the largest solo mileage I've ever managed in a calendar month. Now, I supposed, I could slow down in my journey to… where? Where was I actually going? Was I heading back to the Forth for the winter, or leaving Zoph in Scandinavia? Or even in Holland ? Or Germany. If I was heading back home, why? Was it just for completeness? A bloody-minded desire to say that I'd done the return trip to Russia from Scotland in one season, just because nobody else did. Was that sufficient reason? As always I was plunged into a stupid agony of indecision. God knows how I'd cope if I ever had to take a genuinely difficult, life or death decision.

A naked, gay performer on the rooftops of liberal Copenhagen

Nyhavn, Copenhagen

Hippyocrisy

The timing of my arrival in Copenhagen was spot on and I just had time to walk to the station to fetch Anna. With the small proviso that, given her severe geographical dyslexia, she was unable to say which station she was at.

Arriving back at the boat, she was impressed that we were jammed into such a gratifyingly tiny space, in a proper city centre canal. Old, six storey buildings crowded all round the boat, which was literally wedged between two old tree trunks and nudging onto the quay in an overstuffed canal. Our modest rooms, with kitchen, toilet and balcony over the water, cost about thirteen squid a day including electricity. They were better situated than practically any hotel in the city, in a location under huge demand. We were right in the middle of the capital, yet our bit of canal was as quiet as an anchorage in an archie.

I was impressed once again at Scandian reasonableness. In Britain, in response to the demand, the Council would have squeezed the boat owners dry, charging three or four times that, for such a prime piece of water. I suppose the rent of a bit of canal can't be 'real estate', can it? Well 'pretend-estate' then. As I sat there on my perfect capital city mooring, the rapacious berthing police at Weymouth were chasing twenty seven foot yachts for berthing fees of a hundred and fifty pounds a night to raft up in the harbour. Or, if you couldn't afford this, you were welcome to anchor, out in the wide open, exposed bay off Portland, for as little as eighty two quid a night. I think I'll steer clear of the south of England. The Scandians recognise that boats are driven by ordinary people and add something to the attractions and atmosphere of the city.

An architect designed this thing so that it looks OK from just this one place

We wandered around the city. I had been there a couple of times before, but in winter. I used to supervise three PhD students who were, oddly, sexagenarian senior staff of the Danish Technical University. For some reason they all wanted to do PhDs at a little known, dead parrot university in Aberdeen. (A 'dead parrot university is, of course, an ex-poly-technic). They had shown me round the town on a couple of occasions, but it all looked very different now. Partly because it was summer, but mostly because, instead of taking an hour and a half on Difficultjet, the trip had taken three months from Edinburgh, via Russia and Estonia, at about four miles an hour.

Copenhagen is ten times scruffier than anywhere else in Scandinavia. I wouldn't have thought this was necessarily a positive attribute, but after three months of Scandian spick and span it was quite refreshing. It's Like Hamsterjam, not only because of the canals, but also because none of the iconic sights are huge, overbearing, fuck-off imperial structures, designed to intimidate people. The stupid wee mermaid in particular, of which more later, is the world's single, least impressive, well known iconic symbol of a city. This lack of pompous posturing makes it feel an awful lot more friendly and democratic than more rapacious, imperial cities like London.

One of the scruffiest bits, which is on the tourist route, is the hippy colony at Christiana, a kaftan's throw from Zoph's berth. This is a large, formerly derelict, industrial and barracks area, which was colonised by a load of anarchists, squatters, punks and hippies in the 1970s. After a history of run-ins with the authorities over drugs and the like, things have settled down and there is now even a law, giving an unprecedented degree of administrative independence to the area. Put simply, they get to take drugs and pay no tax, without being hassled by the police. We wandered around the shambolic, haphazard buildings. The earlier ones looked like they were made out of found materials and cheap crap. The later houses looked like rambling mansions pretending to be made out of soil and bark, but actually designed by architects with small willies, for graphic designers with a penchant for the pseudo-organic aesthetic.

The new extension to the National Gallery. Not bad for an architect

I wondered whether the principles on which it had been founded had survived or if, as is usually inevitable, it had just turned into a retreat for middle class, 'lifestyle' seeking aesthetes. I had visited a couple of these types of communities in the past – notably Findhorn on the Moray Firth and Auroville in southern India. In both cases the idealism had quickly been replaced by comfortable nimbyism. Altruism by a concern for property values. Though Christiana was only about a hundred and fifty yards from the boat, it was an age away from our genteel bit of waterfront. It was not as gentrified as Findhorn, where the 'members' of the peace-and-love community now actively campaign to get the dog-on-a-string hippy caravan encampment - which kicked off the whole thing - forcibly evicted. Nowadays you need bucket loads of money and a Grand Design to buy into the anti-materialistic, idealistic community at Findhorn. It could never, however, be as nakedly hypocritical as the worst place I've ever been to in the whole wide world, the European hippy slave colony at Auroville, in southern India. I wrote about that hell–hole in a tale called "Hitchhikers and Eurovillains" in my book "The Front of Beyond".

A wacky tea party near the hippy, anarchist settlement. Yeah... Stick it to the man, Man

The rules of the hippy colony were amusingly ironic and hypocritical. An anxiety to stick it to the man and not live by society's fascist rules, has of course translated itself into: 'I demand the right to make everyone live by my rules'. The hippy central committee has drawn up a set of rules which are displayed everywhere. One of them is 'No photography'. That is what the Police State does. It prevents the subversive influence of photography. Around the world, protesters use photographs to spread information about what the state is doing and to overcome repression. Freedom of information is a key weapon of anyone trying to achieve radical change. But the anarchists and punks and hippies of Christiana have a 'No Photography' rule. Even more surreally they have a 'No Running' rule throughout the 'community'. The only time I have ever seen a 'no running' rule is in the corridors of a school. But the freedom loving society of the peace and love hippies has instituted a 'No Running' rule.

The freedom to camp anywhere you want is enshrined in law throughout Scandinavia. Except in this hippy colony where, honestly, there is a 'No Camping' rule. I saw an explanation for this. To paraphrase: "If we let people camp there'd be no control. Any old Tom Dick or Harry could move in". In the

1970s they crossed the fences and illegally retook the land from the army, for the people. And good for them. Now they do their utmost to keep it for themselves and stop a new generation of people from claiming bits of it.

So how is that any different from normal naked capitalism? They won the land for their tribe and now are fighting off other tribes to keep it for themselves. They have a nice rural bit of Copenhagen to live in, when they head back from working in the city as graphic designers and IT consultants. They probably didn't have to pay for the land and nobody hassles them if they want to smoke dope. As a bit of an old hippy myself, I'm always disappointed at the serial failure of principles to survive age and growing comfort. As always, a breathtaking degree of Hippyocrisy wins over altruistic principles, it seems, every time.

...But within the rules of course. No running, no photography and the only 'no camping' sign in the whole of Scandivania. Right on Man

The one positive you can take from the place, is that it is possible to create interesting, varied and pleasant built environment, without having recourse to architects. Give everyone a bit of land covered in trees and let them do what they want, within a human scale. Houses made of bits of wood, corrugated iron, rusting steel, bicycle frames and painted up shipping containers, are more or less randomly arranged, amongst rotting barrack buildings. Yet they manage to look quite appealing and create a liveable environment, without an architect's master plan. Only the later, Grand Designs houses look like they have involved an artifartitect.

We explored the more institutional parts of town. The National Gallery was worth a look. It has a massive new extension, which is actually quite striking. Most of the recent work in it, however was of the 'I have a small idea which I can't express properly, but I have enough money to get loads of people in China to make it for me, which is handy because I have no craft skills' variety. One such brilliant work of artistic genius, by the hard of thinking, was a couple of large clear plastic spheres, each with an air plant growing in it. As we approached I suggested to Anna that this piece of nonsense looked like the work of an architect – it was particularly poorly made and lacking in craft

Zoph literally wedged between two tree trunks

and beauty. The blurb said that it could be "...viewed as models for alternative types of social spaces and habitats for people". It went on to say that the artist had trained as an architect. Hurray! Well done. As stupid a statement as I have come to expect from an art school trained architect who has never been called upon to build anything.

A few lazy days in Copenhagen and we began to get port-bound. The prospect of the big, bad sea seemed a frightening one. The forecasts were for strong stuff for a day or two, so we stayed for four nights, wedged between our tree trunks – a day or two longer than intended. But on August the third we headed out of town up the channel. We passed some astonishing, huge sand sculptures, which had been produced as part of a competition and were now a temporary tourist attraction. From the land you had to pay to see them. From the water we could browse slowly along the quay, having a squint at them. Like most things in Copenhagen it appeared to be sponsored by Audi. It seemed that they could erect any sort of daft, logo-themed plastic crap temporary building, anywhere in Copenhagen, to obscure any historical monument they wished. Presumably they paid a lot of money into the city's coffers. Or gave the leader of the Council a free Audi, or something.

Christianshavn

The Old Custom House, Copenhagen

We approached the daft wee mermaid statue and pottered over to have a look. From the land side this statue of a wifey, about full size, sitting on a very unremarkable rock ,on a very unremarkable stretch of waterfront, was thronged with touros at all times. It is of no great historical significance and neither particularly old nor impressive. It was just commissioned by the head of Carlsberg in 1909, yet has achieved astonishing iconic status. From the sea side, her rock is in reasonably deep water, so we approached as close as possible. As I say it really isn't much of a statue, so why the Danish police should be so concerned about the bloody thing being rammed by a twenty seven foot yacht is beyond me. Anyway, we didn't do a lot of damage and got some photos, so what the hell are they worried about?

(For the avoidance of doubt, and should you be a member of that fine body of men and women, the Danish Police Force, we didn't actually ram the little mermaid in Copenhagen. It was just a joke. Honest).

We headed south. A British flagged boat passed us heading north. It was the biggest boat we had seen for weeks. A huge, hundred foot, grey superyacht. It's amazing how often the superyachts are British flagged. Presumably it's to do with the concentration of wealth in the UK. In Scandia most of the population can afford a second hand yacht of about thirty feet, costing thirty or forty thousand quid. In Britain, a thousand bankers can each afford a superyacht costing thirty or forty million. The rest of us can go and screw ourselves.

Ramming the Little Mermaid, if you'll forgive the expression and I see no reason why you should

In six to twelve knots of breeze from the west, the engine went on and off at least four times, as we tried to sail at a sensible rate. The breeze was fickle all day in the open water, but we had some pleasant, gentle sailing in the sun. Latterly we were chased by a blue hulled yacht with a 'GBR' sail number and a blue ensign. As it drew nearer we could see that she was called 'Clemency'. What with the name and the posh ensign I deduced that she was the property of an English lawyer of some description. Celebrity was about a thirty eight footer, so of course she caught Zoph, but not very rapidly. Indeed Zoph seemed to be just about as close winded as Celeriac. As we approached the harbour at Rødvig we noticed a whole pile of fish sticks littering the sea. These twigs, sticking up out of the sea, to hold longshore nets, are quite a hazard in this shallow sea. They are often a long way from shore in quite deep water and it's not always clear which side of them you should pass. They are a particular pain when placed in front of harbours. As at Klintholm, months before, the many boats approaching Rødvig seemed uncertain how to proceed.

We made it into the harbour however, and secured a large space between piles, then watched the harbour fill up. I chatted to the crew of Calamity, which turned out to be a Finngulf thirty nine. The boat had been based in the Baltic, of course, but was now being sailed home to be sold. I could tell this was a Baltic boat before I asked, by the reel of luggage tape fixed to the stern as an anchor warp. This is a ubiquitous Baltic arrangement. Rødvig was a small, fairly nondescript but nonetheless pleasant commuter town with, of course, the inevitable tourist industry for yachts. We wandered the town for a while in the warm evening.

Joy Spring

The next morning we headed out, into a gentle breeze, and sailed towards the shallow, sandy channels leading westwards over the north side of Møn. These were the channels that I had avoided on the recommendation of the stupid pilot book in May, on the grounds that they were dangerously shallow and subject to strong tides. Naturally this now seemed ridiculous as we joined the massed ranks of Danes and Germen, heading south and west.

The breeze backed slowly round from south west to south east, which was handy as it allowed us to sail pretty much all day through the winding, complicated buoyage. The British yacht Catastrophe headed off south, but we followed a constant procession of boats down the shallow channels. As we approached the starboard hand buoy marking the start of a channel, we were neck and neck with a rather nice looking Germanian yacht called 'Joy Spring'. A glossy maroon colour she looked like a fairly traditional long-keeler. She turned out to be an Amigo 33, crewed by a couple of jazz musicians – the name apparently refers to a jazz album.

It was entirely clear to me that the Germen were racing us. It was just obvious. We passed the buoy about five metres ahead of them, then continued what was obviously a race for the rest of the day. Anna was unconvinced. She felt it likely that I was the only person involved who thought that a race was in progress. The fact that we were winning – which slow old Zoph never does – lent weight to her argument, but I chose to ignore her. Clearly he was racing. He turned hard round every channel buoy, when there was clearly plenty of space to cut the corner outside the channel. Obviously the actions of someone involved in a race.

After a couple of hours we were headed on one stretch and had to motor. Joy Spring immediately cut a huge corner across the shallows outside the channel. Then we were able to bear away and he was back to staying strictly on the race course. Astonishingly we stayed ahead of her all day. She was a little closer winded than Zoph – practically every boat is – but we sailed just a tad faster. It's not often that Zoph can beat anything – apart from a Bavaria, of course.

The sun disappeared in the afternoon and we had heavy showers after four, The rambling and scruffy marina at Vordingborg looked full at first, with boats rafting up on its outer pontoons. As usual however, there was plenty of space inshore, in the narrow slots between piles and in the shallower water. Zoph was spoiled for choice. The lawyers on Celibacy turned up later. They seemed to have taken the much longer route round the south of Møn. They had probably read the Imray pilot

We wandered around the pleasant commuter town, with its historic centrepiece of a brick tower in an attractive park on the site of old fortifications. We got an inkling as to why the Scandians all head off to small islands for barbeques in the summer. It was a Saturday evening in August. From about eight to ten in the evening we wandered around the substantial main shopping streets of the town. Everywhere was completely dead. Hardly a person was to be seen on the streets. The odd, shifty individual scurried past on the way home. All the bars and restaurants were empty and apparently shut. The only signs of revelry came from a flat above the shops, where someone was having a small, hushed party. It was a pleasant enough town but just too sanitised and, frankly, dead.

The next morning we motored off towards the execrable island of Vejrø, Denmark's biggest rip-off. We were helped by nearly a knot of tide pushing us through the bridged narrows. I still hadn't worked out whether these tides were driven by the moon – and therefore likely to change every six hours – or the wind. You'd think it would be an easy thing to establish, but the Scandians all have a blind spot of stupidity when it comes to tides. After a couple of hours motoring, the breeze got up a bit and we sailed, first on a broad reach then dead downwind. The spinnaker pole was deployed, for the first time that year, to pole the jib out. A preventer went on the main, the staysail came down and we cruised gently downwind at five knots in twelve knots of true wind. It is testament to how lazy I am with the rig that Anna claimed never to have seen this configuration in operation before.

We gave Vejrø a wide berth, of course. We followed several yachts and a ferry round the north end of the island of Omø, then hardened up and sailed to the entrance to its little harbour. The tight, well sheltered harbour was filling up, but once again there was plenty of space for a small boat with a relatively shallow draught.

Omø is a small, flat, sandy island a couple of miles long, with sandy beaches, holiday cottages and a large camp site next to the marina. There was a jolly, holiday atmosphere and the smell of barbeque pervaded everything. Presumably this was where all the denizens of Vordingborg were this weekend.

After three months of watching everyone else barbequeing I decided to manufacture my own. While Anna improvised beef burgers from the contents of the fridge, I constructed a barbeque from the lid of Zoph's charcoal stove and various bits of metal I found lying around. Ashore we joined the massed ranks of the Scandian and German barbie enthusiasts with their huge, gleaming, stainless steel gas or charcoal barbequeing devices. God knows where they find the space to store them on board. For some reason, people looked askance at our six inch diameter tin lid. They smiled nicely, if somewhat condescendingly, and seemed somehow to smirk at one another as they passed us tucking into our excellent burgers. I've no idea why.

We left early the next morning, as the weather was due to break later in the morning. We started out under full sail, on a broad reach, round the top end of the appropriately named island of Langeland, then hardened up to sail south on port tack, against a knot of tide. After a while, the twenty knot breeze dropped and headed us from the south. Within half an hour, in the pissing down, driving rain, the breeze had gone right round to the west and we were hard pressed, on starboard tack, in a force five. We beat to the start of the winding sound which the pilot book bills as the 'Danish Riviera', then motored down it, against the twenty knot breeze and fully two knots of tide, in this tideless sea, to the town of Svendborg. In the full harbour, rafting up was the order of the day, but just as we were eyeing up a victim to tie to, I spotted a spare stern buoy across the harbour, amongst some local boat club moorings. We settled down to the fine, spectator sport of watching everyone else fight for spaces. We were getting closer to Germania now and I had been told that the Germen tended to take their holidays in August. I would estimate that sixty to seventy percent of the visiting boats were German.

The Germany and Denmark Imray pilot simply referred to Svendborg as 'sprawling', which didn't do justice to this pleasant, hilly old town, with cobbled streets and nicely ramshackle old buildings. There were a lot of tall ships and old sailing boats in the harbour. The town has a lot of wooden shipbuilding and a part of the harbour was dedicated to a sailing museum, with a selection of fine looking old craft of various types.

It was unsurprising to find that the city had invested huge amounts of money in a plush new visitors' harbour for yachts. It was surprising to find that it was a bit of a rip-off and hugely badly organised. I suspect that the arrangement of moorings had been designed by an architect, since there were all sorts of bits which could have been used for moorings, but appeared to have been designed for the visual appearance of the pontoons, as opposed to optimising the number of boats they could accommodate. It was an extraordinarily posh facility, with a plush new floating bog, shower and office block. It had overtones of Britishness, on the other hand, in as much as they wanted a king's ransom for electricity. Happily, where we were, amongst the local boats, there were unmetered leccy outlets, strictly for the use of local boats, which of course I wouldn't have dreamed of using.

The next day's forecast was for near gales from the south west, so we decided to stay in Svendborg for two nights. I was getting lazy. We had only done four days' sailing since our last long sojourn in Copenhagen. But the wide shallow bay to the west of Svendborg was rumoured to get quite choppy in westerlies and the near gale would be right on the nose. I noticed that the strong tide running through a part of the harbour turned later in the day and ran, as you would expect from a normal tide, in the other direction. Clearly this was not wind generated tide. I mentioned this to a chatty bloke on a Danish boat which turned up the next morning. I asked how locals knew which direction the tide would be flowing as any particular time. He looked puzzled and asked why they would want to know such a thing, since they couldn't change it. I rabbited on a bit about passage planning and the fact that they could choose to exit the harbour in either direction, depending on the tide. He just sort of glazed over and asked again why anyone would want to know about tides. A very strange, fatalistic view, which doesn't seem to extend to other natural phenomena, like the weather.

One other British boat was in port. A chunky motorsailer called 'Baltic Bear'. They had just arrived from the UK, it seemed, but weren't intending to go back this year. As the name suggested, they would be based in the Baltic.

After two nights we headed out of the perfect shelter of Svendborg and down the choppy, windy channel to the west, into the teeth of a good force six. With a knot of tide with us the channel was choppy, with white spume blowing off the waves. The wind was a little north of west, so we beat down the channel, with two reefs in the main and just the staysail, in company with a few relatively hardy souls. Soon we turned, through ninety degrees to the south, and had a fast reach across the shallow bay between islands. For three or four miles there were quite large, steep waves and boats heading north were struggling as they battered into them.

On the final approach to Marstal we passed a Dutch tall ship edging down the channel. I was expecting the large marina at Marstal, on the eastern edge of the island of Ærø, to be full, but though there were a lot of boats on passage it was no more than half full and we got a large space, facing to windward, between widely spaced piles. 'Joy Spring' was in port. Her skipper was a Vanc. enthusiast and after I'd shown him round scruffy, dirty, world-weary Zoph, I was invited on board his boat for a beer. I marvelled at the gleaming, scrubbed, perfect nature of everything on board. The Joy Spring boys were gracious enough to confirm that they had indeed been racing the other day, even though they had lost. They also confirmed that everywhere was quiet for the time of year. On previous years it had been much busier. Back on Zoph we listened to the wind whistling in the rigging. This was supposed to be after the near gale had passed through. The forecast was for quite light breezes, but Zoph's anemometer still showed up to thirty one knots.

We wandered around the pleasant wee holiday town, population two thousand with, of course a huge dry dock and shipbuilding facility. We stopped for a beer in the only place with any life, an Irish pub. These edifices are of course now ubiquitous throughout the world, but this one was actually owned and run by a genuine Irishman. God knows how he had wound up in this wee, out of the way place, but he was doing a good job of being a professional Irishman and seemed to be appreciated by the punters. A rather good professional Northern Irish folk singer was on the books and played a really rather good set with his guitar. It is strange how Irish and Scottish music manages to pervade so many other cultures. It seems instantly recognisable to Scandians and Germen as well as people from other parts of the world. Somehow the passion of the less rule bound, conformist Celts seems to appeal to a lot of foreigners and make an easily identifiable export, along with whisky and CQR anchors.

Twinned with Hull

We left early in the morning, for the thirty-odd mile trip over to Germania. There were a couple of other boats out, but I was surprised there wasn't more of a mêlée. Nobody would have made the trip in the previous two days of strong winds. From the start we had a perfect sail, in about eighteen knots from the west north west, under full sail. As usual I found a reason not to go in a straight line. We headed twenty degrees off course to the west, as an insurance policy against the wind backing and increasing and making a passage west of south difficult. In the event the breeze dropped slightly and didn't back as predicted and we had a very pleasant, quite fast sail to Germania in the sun.

As we raised the German coast we were treated to a salutary lesson in the dangers of relying on high tech, electronic navigation aids. We passed a huge, sleek, posh ketch motoring in the opposite direction, towards Marstal. It had a flag which I didn't recognise, so later I looked it up on the interweb. They were, it seems, from the Marshall Islands, a series of low atolls in the middle of the Pacific. They are just about the most difficult place on the planet to get to Marstal from. You'd need to sail at least fourteen thousand miles, via the Panama Canal, or sixteen thousand, via Australia and the Cape of Good Hope. It was obvious what had happened. Somebody had mistyped the word 'Marshall' into a sophisticated navigation aid. They were going to be bloody furious when they arrived in Marstal and found that it wasn't a tropical coral island.

We were nice and early arriving in Kiel so went straight along to the canal entrance, where I made an arse of stopping against the horrible, low, solid pontoons with metal spikes on them. This was my third, passage of the Canal but the first time I'd had crew, so it was possible to pay the canal dues which Anna, unbidden, did. I was almost disappointed to find that the dues I had successfully avoided in the past were only about a tenner anyway, which makes this massive shortcut fantastic value for money.

I can understand any city not wanting to be twinned with Hull, but it did seem a massive missed opportunity that Kiel wasn't. After all a kiel's not much use without a hull and versy-vicar. We motored another three hours or so, to Rendsburg, past the massive floating sheds where the Germen build superyachts. I was confidently expecting this, the only

Beach huts in Marstal

marina in the whole fifty mile canal, to be mobbed, but in fact it was less than half full. Everywhere, it seemed was having a lean year. Of the boats that were in port the Dutch were much in evidence. A huge, chunky ship of a gin palace called Rudolph Diesel was also in port. We'd seen her back in Svendsborg days ago. Once again there was a boat which travelled immeasurably faster than Zoph, yet ended up in the same places and didn't actually go any further than her.

We had an excellent meal in the restaurant on the marina that evening. Sitting outside, on hard chairs, the waitress suggested a Sitzkissen. I pointed out that there was no need for that kind of smut and that Anna was sitting there, in full earshot. But apparently a Sitzkissen is a species of cushion. As we left Scandinavia behind and food was getting cheaper it was, paradoxically, going to cost us more. The moorings in Deutschland and Dutchland aren't on uninhabited islands but in pleasant urban centres. We were inevitably going to be eating out more often.

Svendborg

I really, really don't want to know what this means

In 2007 I had left Zoph in Rendsburg for a couple of weeks. As we were leaving in the morning I realised that, back in 2007, I had left Rendsburg for Brunsbuttel on exactly the same date. It was good to have crew for the boring old run down this canal for once. The steering is easy down the wide channel, but you still can't afford to leave the helm for more than thirty seconds or so. Not long enough to make a sandwich.

In the late afternoon we arrived at the packed little visitors' harbour at Brunsbuttel, in the rather industrial area at the western end of the canal. We rafted up on a German yacht, crewed by a slightly eccentric solo sailor in a cowboy hat. Another German boat, with a old skipper and his sons, promptly rafted up on us. Amazingly, this was the first bit of rafting of the whole summer. Brunsbuttel is not the most gorgeous of places but on this occasion it was truly bizarre. Within five yards of the boat was a huge, flashing Ferris wheel, unnecessarily advertising itself with loud, crappy music blaring from distorting speakers. Behind the big wheel was a long, straight, usually quiet shopping street. Now it was packed along its whole length with the naffness of an old fashioned fair. There were ghost trains, shooting games, candy floss, dodgems and heavily tattooed blokes ripping off the locals with the tempting promise of winning a crap, badly sewn, pink teddy bear. Each of the rides and stalls was competing with each other for custom with massively distorted loud music.

A few other boats arriving from the east went straight into the lock out to the Elbe. Since the three knot tide was in flood I assumed they were all heading up river, but wandered along to the inaccessible, security mad lock to take a look. A couple of the boats started heading down stream, which seemed a fruitless task. But they hugged the east bank of the river and disappeared across a muddy bank into what looked like a shallow ditch on the east bank. I followed them along the ditch into what turned out to be a substantial marina, lining both sides of a narrow creek. It was deliciously quiet, a short walk from the town and had visitors' berths. Bollocks, we should probably have gone in there. The walk back from this marina was through genteel streets of deathly quiet, middle class, detached suburban houses with fine, secluded gardens.

The motorway to Marstal

I wondered about heading out through the lock at high tide. I had just decided against it, on the grounds that it would make us rather late down at Cuxhaven, secured the boat for the night and cracked open a beer, when all the Dutch boats in the marina suddenly cast off and buggered off through the lock.

Back in the madness of the fair, a marching, uniformed oompah band blocked the street and all the vest wearing, tattooed, attack dog owning Rab C. Nesbitts stood watching. Trying to enter in to the spirit of the thing we had a couple of beers, out of plastic cups, from a small trailer as we listened to the local bands on a mobile stage. Back on the boat we listened to the six hundred foot long cargo ships pass slowly through the locks, twenty yards away, throughout the night. I liked the ship called 'Nordic Nora'. The throbbing of their huge diesel engines through the water was infinitely preferable to the dreadful karaoke oompah wafting across from the fair, from a uniformed gang of tone deaf, geriatric German 'singers'. I waved a greeting to the Filipino crew of one ship as it edged slowly into the lock, passing a few yards away from the Ferris wheel and all the fun of the fair. After battling the oceans, through winter gales, from the other side of the world for most of their working lives, what must they think of this surreal scene, ghosting past a brightly lit funfair at night. Even if they weren't just passing straight through to the North Sea, they probably didn't have visas to wander around eating candyfloss like everyone else. Though a motorboat nearby ran its generator all night, for once this wasn't annoying as I couldn't hear it for the rest of the racket.

The ships locking out of the redundant canal throb past the visitors' moorings all night

The next morning we considered a number of possible passage plans. It's only about fifteen miles from Brunsbuttel down the river to Cuxhaven. With a favourable tide in the river ,it doesn't take much more than a couple of hours. But it's sixty five miles from Cuxhaven to Norderney, the first all-tides destination in the German Frisian Islands. It would take up to an hour to get out of the canal through the lock. We would be arriving in Norderney well into the night and crossing the bar in the dark. Not fancying this we decided just to head down as far as Cuxhaven.

The ebb tide wasn't due to start until about half nine, but typically, at eight in the morning, all the Dutch boats still in ports upped sticks and headed for the lock. Did they know something I didn't? We headed for the lock. The larger of the ship locks is three hundred and thirty metres long. They handle about a hundred and ten ships a day. At an average of a hundred and fifty metres per ship that's ten miles of ship a day. I riffled through Griff Rhys Jones' book again to find the bit where he describes the canal as being redundant and wondered if his farty little ports in Suffolkshire could match that.

The Dutch boats didn't know better than me. We stemmed the flood tide for fully an hour and a half on the way to Cuxhaven, following six or seven other boats. By the time we arrived the ebb was in full flow and we were motoring at nine and a half knots over the ground. We arrived much earlier than I had been expecting and motored across the tide and into the marina. None of the Dutch boats were in. They were clearly planning on going all the way. It felt stupidly early to be stopping. We would just have to sit there all day, watching other boats sailing past. Finally making a decision, I motored back towards the entrance. A German Halberg Rassy 34 called, oddly, 'Blue Belly' was just motoring in with her main up. I turned to starboard a bit to avoid her. She turned to port to maintain the collision course. I turned further to starboard. They turned further to port. Eventually I had nowhere else to go. We were heading straight for the harbour wall whilst Blue Arse bore down on us. I jammed on the brakes and turned hard to starboard, describing a 270 degree turn. The air was bluer than the Halberg's belly as I swore at the bugger at the helm, who just looked vaguely bemused. The international coll. regs are something of a mystery to a lot of Scandians and Germanians.

Back out in the strong tide we headed north. It would be too far to go to Norderney, so we would head out into the North Sea to Germany's only rocky island, the tax-free-booze-port of Helgoland, around forty miles away. We motored with the main up across the main shipping channel. then eventually down a minor channel through the sandbanks to the north. The sandbanks and shallows of the Elbe estuary stretch many miles from the shore and you are still negotiating the buoyage of the channels when out of sight of land. The sea had a glossy sheen in the hazy sun and the calm. The horizon was only punctuated by the odd channel buoy, the occasional yacht heading, perhaps, for the same place as us and a procession of fast ferries, taking thousands of Germen to the delights of Helgoland for their duty free. At about three in the afternoon a small breeze cut in from the north east and we had a bit of a motor sail. But by then the tide had changed and we were again stemming the current, albeit only about a knot of it.

Eventually the lump of Helgoland appeared on the horizon and slowly grew larger. We entered the large outer harbour, about half the size of the island itself, then the inner harbour, also pretty large. Big it is but organised it isn't, the Helgoland harbour. With room for the world's largest marina they actually have only one long pontoon. So we rafted up on three other boats – the smallest raft available – then watched as four more boats rafted up on us. We had a leisurely beer in the sun then went off to explore the strange island.

Back under Europe's daftest bridge

Last of the Summer Bulk Carriers

Mingunauld

Helgoland – Heligoland to the Victorian Brits – was a British island from the early nineteenth century, having been nicked off the Danes. The inhabited island is less than half a square mile in area. In an unequal exchange, the Brits swapped it with the Germanians for Zanzibar – a group of islands with an area of over a thousand square miles and a population of a million – in 1890. The Brits revisited the evacuated island with lots of bombs between 1945 and 1952. The air force used it for target practice and detonated explosions large enough radically to change the shape of the rocky island. It has a tax haven status and the summer ferries clearly bring thousands of thirsty Teutonic types over for cheap beer. For this reason, I suppose, the Germans are terribly fond of the wee speck of island, thinking it a rare beauty spot.

I imagined that reselling mainland German beer to mainland German trippers, might provide an economic basis for a population of a couple of dozen summer migrants. Bizarrely, it seems that well over a thousand people live on the island. Behind a row of slightly tatty looking hotels, guest houses, bars and cheap booze outlets, the population is all housed in the drab, institutional houses of what looks like a 1960s new town. All the housing stock having been destroyed in the war, it has all been rebuilt on exactly the failed urban format of Runcorn or Telford, but in miniature. The new town architecture occupies the majority of the tiny scrap of land area, both low down near the harbour and high up on the slopes of the upper part of the island. God knows what the people find to do. There's scarcely enough room for them to be employed doing anything gainful. I can only assume that the tourism generated by the tax breaks is enough to keep the wolf from the door. But for over a thousand people! Given the tax haven status, I had half expected millionaire mansions, or at least the offices of tax accountants and the fronts for dodgy businesses. But in fact it's like a good old working class, miniature 1960s new town, in the physical environment reminiscent of one of the outer Hebrides. It's the town of Cumbernauld on Mingulay. Cumberlay, in fact. Or perhaps Mingunauld.

Despite its oddly urban atmosphere, it was playing on its wilderness credentials. Adverts for rooms outside guesthouses extolled the virtues of staying there during winter storms, just for the experience. Its unloveliness extends to the social atmosphere created by some of its odd laws. There's a special 'Island Tax', which all boats have to pay to keep the Mingunaulders in the style to which they have become accustomed, for example. Ironic in a place which is exempted from paying the normal taxes that the rest of the EU pays. One of the more bizarre of the many control-freak local laws is that bicycles are banned. I wonder if this is the only bit of land in the world – well, outside america anyway – where this is the case.

Back aboard, the air was rent with the sound of half-pissed youth, on various boats, working at getting completely pissed. There seemed to be quite a number of very young, laddish crews, in particular on the larger boats rafted up outside us. I wandered around the massed partying boats. Of particular note was the world's oddest looking catamaran, a huge affair with a geodesic dome instead of a cabin and a huge sail area but no mast. Or rather, the 'main' was on a genoa furler suspended vertically from two aluminium space frames. Very eccentric indeed and probably designed by an architect. Other oddities were a brand new workboat with a Welsh dragon painted on the side, from Beaumaris, and a huge seagoing lifeboat giving birth to a little baby lifeboat. The massive search and rescue craft had a wee mini version of itself, stored inside it, on a ramp in the stern which could, presumably, be released at sea. Think Virgil in Thunderbird Two, releasing the useless part-timer, Gordon, aboard Thunderbird Four, and you've got the picture.

The boats inshore of us on the raft were leaving early in the morning, so we agreed to cast off at the same time. The bleary eyed youths, on the piss-up boats outside us on the raft, took a fair bit of waking at half past seven. Eventually they were roused however and we headed off. It was full sail from the start, as we easily passed the German yacht 'Tramp' in a slowly increasing easterly force three. This was the boat we had rafted on in Brunsbuttel, which had anchored off the beach at Mingunauld to save money. She seemed eccentrically driven and sailed on a winding, half pissed course, with sails flapping.

We were passed by another yacht from our raft, 'Lisa' and three others, as we headed south-south west, to pass just south of the Elbe Approach Traffic Separation Scheme. Annoyingly this course had us almost heading back where we had come from the previous day, for a while. Right on cue, as we turned further to the west round the end of the scheme, the wind increased to the upper end of a four and we kept up a six knot average all day. As the breeze increased to a force five we got rid of the staysail and rigged a gybe prevented on the main. Eventually, in the increasing breeze, we furled the jib and barrelled downwind under just the main. The swell grew worryingly steep as we crossed the shallow bar in the eastern approach channel to Norderney. The five foot swell over the ten foot deep bar was on the point of breaking as we almost surfed in.

Our timing was good in that the wind was increasing all the time and due to do so for the next twenty four hours. Norderney Marina was particularly busy. We were also just in time to get practically the last pontoon berth in town. The folk from 'Lisa' recognised us, and beckoned us into a berth, which was marked with a red square – meaning unavailable. But they had established that the owners were away and that the berth was, in fact, available. This was something of a lucky break, as later boats were forced to raft up on the harbour wall.

Back from the Baltic to the Netherlands

Norderney was just as old fashioned a Victorian holiday resort as it had been in May, but this time with added, old fashioned, traditional touros. All manner of traditional Germanian families wandered around, eating ice creams in the traditional streets. Their sprogs ran amok in a traditional, rosy cheeked, Germanic sprog-like way. When the little darlings had exhausted themselves with lashings of dashing about, their parents pulled them home in brightly painted little four wheeled wooden carts, with big thick pneumatic tyres. They were like vehicles from a German cartoon about the good old days. I was unclear why, if they were keen to have their sprogs exercise, they couldn't just get them to walk home. I'm sure the Victorians would have done.

Norderney seems so old and traditional it is truly bizarre to think that it didn't exist at all, in the year twelve hundred. It's just a smear of sand deposited in a gale by a particularly high tide. It was a resort back in the eighteenth century, when most of the actual land was only three hundred years old. Yet it seems somehow timeless. By contrast the ancient rock at Helgoland feels like it was created by an edict of the Wilson government. The apparent old tradition of the shifting sand dune is, somehow, much more pleasant than the brash twentieth century old rock.

The friendly couple from Lisa who had helped us to a mooring continued their helpfulness by inviting us on board that evening for a beer or two, or three.

The cool and trendy strandkorb crew

Making polders the old fashioned way

The next day we thought about heading off in the morning, but with a force six or more forecast and gentler conditions the following day, we decided on another day in port. One of the problems was the timing of the tide. It's possible to take the rising tide across the inner, shallow route to the Ems, behind Juist and Borkum. But you need to make the most of the flood, by crossing the shallowest patches as early as possible on the rising tide. That day this would have meant leaving Norderney at around five a.m. In the middle of August, almost two months after the solstice, this would have been in the dark. The drying inner channels are only marked by unlit buoys, and withies stuck into the sand. These would have been impossible to follow in the dark. So the only real option was the long trip west, round Borkum and back up the Ems. We decided to wait for more benign conditions for this.

Meanwhile I annoyed Anna by hiring a bike. With two bikes between us she had no excuse and had to do a cycling tour of the island. Norderney made Scandinavia – and even Holland – look like Helgoland when it came to bikes. It was as though its population, and all its visitors, had reacted violently to the anti-bike law on Mingunauld, vowing never to go anywhere at all, without at least three bikes each. We had to climb the sandy dunes from the low lying, sea level grazing land, to see the long white beaches and the sea. At every access point through the dunes, the number of bikes had to be seen to be believed. Rank upon rank of them stretched for hundreds of yards around. You needed a bike, just to get from one end of the bike park to the other. Most of them were hired bikes, and many were ridden by people who looked more like models for Beryl Cook postcards, than your average, stringy cyclist. Some had not yet mastered the fine art of steering a bicycle. They had presumably been installed aboard by the bloke they hired them from, then given a shove downwind towards the opposite end of the island. When they encountered us, coming the other way, it often seemed like this was the first time they had been called upon to attempt any sort of manoeuvre. I would have felt marginally more secure cycling the wrong way round a grand prix circuit during a race.

Bikes, bikes, bikes, bikes, bikes, bikes

This picture was taken in 2012, not 1912

In the morning we left as part of a procession of boats heading west. With a forecast of a force six, albeit from the south east – the best possible direction – we started out with a reef in. In the event the wind was never above a force four and we had a pleasant broad reach for about five hours. I was however in a haze of indecision, with about fourteen possible passage plans floating around in my brain. The basic idea was to take the ebb along the coast, past Borkum, then the flood up to Delfzijl. But this would mean heading straight into the otherwise favourable wind up, the Ems estuary. Another option was to stop in Borkum. Third, fourth, fifth and sixth options were to keep heading west, and nip in behind the Frisian Islands at one of a number of places, the leading contender being Lauwersoog.

As so often the problem was information. The useless Imray pilot – sorry to bore you with this constant refrain – was, as its name suggests, useless. The bloody thing is arranged in a 'What I Did on my Holidays' format. That is to say, it follows a particular chosen route, in a particular direction and tells you at what stage of the tide, for example, to start. If you are going somewhere else, or in the opposite direction, it's about as useful as a pilot book as this drivel. It gave absolutely no clue as to whether the channel to Lauwersoog – where there is a lock into the inland waterways – was all tides or drying, or what the currents were like. On the chart plotter there were few depths shown, but at least the channel was shown as water, so we should be able to get in on a rising tide. This would save us at least a day of motoring down canals. We decided to head west for Lauwersoog.

Then I looked at our paper chart. It also had few depths marked, but it coloured the channel to Lauwersoog brown. It was clearly shown as a drying channel. Coupled to this, it seemed that the current was not behaving as our best tidal information suggested it should. It looked like the tide was a couple of hours later than it ought to be. I spent an hour or so completely confusing myself, by trying to work out whether the use of different time zones could be causing the problem. We decided against Lauwersoog. Over a period of three hours or so, I swithered back and forth between the options, in a stupidity of indecision. In the end, having driven Anna more or less to distraction, the entrance to the Ems appeared and a decision had to be made. We turned left towards Delfzijl. Naturally, of course, every other boat we saw kept heading west for some unknown destination.

We ought to have been at the Ems entrance at around slack water, but we were still plugging against the last of the ebb for nearly two hours. The piss-paucity of our information could have been a problem, had we continued to Lauwersoog. The wind was on the nose, but with only a force four coming off the land there was no real sea to contend with. Eventually the tide turned and we finished the sixty mile passage doing eight knots over the bottom. Surprisingly the wind, blowing against the three knot tide, didn't really throw up anything nasty. We motorsailed past the docks, tanks and pipes of the large refinery facilities and, at eight p.m, we arrived at the marina in Delfzijl.

Fan

This was the third time I'd been in Delfzijl and I had steeled Anna not to expect much. After all, it is an unprepossessing oil port town. A small working city with nothing to attract the visitor, whose inhabitants work in oil refineries and chemical plants. As I've said before it's basically a Dutch equivalent of Runcorn or Grangemouth. And yet, of course, it isn't. Like everywhere in The Netherlands it's a perfectly pleasant, liveable place, with a low key 1960s shopping centre which does not have boarded up windows or large amounts of graffiti. It looks, sort of, like a 1960's planner might have hoped that Runcorn would look in 2012. It's got canals of course, and a large windmill in the middle of town which houses a small museum. Like most places in The Netherlands it is not dramatic, but like everywhere the thought of living there doesn't fill you with horror.

In the evening we wandered into the town in search of a beer. One pub looked reasonably lively. It was a large, pretend half-timbered affair, standing by itself in what amounted to a car park. I remembered such edifices from being forced to drink in Manchester. There the route to the pub would be fraught with danger, across several lanes of traffic. Which is fine, because going into the god-awful hole would be fraught with even more danger. In the Delfzijl equivalent, we ordered a beer and sat outside on a balmy evening, at the edge of a perfectly pleasant car park, in a perfectly pleasant town. The locals were all old blokes – retired refinery workers out at the boozer. But all of them sat, two to a table across the wide paved area, quietly playing chess. Yes, chess. I may be wrong, but I suspect that scene was not mirrored that night outside the pubs of Grangemouth.

Back aboard the next morning, a local bloke was doing what I do in marinas, wandering along all the pontoons looking at all the boats, on a hunt for something exotic. Apart from the local Dutch boats, Delfzijl had a lot of German yachts. These were mostly quite small, local ones, probably used mainly to cruising the estuary and a few of the Frisian Islands. So Zoph was, I suppose, at least slightly exotic. He stopped next to her and appeared to be examining her in some detail. I was just going ashore so I nodded and said hello as I passed. "Are you the man who writes books on the internet?" He asked. "What?" I asked. He repeated himself. Was I the bloke who wrote accounts of his sailing trips and published them electronically? I replied

Groningen

that I was certainly a bloke who did that. I would hesitate to claim to be the bloke.

He had, apparently, read all my previous tales for e-reader and – incredibly – enjoyed them. I was completely, as they say, made up. This might not seem such a big deal, but these accounts don't exactly fly off the shelves. To have anyone read them at all was an achievement. To be accosted by a 'fan', of sorts, in a marina in a random oil town in a foreign country, so far from home was, it seemed to me, remarkable. I was conspicuously chuffed.

In the morning we motored off down the long, dull, straight canal. We skirted Groningen, sightseeing only from the boat, which is not a bad vantage point for seeing this town. After a slow passage through the many bridges we headed north and passed through one of the Netherlands' very few locks with a significant vertical component. This time, disconcertingly, having risen only marginally from the sea at Delfzijl, we plummeted downwards over a metre.

The fishing fleet miles from the salt water in Zoutcamp

A traditional clogging

Entering the fresh water again was the crowning glory of my 2012 Barnacle Confusion Strategy. I aimed to confuse the hell out of the marine fauna and flora which tried to get a toehold on Zoph. To do this we had started in a salty North Sea, at about four degrees. We had gone into fresh water, then salt again, then fresh, then marginally less salty than the North Sea, then fresh, then brackish, then increasingly less salt, then increasingly more salt as we came back west, then fresh, then full saltiness. Finally, at Delfzijl, we were back into the fresh water again. Any organism that could survive that is probably a mutated super-barnacle with evil plans for world domination.

Everyone wants to get onto the water in Holland and the canals in August were full of a motley collection of craft. From world-girdling yachts and gleaming gin palaces, to knackered, smoky motorboats, rowing boats, speedboats and canoes. Families were out for a potter up the canal, from one commuting village to another, in wee open boats. They couldn't boast the Scandians' million perfect island anchorages, but they did the best with the resources they had. The daftest craft I had yet seen were hanging around the lock entrances. They were, basically, half a dry suit attached to a lorry inner tube. Blokes floated about in the canal in these suits, buoyed up by an inflated rubber ring, dangling their fishing rods in the water. They paddled themselves from place to place using just their hands. Quite a few folk seemed to have taken up this activity, which they mostly chose to do in the most awkward of places, just as boats were trying to manoeuvre. For once, Zoph was the supertanker, with restricted manoeuvrability, dealing with the pesky, smaller craft.

We stopped at the first wee marina after the ship lock, mooring in one point two metres if water, in the mud between piles. In the small commuter village of Garnwerd, below the level of the canal, was a knot of the most aesthetic little houses, three restaurants – posh, middling and scummy – a caravan site, a sandy beach, a swimming pool, ponies for hire and a marina. One of the restaurants had bike racks for twenty four bicycles, each of which had – get this – an electrical point, for the free recharging of your electric bike. Why the hell they need electric bikes, in this perfectly flat country, is beyond me, but I don't suppose there's a single bike rack in the whole of Britain with as good facilities for bikes as that random wee restaurant. On a random bit of artificial canal was an artificial beach with a pool cut out of the banks. The massed bands of the Dutch sprogs leapt in and out of this pool in this tiny, Toytown resort and generally acted as though they had been treated to an overpriced holiday in Centre Parks. The Dutch holiday resort is an odd – but appealing – place. To me a bona fide rural retreat ought to be set in genuine countryside, with something that at least looked like it might be genuine wilderness nearby. The Dutch, of course, don't have any wilderness, so they get away from it all to the suburbs.

We pressed on in the morning, motoring down the canal then, sailing a bit on the Lauwersmeer. We'd have been leaving the sea here two days before, if we had kept heading west after passing Borkum. We messed around, looking for lunchtime anchorages on the wee artificial islands on the meer. We managed to run gently aground in the approach to one. A shoal draft boat is a real boon in these waters and a lot of the large Dutch barges sail where we never could. We managed – with difficulty – to reverse off however and found a slightly deeper quay to tie up, for lunch and a swim in the twenty degree loch. The thing looked pretty muddy and poo-filled, but half of Holland were up to their necks in the foetid swamp, so what the hell..

Later I was gunning the engine a bit, to try and get to the opening bridge at Dokkum, before the bloke went off for his scheduled afternoon nap. Zoph was zooming along at a good six knots, when we passed a group of small gin

Lunch in the Lauwermeer

palaces, moored at the side of the canal. I was almost pleased when one pissed off old bloke on a motorboat shook his fist at us, as our ripple of wash hit him. Just for once the boot was on the other foot and slow, placid old Zoph was annoying the speedboats. We moored alongside, in one of the few places left, in the pictureskew old town of Dokkum. A pleasantly quiet place, yet with a few waterside bars and eateries at which we indulged ourselves. We were really slowing up now and the cruise had taken on a very elderly complexion.

Dokkum

Dokkum

We were even slower and more elderly the next day as we motored onwards. At the first clogging Anna short-changed the clogger by miscounting the Euros. This led to some comedic manoeuvring under a narrow bridge, as I tried to keep an unfendered Zoph stationary, while she sorted out the right change. At Burdaard we underwent another clogging, then pottered on to the centre of Leeuwarden where, this time, we got a plum position in the park, instead of a wet canal bank in an industrial estate.

We were early after just half a day's trip. The sun was out and it was proper summer in the park. Half of Leeuwarden was picnicking and we had our own spot on the lush lawn, a foot away from Zoph's toerail. In the afternoon we wandered the town in much better weather than I had seen it in, over three months before. Again I marvelled at the sheer amount of money which had been poured into this prosperous, regional centre, which I had never even heard of before. If I had criticisms they would be of the automated, far too high-tech. payment system and the total lack of any tourist information, in a town liberally sprinkled with visiting touros. I chatted to an English bloke aboard a large, chunky, British flagged barge. This was a wide beamed vessel of Dutchlike specification and, of course, permanently based in The Netherlands.

It was still proper summer the next day, as we motored through the bridges and paid another clogging on what was, potentially, the last day of the cruise. I had been in the sort of ludicrous agony of indecision that only someone with no life or death decisions to make can be. Would I take Zoph home to the Forth for the winter, or leave her in The Netherlands? The only real reason to take her home was just for completeness – to say that I'd done it. That and an irrational fear of becoming part of some elderly, probably golf playing, ex-pat community.

Of course I would miss the autumn and winter sailing in Scotland but, over the past few seasons, there had been precious little winter sailing, and I could always fly from Edinburgh to Hamsterjam by Difficultjet a couple of times, in September and October.

The main mast-up channel through the Netherlands

A misguided straw caravan.

I smell a hippy architect

There was also the little matter of cost. Dutch marinas are eight times more efficient, four times more pleasant and half the price of Scottish ones. Even the crappy east coast Scottish ones. Leaving Zoph in The Netherlands would also, if I was planning to go anywhere outside the UK or Ireland next year, save me two, fraught, cold, probably unpleasant, North Sea crossings. This season I had only just found a window to cross whilst I had a crew. I had heard several tales, from other sailors, about a planned cruise to Holland or Norway which had been cancelled altogether, due to contrary winds in early summer. It was, finally, decided then. I would leave Zoph here. The next question was, of course, if I was going back to Scandinavia next year, why the bloody hell had I sailed all the way back to Holland? But never mind that. It was a fait accompli.

Having decided to overwinter in the Netherlands I had settled on the small town of Lemmer as our final destination. Practically any village in the country would have done. They all have at least two marinas and all the facilities for boats you could want, but Lemmer had a ridiculous concentration of both boats and stuff for boats. The idea of overwintering in The Netherlands seemed particularly appealing on that hot, hot August Saturday. This was a proper summer weekend and the whole country was out on the water. I'd seen busy waterways in Scandinavia that summer, but nothing to compare to the fifteen million Dutch, each of whom owns a boat of some sort, all crammed into their network of canals and puddles.

I deliberately took a wrong turn on the Staande Mastroute, to go back through Warten. As we waited in a queue of flotsam and jetsam for the old gadgie to finish his lunch and lift the bridge it didn't look quite as idyllic as it had done in May. The village was preparing for a summer fete. This preparation involved testing a five hundred gigawatt sound system, by blasting crap, middle-of-the-road American rock through it, at full volume. It rather disturbed the rural tweenery. We pressed on. After taking another wrong turn for a few miles – this time accidentally – we were swept by the milling throng of boats into the Sneekermeer.

It was far too nice a day to waste in a town, so we joined the Piccadilly Circus of craft sailing randomly around the lake for a while, then dropped anchor, amongst an even scattering of boats of all kinds. Since the whole two mile long lake is all exactly one point eight metres deep, with a muddy bottom, it scarcely matters where you anchor at all. If a strong wind was forecast you might want to err on the weather side, but basically there was no serious decision making. You just dropped anchor whenever you got bored with sailing. The Dutch have got it even cushier than the Scandians, if anything. We had a leisurely evening, with a dip, a G&T or two and a meal watching the sunset. It was probably the properly hottest day of the year and it felt a bit daft to be coming to the end of the cruise and thinking about autumn. Nevertheless we had a plane to catch.

The leaning tower of Leeuwarden

Picnic in the park in Leeuwarden

Lemming

In the morning we headed towards Lemmer. First we took a side trip to the theoretically pictureskew town of Sneek. It was late on Sunday morning and yesterday's Saturday crowds paled into insignificance, beside the hordes rushing along the canals here. Most of Friesland seemed to be motoring out of Sneek. Today, this was approximately a six lane canal – three lanes in each direction. The wash thrown up by the thousands of boats, albeit mostly small and slow ones, made the water really quite rough and the banks untenable for mooring. In the end we didn't bother stopping in Sneek. Everywhere looked like too much hassle. We turned round and motored towards Lemmer.

Soon we entered the small Koevordermeer. In the gentle breeze old barges, yachts, dayboats, dinghies and wind surfers sailed backwards and forwards across the lake. Gin palaces, speedboats, traditional motorboats, rowing boats and canoes pottered around randomly, dropping their anchors wherever they saw fit. Often a sailing boat, its crew hungry for lunch, would just drop an anchor in a random bit of the middle of the lake. The whole scene was dotted with hundreds of boats of all kinds, under way and anchored. It was much busier even than Sneekermeer had been yesterday.

As well as the boats there were a lot of other, smaller dots. Perhaps they were fishing net poles, or ducks. As we got closer we realised that they were people. All over the calm lake in the hot sun people stood about in the water. They had waded and swum away from their boats in the two foot deep water and were standing about, cooling off, as barges and yachts criss-crossed around them under full sail. It was one of the more surreal sights of the summer.

The new Friesland Museum

We motored on and soon approached the outer suburbs of Lemmer, where Simon and Gordon had left the boat at the start of May. We passed the rows of holiday homes with their own private docks, the unremarkable suburban houses with their ocean goings yachts tied to them and two or three of Lemmer's twelve marinas. We underwent the last clogging of the cruise – in this case a lemming – and tied up outside a restaurant on the main street. We cracked open a beer from our dwindling stock and toasted what felt like an anticlimax – the end of Zoph's 2012 from the Forth to Russia and most of the way back. Because we were stopping in a more or less random Dutch town, there was none of the fanfare of arrival I'd experienced on previous cruises. We weren't home yet and it didn't feel like an ending at all. It was only August the twentieth and there was plenty more sailing to do. But you've got to stop somewhere, draw a line under it and say "that's it, the final destination in the year's cruise".

Posh bank headquarters in Leeuwarden

Zoph had come 3048.8 miles since leaving her berth in Port Edgar a hundred and eleven days earlier. In that time she had travelled for a total of eighty seven days. I would return three times that autumn and get another twelve days sailing, enjoying five hundred miles under sail in the genteel surroundings of the old ports that line the Ijsselmeer and the Markermeer. But each time I returned to Lemmer, which was effectively the end of Zoph's cruise for 2012.

I cycled around the wee town. It was clear that, on a summer Sunday, every available inch of the land, within half a mile of Lemmer, was used as car park for the millions of punters who thronged the beach. I can only assume that these sandy beaches, formed when the Ijsselmeer was the tidal Zuiderzee and filled with marine life, are now temporary phenomena and not long for this world. That night we had a last, celebratory meal. Disappointingly, it was in a 'British pub' twenty yards or so from the boat, complete with a plastic rozzer in a tall blue helmet and a miniature red telephone box. An authentic touch of home was provided by the myriad grocers' apostrophes which littered the menu.

In the morning I sounded out a few of the twelve marinas, some in the Ijsselmeer, some through the lock in the even lower canal system, comparing facilities and prices for winter berthing. Without really shopping about much – and in this expensive corner of the country – I soon agreed a price for the winter, with a friendly chap, in a family run marina, in perfect suburban shelter, next to the village. It was about half what I would pay at home, and in agreeing it I suffered neither the abuse nor the incredulity, which would be standard practice in the UK.

Waiting for the bridge at Wartena

Vehicles of all kinds at Sneekermeer

Sublime to...

In the autumn I learned just how efficient and well organised the Dutch system for overwintering boats is. Everywhere has the same, standardised system of chunky steel cradles. These can all be lifted and trundled about on standard road trolleys. In October the roads around Lemmer are thick with yachts zooming around on their standard cradles, being transferred from marinas, to overwintering sheds, to repair yards, to people's back gardens. The standardised cradles are even all painted the same colour. I was sure that old Zoph would be snug and comfortable in her winter home.

So where would we go next year? It had, of course, to be somewhere which would afford me a small frisson of adventure, whilst at the same time being fantastically easy and safe. I wanted pseudo-real adventure, not just the virtual kind. I couldn't stand the thought of just getting my adventure from theme parks, or watching the telly, or playing computer games. It had to appear intrepid whilst actually being extraordinarily wimpy. It's hard for an abject coward, with a thirst for adventure and an aversion to the virtual

The Dutch are a peculiarly cruel and sadistic people

...Ridiculous

I could head for the Gulf of Bothnia. I could go back to Santio and, this time, press on to the Finnish lakes. I could find a way through the European canal and river system to the Mediterranean. I could try for the Black Sea, via Poland.

More ambitiously, I could try for the Russian river systems up to the White Sea, then head round the North Cape and back south to Scotland. Whatever it was, I knew it would need to involve a bit of exploring. And when would I stop exploring? More to the point, when you stop being an explorer do you become a plorer? Or is ploring something you could only do before exploring? Or am I just talking nonsense? Wherever I choose, there's a whole world of water out there, waiting for Zoph.

This is one of four books so far describing Zophiel's cruises.

"***Skagerrak and Back:*** *Zophiel's Two Summer Cruises in 2007"* is the first one and is a relatively short account of a North Sea circuit.

"***Floating Low to Lofoten***" describes her trip from Edinburgh north to the Norwegian arctic and back in 2008.

"***A Gigantic Whinge on the Celtic Fringe:*** *A Total and Complete Circumnavigation of Ireland and Britain by the Slightly Truncated Irish Route"* is, if you can get past the misleading title, just about a trip around Ireland in 2011.

"***Bobbing to the Baltic***" is the tale of her 2012 trip along much the same route as described in Griff Rhys Jones' book 'To the Baltic with Bob', but with a pile more photos and descriptions of a lot more good places to stop.

I have also written two books about my travels – without Zophiel – in parts of Asia, Africa and Central America little frequented by Europeans. They are entitled "***Travels with my Rant***" and *"**The Front of Beyond**".*

There's more sailing tales at **http://www.edge.me.uk/Sailinghome.htm**, where you will also find the colour photos contained in these volumes.

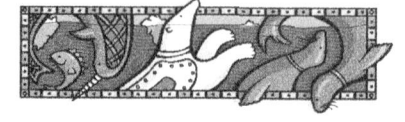

Printed in Great Britain
by Amazon